Book Talk

Book Talk:

Essays on Books, Booksellers,
Collecting, *and* Special Collections

Edited by
Robert H. Jackson
and Carol Z. Rothkopf

OAK KNOLL PRESS

NEW CASTLE, DELAWARE

2006

First published in 2006 by Oak Knoll Press
310 Delaware Street, New Castle, Delaware 19720 USA
Web: http://www.oakknoll.com

ISBN: 1-58456-188-2

Title: Book Talk: Essays on Books, Booksellers, Collecting, and
Special Collections

Typographer: Scott J. Vile

Dustjacket Design: Scott J. Vile

Publishing Director: J. Lewis von Hoelle

Copyright © FABS (The Fellowship of American Bibliophilic Societies) 2006
All Rights Reserved

The CIP record for this book is available from the publisher.

ALL RIGHTS RESERVED
No part of this book may be reproduced in any manner without the express
written consent of the publisher, except in the case of brief excerpts in critical
reviews and articles. All inquiries should be addressed to:
Oak Knoll Press, 310 Delaware St., New Castle, DE 19720.
Web: http://www.oakknoll.com

This work was printed and bound in the United States of America on archival,
acid-free paper meeting the requirements of the American Standard for
Permanence of Paper for Printed Library Materials.

Contents

Preface	*Robert H. Jackson*	i
Foreword	*John C. Carson, MD*	v
Introduction What is the Fellowship of American Bibliophilic Societies?	*Lawrence N. Siegler*	vii

BOOKS

The Past, Present, and Future of the Book	*Jason Epstein*	3
"Only Copy Known": Random Reflections on Rarity	*Bruce Whiteman*	11
Books That Everyone Has Forgotten: Some Preliminary Notes on Low Spots In Literature	*Garrett Scott*	29
The Pre-Socratic Project and Remarks on the Philosophical Side of Fine Printing	*Peter Rutledge Koch*	39
The Woodcut in Ferrara in the Late Fifteenth Century	*Daniel De Simone*	57
Aurora Australis (1908), Edited By Ernest H. Shackleton: A New Description of the First State of the First Book Published on the Antarctic Continent	*Martin L. Greene*	69

BOOKSELLERS

The Messiah Factor in Bookselling	Tom Congalton	83
The American Antiquarian Book Trade: Yesterday, Today, and Tomorrow	John Crichton	95
Adventures of a Bookseller	Priscilla Juvelis	109
Roxburghe to eBay: A Brief Survey of the Way Books Change Hands	Peter Kraus	123
Some Thoughts on the Maturing of the Rare Book Market	Ken Lopez	139
My Adventures in Academe	Anthony Garnett	155

COLLECTING

Will the Book Collector of Today be the Donor of Tomorrow?	Robert H. Jackson	169
A Book Collector Builds A Life	Arthur L. Schwarz	183
The Future of Book Collecting	Paul T. Ruxin	195

SPECIAL COLLECTIONS

What Can A Librarian Do?   *Roger E. Stoddard*   205

An Embarrassment of Riches: Collecting Trends
     in Institutional Special Collections   *Samuel Streit*   223

I Didn't Know You Had That!—
     Resuscitating Special Collections   *Geoffrey D. Smith*   235

Contributors   245

Index   251

Preface

Robert H. Jackson

D<small>R</small>. A. S.W. R<small>OSENBACH</small>, perhaps the best-known and most successful American dealer in rare books of the twentieth century once said, "the greatest sport, next to love, is book collecting." This sentiment still rings true to many collectors. While its charms will always remain a mystery to the majority, rare book collecting has, in recent years, begun to entice a growing band of admirers. This is happening despite the fact that for a long time, the supply of older material has been shrinking, as books, manuscripts, and ephemera are retired from the marketplace and enter institutional collections.

Once the preserve of the male elite, book collecting now appeals to a more diverse group. As collectors have changed, so have dealers. Today's dealers can no longer rely on one or two wealthy individuals for their livelihoods. Gone are the days when book dealing was the incidental pastime of a bored dilettante. Today's successful book dealer is an aggressive, full-time business person, applying the latest marketing, financial, and promotional techniques to the work at hand. The Internet has become the book dealers' most valuable tool, creating a broader market of book collectors, and permitting even more dealers to flourish.

Interest in book collecting has been further increased by regional and national book fairs, trade journals, and the active involvement of major auction houses. Recently, a series of regional auction businesses have dramatically emerged, as the major auctions raised their minimum lot prices. With the diminishing supply of traditional rarities, dealers and collectors have sought new hunting grounds to fuel the natural pleasure of the chase. Book clubs currently evolving and flourishing throughout the country provide another important venue for book people to indulge and expand their interests. Once arcane specialties such as political propaganda, pop-up books, regional history, unusual bindings, or eighteenth-century French cookbooks, now supplement traditional favorites such as sports, color plates, incunabula (books from the dawn of printing), topography, maps, and English and American literature and science. The constant pursuit of new specialties and the revival of old interests is creating an air of vitality and excitement that had recently disappeared from the field.

Book Talk: Essays on Books, Booksellers, Collecting, and Special Collections reflects some of this heady new atmosphere. Most of these essays originated as talks given under the sponsorship of the Fellowship of American Bibliographic Societies (FABS) from 1997 through 2005. These symposia and book study tours were designed to take place in different cities each year to as a way of providing opportunities for rare book collectors, librarians, dealers, and others interested in the Book to gather outside the usual book fairs, occasional rare book conference, and the annual "rare book schools" at the University of Virginia and in Colorado Springs, to view a wider variety of public and private collections. People who are passionate about books need more places to meet, express themselves, and exchange ideas, information and, of course, gossip about the book world.

Book collecting — a field whose currency is knowledge and communication — ironically enough produces little information about its own standards. FABS members are expanding book study groups and European sponsored trips are appearing. In the past

Preface

twenty years, there has been, however, such an explosion of information about its economics and history, that it is difficult to separate out the most meaningful material. There are several books to recommend to people interested in this field whether they are novices or veteran collectors. *New Paths in Book Collecting* (1935) and *Taste and Techniques in Book Collecting* (1949), by the well-known English bookman John Carter, are indispensable. Notable successors include *Book Collecting: A Modern Guide* (1977), *Collectible Books: Some New Paths* (1979), edited by Jean Peters, *ABC for Book Collectors* (2004), John Carter and Nicolas Barker, co-editors, 8th ed., 2004, Anthony Rota's *Apart From the Text*, 1998, all of Nicholas A. Basbane's innovative series of recent books on the multi layered book world; and the newly released, *The Literature of The Book* (2005), a useful bibliography as a guide for the world of books about books. In recent years, Delaware-based Oak Knoll Press has emerged as the premier international publisher of a broad spectrum of volumes on book topics such as printing history, typography, bibliography, book design and fine presses, and book illustrations. Magazines including *The Book Collector* and *Rare Books* (published in England), *Fine Books and Collections* and *Firsts* in the United States provide an interesting and improving flow of information and notices on recent scholarship and happenings in the field.

Book Talk addresses the sharing of information, and takes the reader on a tour of some major ideas and controversies now current in the rare book world such as the future of the book in a printed format and of special collections, the book trade and the Internet, and collecting trends. While all kinds of sources of information for collectors are available, this volume provides a unique compilation and overview of the field today by prominent writers. The contributors have an active personal involvement in their topics, which range from fifteenth-century Italian methods of textual illustration to book dealers' strategies to scholarship to how book dealers stoke the passion for collecting.

Book collecting today is as exciting and absorbing as it has ever been; perhaps, even more challenging and competitive. No single volume could contain all the concepts, observations, and fresh notions being generated both by newcomers and veterans in the field. But if *Book Talk* interests, challenges, stimulates, or inspires you, it will have fulfilled its mission.

Carol Rothkopf, my insightful and knowledgeable co-editor, was a delight with whom to work. Larry Siegler, in his introduction, identifies our co-founders who helped form FABS, I am grateful for their support and steadfastness. Further, I want to thank the writers for their willingness to revise their talks into articles as only in the last few years, when the idea of this book began to crystallize, did I request the contributors to transform their talks into essays. Heather Miller, formerly Humanities Acquisition Editor at The Ohio State University Press, was of great assistance in preparing the manuscript for publication. My secretary of thirty years, Jan Shanley, in addition to her multifaceted responsibilities, also prepared many aspects of this manuscript. To my wife, Donna, my best friend and travel companion, personal editor and constructive critic, my love and well-deserved thanks.

Foreword

John C. Carson

THE STORY OF American book collectors' associations has its roots deep in our nation's history.

As early as 1731 The Library Company of Philadelphia was founded by Benjamin Franklin and some of his fellow members of the Junto, a discussion group that often needed printed references to settle differences of opinion among them. The members could not afford to build a library of such materials separately so they pooled their resources to establish and support this, now the oldest of the subscription libraries in the United States.

Other scholarly and bibliophilic foundations soon followed, notably The American Philosophical Society (1743), The Charleston (South Carolina) Library Society (1748), The New York Society Library (1754), The Library of Congress (1800), and The Boston Athenæum (1807).

In the latter part of the nineteenth century, clubs were established exclusively for bibliophiles. The oldest, The Grolier Club in New York City, was founded in 1884 and is renowned to this day for its exhibitions and publications. Other bibliophiles clubs were soon established elsewhere in the country: The Rowfant Club in

Cleveland in 1892; The Philobiblon Club in Philadelphia in 1893; and The Caxton Club in Chicago in 1895.

As other bibliophilic groups were formed in the twentieth century, it remained only to form an umbrella organization that covered the entire nation. This was, of course, the now familiar Fellowship of American Bibliophilic Societies, which was created in 1993 and whose history is told by Chairman Emeritus Larry Siegler in this volume–the first in what we project to be a series of contributions to the world of books. This volume, *Book Talk*, in its conception, planning, and execution owes everything to the foresight, talent, and energy of Robert H. Jackson. The articles included in this volume first sparkled when heard as talks at various symposia held in Detroit, San Francisco, Cleveland, Chicago, Pasadena, New York City, and St. Louis. We think they shall continue to sparkle in their written versions.

Introduction

What is the Fellowship of American Bibliophilic Societies (FABS)?

Lawrence N. Siegler

I

MAN HAS ALWAYS sought explanations. So it is fair to ask: what is FABS' raison d'être? What great satisfaction made FABS thrive and attract over thirty clubs in its brief history? Why are over 5,000 people associated with this nonpolitical and noninvasive association? The reason is more obvious than one might think. Simply stated, FABS supplies a vivid and effective association with our civilization. Western civilization, though sometimes harshly criticized and rudely challenged, has impressively demonstrated enormous beauty, vivid imagination, and profound spirituality as well as compassion, justice, and with a high degree of *gravitas*, a sense of community. People have permanently recorded in books (until relatively recently almost exclusively in books), their achievements, thoughts, and fantasies. FABS and its associated clubs supply to book lovers an important channel for deeper involvement and passion for their civilization.

Human nature provides the foundation for collecting. We have inherited, from many generations of our hunter/gatherer ancestors, a drive to collect. It is not uncommon to hear collectors refer to their quest for books as "the hunt" or speak of the "thrill of the chase." The drive is indeed inbred.

Books do more than preserve and record. They explain, convince, provoke, amuse, delight, improve, and soothe the spirit. Reverence for books develops as humans appreciate these powerful attributes. Collectors revere books and accumulate them because of their various messages, their manifold stimulations and associations; and quite often as exquisite expressions of beauty and feeling.

Future innovations will occur: books will talk, emit music, provide fast and easy links to references, and project supplemental pictures to the text. Electronic books soon will be more legible, portable, interactive, flexible, and have many other amazing and I hope, artistic attributes. This merge of multimedia and rapid retrieval will make the book even more powerful.

Freud defined the *Sammler*, or collector, as anal-retentive. Whether asinine or merely retentive, the psychic drive to collect exists in many of us. Clearly, there will still be books, providing a private communication with the reader—a direct message to the brain through its consciousness, its libido, its synapses, and other almost mystic processes. Among us FABS members, there are many whose pride, joy, inquisitiveness, acquisitiveness, aggression, and other drives push us to collect. Expressed in positive and unambiguous terms, it is our innate quest to understand, recall, and celebrate our civilization that drives our keen interest in books.

Though some books perversely inspired Don Quixote, bothered Saint Augustine, and sent Dante's Paolo and Francesca to Hell, many more books have made most of our lives fuller and richer. Whether temptation, transmogrification, or totem, the desire to possess these significant and powerful items will always exist. There have been collectors since the very beginning of book production. Books of course, include tablets, scrolls in papyrus, ephemera, and various codices. Early collectors were relatively few, because books were rare and expensive and literacy very limited. Until the nineteenth century, there were hardly enough collectors to form associations in any one country or city. Even among the aristocracy,

Introduction

collectors were few. However, by the late eighteenth century, a number of factors aligned that spurred growing interest in reading and collecting books. These factors were mainly increased literacy, cheaper and more readily available books, and much more disposable income in the hands of more people.

Humans, like their simian ancestors, are gregarious. This gregariousness forced the gathering together for such mutual needs as nourishment, defense, and communication. It is noteworthy that the word "club"—an association of people with a common purpose—is also defined as a weapon for defense, offense, and hunting. For millennia, people have joined guilds, clubs, and other groups, for work, leisure, self-interest, and enjoyment. For many, these gatherings were a place to find like-minded peers, where collectors could exercise power and control or merely trumpet their own achievements. It follows that when book collecting became widespread, people banded into clubs.

By the last quarter of the nineteenth century, there were many more potential collectors. A growing and educated middle class came to appreciate and enjoy reading books. Of these people, some began collecting rare, beautiful, and important volumes, sometimes with significant associations, rare autographs, and interesting inscriptions. The commercial book trade began to grow accordingly. Book dealers set standards of value and taste for an increasing number of collectors.

Collecting was an adventuresome quest during the 1800s. In the nineteenth century, antiquarianism, accumulating memorabilia, and especially seeking the unusual became more common and easier than ever before. The then new technique of photography and safer and speedier travel made the entire world more visible and accessible. Increasing numbers of collectors gathered ever more books, both rare and popular. In this country, book collectors' clubs were first established in the 1880s. The oldest is New York's Grolier Club, (1884), which was followed by clubs in Boston (1886), Cleveland (1892), Philadelphia (1893), and Chicago (1895). Today, the social and cultural milieu for bibliocentric clubs continues to flourish. By extension, FABS, as a networking association of geographically scattered book clubs, is essential as the book-collecting trend continues.

II

What about the Fellowship of American Bibliophilic Societies? What can a loose and informal association of book clubs do that each cannot do for themselves? To answer these questions, an outline of our objectives and how they have been achieved must be presented.

Although each book club in the FABS confederation is unique, all member organizations possess similar basic purposes and methods. All celebrate the book in its various manifestations and capacities to please the mind of man. Discussions, lectures, exhibits, and publications express club members' appreciation for their shared passion. Large or small, member clubs can learn from each other. Each club has an identity, history, and organization all its own. FABS has no direct influence on each club's composition, rules, or activities. Any bibliophilic club can seek to affiliate. FABS gives members of book-collecting clubs an opportunity to meet with each other and exchange ideas. Annual trips and a bi-annual newsletter have fostered gratifying and vibrant comradeship among bibliophiles for over a decade now. A positive outcome of these activities is that some people seek membership in other clubs. Grolier, Caxton, Rowfant, Book Club of California, and others have gained new nonresident members. Many of the founders and organizers of FABS belong to several clubs and find it very gratifying.

A primary objective of FABS is to share information. This might entail using other clubs' programs, exhibits, publications, funding, and administration as a model for themselves. However, ideas are often reciprocal. Clubs may find out about outstanding speakers from other clubs, or clubs might learn how best to arrange

Introduction

travel projects from those who have already gone through the process. Some clubs, following the lead of The Zamorano Club and The Book Club of California arrange annual meetings in each other's cities.

FABS is also instrumental in promoting individual club newsletters. Clubs exchange newsletters so that each can learn and observe the various styles, ideas, and compositions of other newsletters. Robert Cotner, who for many years produced a superb monthly newsletter for The Caxton Club, wrote a very lucid and helpful article about the role of club newsletters in an early FABS newsletter. The FABS newsletter has been printed since 1995. The original issue was a two-sided page edited by Eliot Stanley, from The Baxter Society, and Larry Siegler, a member of The Rowfant Club. Scott Vile, a prominent designer from The Baxter Society produced an enlarged and elegant newsletter for several years. We now produce a glorious thirty-two-page bi-annual issue edited, managed, and published by The Bixby Club's Kay Kramer.

The FABS newsletter contains articles of mutual interest to collectors and their clubs. Since the demise of *Biblio* magazine and *AB Bookman's Weekly*, there are far fewer publications directed to bibliophiles. The FABS newsletter's circulation is over 6,000. The newsletter is shipped in bulk to each club. The club then distributes the paper to its members. In this way, the names of each club's members are kept confidential. Advertising revenue is good enough to support the paper. Clubs are not charged for the newsletters.

Articles submitted by various collectors and book arts practitioners are exceptionally interesting, pertinent, and useful. Each club submits information on their activities, publications, and exhibitions. Sometimes members of FABS clubs who find themselves in a club's city might attend some of their events. Club publications are announced in the newsletter and offered for sale. There is no charge for a club to list its publications for sale.

For several years beginning in 1995, The Grolier Club, The Caxton Club, The Book Club of California, and The Roxburghe Club organized receptions in conjunction with major Antiquarian

Booksellers' Association of America (ABAA) book fairs in their cities. In recent years, FABS club members have gathered informally at the local club where a bookfair is held.

Another major objective of FABS is to organize yearly trips to cities where there are bibliophilic clubs. Here it is possible to meet other FABS members and enjoy with them bibliocentric sites in these cities. The local host club and their FABS representatives organize these trips, which are held from Thursday to Sunday, generally in the late spring. So far, there have been seven successful and overbooked annual trips. The leaders and organizers of each of these trips kept costs low and consistently provided extraordinary experiences for the travelers. The FABS trips provide a grand opportunity to meet and enjoy the company of members of other clubs. Among these local club members and travelers are collectors, dealers, librarians, authors, publishers, designers, restorers, curators, and involved book-lovers. There is always much to share among the participants.

The first annual trip was in Philadelphia and Delaware in May 1998 and was put together by Rowfant's Robert H. Jackson, Jack McClatchey, and Robert Targett, Bruce McKittrick and Gordon Pfeiffer acted as local club hosts and guides. The next year, we gathered in Detroit with Sam Gatteño as our local organizer. In 2000, we were in San Francisco with Jerry Cole, Larry Siegler facilitated Cleveland in 2001. The 2002 Chicago trip was led by Hayward Blake. The Los Angeles and Pasadena trip in 2003 had John Carson in charge, and Paul Romaine led the New York City trip in 2004. In 2005, we visited St. Louis, with John Hoover, in 2006 Seattle with Martin Greene, and Washington, D.C., with Leslie Overstreet, in 2007.

A typical trip includes an opening evening reception for those who arrive on Wednesday evening before the FABS gathering. On Thursday, we see local private and public rare book collections. Curators, librarians, and private collectors show and discuss the highpoints of their collections. Visiting these collections is an experience the travelers eagerly anticipate. Local booksellers and/or the ABAA often host receptions and dinners on Thursday. On

Introduction

Friday, we continue to visit additional bookish sites. Access to these sites is not usually available to the ordinary traveler. Organizers select places in their hometowns that are most often both extraordinary and unexpected.

During each trip, Robert Jackson has organized a symposium held on Saturday morning, which lasts for three hours with one short break. Experienced collectors, well-known book dealers, and other knowledgeable book people present twenty- to thirty-minute talks. After the talks, there is a question and answer session. The symposia are stimulating and informative events. Fortunately, some of the best of these talks are preserved in this volume.

On the final evening, the travelers attend a dinner organized by the host club. There are additional events on Sunday for those who choose to stay on. The host clubs are happy and proud to show their local bibliophilic gems and the travelers are delighted with these rare experiences, otherwise not accessible. Not the least pleasure is the warm and cordial friendships that are formed during these trips.

In 1997, Jack McClatchey produced a comprehensive and periodically updated directory of FABS clubs. It contains each club's officers, number of members, founding date, and contact information for FABS representatives. George Singer, who succeeded McClatchey, has continued to update the directory.

FABS is a nonprofit entity, ruled exempt from federal income tax under section 501(c)(6). No salaries are paid to officers of FABS. Annual dues are approximately $1.00 per member for clubs with between 100 and 500 members. For smaller clubs the cost per member is slightly more. For example, for a club with 50 members the cost per member would be $2.00. For clubs of over 500 members, the cost per member declines because our maximum dues are $500. There has never been any assessment or special charge to the clubs. For several years, FABS has made contributions from surplus funds to various nonprofit libraries and some Library of Congress projects.

III

I had the honor of being elected president of Cleveland's Rowfant Club in 1992. It was the Rowfant centenary. We planned to celebrate our anniversary gloriously and tastefully. To this end, we gave all members a commemorative rosette, we produced a pamphlet meant to inform new members and visitors, a handsome keepsake volume was published containing essays about the club's history, clubhouse, and its members, and we produced a leather keepsake bookmark. We organized a trip to Rowfant Hall in Suffolk, England. Also in 1992, Rowfant presented a commemorative centennial dinner. Representatives from some of the oldest and largest bibliophilic clubs in this country were invited to speak. From New York's Grolier Club came Martin Antonetti, Hayward Blake came from Chicago's Caxton Club, Philadelphia's Philobiblon Club was represented by George Allen, Jeremy (Jerry) Cole came from San Francisco's Book Club of California, and Eliot Stanley represented The Baxter Society of Portland, Maine. Each speaker gave a vivid account of their club's history and current activities.

Meeting and getting to know these prominent bibliophiles made it clear that we had much in common, and more contact between the clubs would be of significant mutual benefit. It was also clear that the camaraderie we enjoyed that evening could be happily replicated with members of other clubs. It also became obvious how similar in purpose we are in spite of our different locations and sizes. For example, only a few of us have clubhouses of our own and some clubs are much smaller than others, but, on balance, we have almost the same problems and objectives and there is much we can learn from each other.

Not wanting to lose the momentum we were gaining, The Rowfant Club created a "liaison committee," of Robert Jackson, John McClatchey, and Larry Siegler. We held discussions with the five book-club leaders who originally spoke to The Rowfant Club in 1992. A meeting was held at The Grolier Club on November 5, 1993. Four of the five speakers at The Rowfant Club attended. Also at the

Introduction

meeting were Paul Birkel and Sandor Burstein of San Francisco's Roxburghe Club, Rodney Dennis and Charles Warner from Boston's Club of Odd Volumes, and McClatchey, Jackson, and Siegler from Rowfant. We appointed pro-tem officers and committees. We discussed the mission of an umbrella association, membership, publications, places for future meetings, and annual trips together. Burstein devised our name and acronym, FABS.

In April 1994, we met again at The Grolier Club. Of those that met at the prior November meeting, were Martin Antonetti, Eliot Stanley, and the three Rowfanters, Jackson, McClatchey, and Siegler. In addition, Arthur Cheslock from The Baltimore Bibliophiles attended as did Bruce McKittrick, a member of the Caxton, Grolier, and Philobiblon clubs. Joanne Sonnichsen represented The Book Club of California and Roxburghe Club; Francis Weber represented the Zamoranos of Pasadena and Los Angeles. Carolyn Smith from the Grolier, John Lannon from The Club of Odd Volumes, and Tom Whitehead from the Philobiblons were also present.

Except for meetings in 1995 in San Francisco and in 1997 at Chicago's Caxton Club, all annual meetings were held at The Grolier Club on the opening afternoon of the annual New York City April ABAA bookfair in that city. Grolier Club presidents, William Warren, William Buice, and Carolyn Smith, and their librarians, Martin Antonetti and Eric Holzenberg, were extremely helpful in providing a location for our meetings at their clubhouse.

FABS elected officers at the 1995 San Francisco meeting. Larry Siegler became Chairman, George Allen First Vice Chair, and Jerry Cole Second Vice Chair. The meeting provided a fine opportunity to meet members from clubs in Sacramento, Los Angeles, and Seattle who attended the reception at The Book Club of California.

At the 1997 meeting in Chicago, Robert Cotner, Karen Skubish, and Mr. and Mrs. Richard Carreño, represented Caxton. Eric Holzenberg came from the Grolier and Bruce McKittrick was there from Philadelphia. Jerry Cole came from San Francisco. Arthur Cheslock from Baltimore and three members of The Book Club of Detroit attended: Sam Gatteño, Annie Brewer, and Lee Kollins.

Articles of Incorporation were prepared by Jack McClatchey and approved. Bob Jackson discussed a trip to Philadelphia and Delaware. Bruce McKittrick was an active participant at the meeting and was appointed Membership Chair.

At the 2004 annual meeting, John Carson from The Zamorano Club and Grolier was elected Chairman. Carson assumed the office earlier when Carole Grossman from Denver's Fine Press Book Association had to resign for health reasons. Grossman had succeeded Baltimore's Arthur Cheslock who was elected Chairman in 1998. Cheslock was appointed Chairman Emeritus in 2004. Also at the 2004 meeting, Robert Jackson became Vice Chair. Reelected officers were George Singer, Secretary and John McClatchey, Treasurer.

Many outstanding book people have aided the efforts of the founders. Those not mentioned elsewhere in this report and who come to mind are: John Crichton, a member of The Roxburghe Club, Grolier, and The Book Club of California; Priscilla Juvelis, member of The Grolier Club and The Ticknor Society; Hal Douthit, from Rowfant; Ron Ravneberg and Geoffrey Smith, from The Aldus Society; Joan Knoertzer, Harriet Larson, and Kay McKay of The Book Club of Detroit; Mary Schlosser, a member of the Grolier; Jim Tomes from Caxton; Lee Harrer from The Florida Bibliophile Society; Marjorie Rosenthal and John Woram, members of The Long Island Book Collectors; and Ray Edinger of The Bibliophiles of Rochester. I hope I will be forgiven for forgetting others who ought to be mentioned.

IV

From the history and progress of FABS, it is clear that the association has a very valid purpose. Our objectives of mutual benefit and enjoyment of rare and unusual books together with like-minded colleagues has been successful. More clubs than we ever expected or

Introduction

even thought existed have joined FABS. There are thirty U.S. and Canadian clubs and three overseas clubs (Berlin, Brussels, and Amsterdam) currently associated with FABS. Our total membership now stands at 6,092. We are proud of our newsletter and our trips have been very successful. We are able to support bibliocentric projects and hope to do more.

FABS has made possible events that would not have otherwise happened. Many members of various clubs might not have met were it not for FABS. There would be far less communication dealing with the book world except for FABS. Similarly, the pleasure and excitement of traveling to many bibliophilic sites would not have occurred. Certainly, the opportunity for so many prominent and serious collectors and expert book dealers to meet each other is increased by the existence of FABS.

BOOKS

The Past, Present, and Future of the Book

Jason Epstein

Anyone interested in the history of the book will welcome *The Gutenberg Revolution* by British author John Man, a brief, readable, and sophisticated account of the machine that opened the gates to the modern world. Man shows that the components of Gutenberg's revolutionary technology had long been at hand—"punch-making, casting, metallurgical skills, wine and oil-pressing, paper making," and, of course, the alphabet.* Gutenberg's genius was in seeing how to combine and exploit these components, but he was mistaken about how this new technology would affect his world, to say nothing of the world to come. The market Gutenberg had in mind for his invention was the Catholic Church, which was split at the time by countless schisms, large and small. Gutenberg hoped that a widely disseminated standard missal, produced inexpensively on his press, would repair religious division and make his fortune. The exact opposite occurred. By secularizing the written word, Gutenberg's technology shattered the Church beyond repair and made possible the humanistic, skeptical, scientific culture that formed today's world.

* John Man, *The Gutenberg Revolution: The Story of a Genius and an Invention that Changed the World* (London: Review, 2002), 122.

China also possessed many of the technologies that Gutenberg exploited, but lacked two components, rendering the others useless. Because the Chinese pressed neither grapes nor olives, they had no mechanism with which to imprint wood-block images on paper; more important, they lacked a short, phonetic alphabet from which a nearly infinite variety of words could be assembled. A further hindrance was the conservative Chinese bureaucracy, which feared the disruptive impact of widespread literacy. Although a Korean contemporary of Gutenberg invented a simplified phonetic system, centuries would pass before China's syllabic ideographs were adapted to the press.

Today the components of a second and even more consequential revolution are at hand, components that did not exist as recently as fifteen years ago. Gutenberg himself could not have foreseen in the fifteenth century the cultural consequences of his invention; it is similarly impossible to anticipate in detail the eventual effect of today's even more efficient technologies. Powerful new methods for the production, storage, and distribution of books are likely to alter our contemporary world as profoundly as the printing press changed Gutenberg's. Three things embody the technological revolution: first, the Internet, which permits unmediated transactions at any distance; second, digitization, which allows electronic storage and transmission of texts in all languages and phonetic systems at practically no unit cost; and, finally, secure network software, which finds and transmits selected electronic files on demand to fully integrated, automatic machines now in prototype. The latter creates, in effect, an "ATM" for books, reproducing a file locally within minutes as a library quality paperback identical to the factory-made version but sold at perhaps half the price, since the major costs—inventory expense, physical delivery, traditional marketing, and retail markup—are bypassed. Imagine a worldwide, multilingual Amazon.com without physical inventory or warehouse and delivery expenses, but with (at least in theory) nearly instantaneous access to every book ever written. Moreover, since physical inventory will no longer be a factor, this multitude of titles can be offered in multiple translations stored at negligible cost, transmitted to machines almost anywhere on Earth, and printed in local languages within minutes of ordering.

Such a system permits not only lower retail prices but larger shares of proceeds to authors since an author's contributed value will be relatively greater than that of a publisher, many of whose traditional functions will be redundant when an author's entire work can be posted for sale permanently in various languages on the World Wide Web. The major consequence of these technologies, however, will be to bring a great variety of books not only to millions of readers in the developed world but to millions more who have thus far lived beyond the effective reach of the Gutenberg system. For better and worse, the resulting stimulus to human ingenuity is beyond imagining.

That these explosive technologies emerged at the present time is fortuitous, if not miraculous, for the trade-book publishing industry in the United States and in varying degrees elsewhere. During the past thirty years or so, the business has become entangled in a structural bind from which there appears to be no escape, resulting primarily from the postwar demographic shift from city to suburb not from managerial inertia or competing media (as might be assumed). In the 1950s, the retail market for books consisted of three to four thousand independent retailers (the exact figure depends upon one's definition of a bookstore) located in cities and their major suburbs. Unlike today's packaged subdivisions, which are served by shopping malls with national chains and branded merchandise, suburbs then were culturally distinct settlements much like cities themselves with local economies and central business districts. Suburban independent booksellers occupied inexpensive premises and traded high retail margins for more intangible rewards, such as maintaining large backlist inventories that reflected an owner's personal interests and those of his or her community. These complex, generally slow-moving inventories were costly to maintain. They called for devoted and sophisticated managers for whom books were not mere inventory units but the evolving record of civilization without which we would have no idea who we were, where we came from, and where we might be headed. Independent booksellers in the postwar decades were integral parts of a cosmopolitan literary culture.

By the 1970s, this regionally diverse, increasingly broad, and sophisticated retail marketplace had given way to a few mall-based chains whose thousands of outlets were paying the same rents and were thus governed by the same turnover requirements as the shoe store next door. These centrally managed stores had no choice but to limit their inventories largely to highly promotable, usually ephemeral titles, while the extensive backlists that had traditionally sustained the book-publishing industry were relegated to the dwindling number of surviving independents of which barely fifty carrying one hundred thousand or more titles exist in the United States today. The effect of this tectonic shift was to turn the publishing business upside down. Publishers had traditionally nurtured their backlists much as conservative families husband capital; now, in order to claim their share of costly shelf space in the suburban malls, publishers often found themselves bidding recklessly for the rights to potential best-sellers, regardless of their long-term prospects.

Within this upheaval, agents representing best-selling authors became the key players, while publishers, in order to attract such properties, practiced a kind of triage, letting their potential backlist titles fend more or less for themselves while their marketing departments concentrated each season on a handful of potential "blockbusters" (aptly named after the highly destructive aerial bombs used to smash entire cities in World War II). In effect, publishers became the hired servants of best-selling authors and their agents; however, in this case, the servant guaranteed payment to the master as a condition of servitude, an untenable situation. To stay in place, publishers found themselves running ever faster as backlist sales dwindled and firms that once relied on this predictable income for long-term stability now had to recreate themselves with each new list. The weaker ones dropped out. The survivors joined forces through merger and acquisition resulting in today's awkward conglomerates:

unstable masses of marginally profitable units within a mature, perhaps declining, industry that is caught between ever more powerful agents and the demands for still more discounts from the margin-starved retail chains. To add more fuel to the fire, the customer base for any bookseller is stagnating as readers turn for entertainment to other media.

From this reconfiguration, two distinct and incompatible publishing models have emerged: the dominant, if unstable, method, which supplies the chains' turnover needs; and, surviving interstitially within this model, remnants of the traditional industry living by the marketing rules and at the sufferance of their dominant partner.

By the mid-1980s, mall stores, now in the thousands, had all but exhausted the possibility of further expansion. Facing a future of slow growth, predictable losses, and lower share prices, management sought a new retail format and came up with the so-called superstore. These larger, often freestanding, stores have faced the inexorable trade-off between rent and inventory and, as a result, have not fulfilled their initial promise. Though a few in major cities are well stocked, most are simply larger versions of the earlier mall stores, offering stacks of discounted best-sellers, high-markup remainders, and promotional titles published by the chains themselves. Meanwhile, powerful general retailers, such as Wal-Mart and Price Costco, have entered the market in force, adding to the pressure on publishers.

This is not to say that books of permanent value are no longer being published. They are—as much as ever. With few exceptions, however, there is little publishers can do to promote and sell them. According to Calvin Trillin, their shelf life now falls somewhere between that of milk and yogurt. That occasionally some of these books sell well suggests the determination of readers to discover books of substance and originality despite the rigidities of the market place.

By bypassing the existing supply chain, new technologies—the Internet, digitization, and secure networks—will replace or at least partially repair this broken system, but not without introducing their own distortions. On the one hand, because new technologies enable anyone to be a publisher, the traditional mechanisms that have separated what is publishable from what is not will no longer function. On the other hand, the filters that distinguish readable from unreadable books or what is of permanent value from what is of merely transient interest are functions of human nature and will continue to operate as such. For unknowable and uncontrollable reasons, readers will continue to value the lists of certain publishers over others. As traditional publishing operations become redundant, the web-based publishing companies of the future will consist of a few culturally compatible editors with their own lists of authors, publicists, and website managers. Since essential infrastructure will be minimal, the price of entry will be low. Because operating costs will also be low, the profitability of well-chosen lists should be relatively higher than that of today's industry with its complex operations and large, fixed overheads. Conceivably, literary agents and their stables of loyal clients will eventually bypass publishers and self-publish on the web, foregoing the traditional publisher's guarantee in exchange for a much larger share of the proceeds. Although predictions are chancy, it is reasonable to assume that all authors will eventually have their own websites (as many already do), where their works will be permanently on sale worldwide and in many languages. Moreover, publishers or agents will also link authors' work on websites of related interest, meaning that over time a writer's work may be available permanently on hundreds or even thousands of Internet sites. In this manner, authors will "own" their World Wide Web–based readership, a far more efficient system than the present one in which books are placed haphazardly on sale for weeks or months and then, unless they achieve classic status, eventually disappear, as did some 60,000 titles in the United States last year.

    I have attempted here to imagine the electronic future within a very narrow range of possible outcomes. What the actual future holds is anyone's guess, though the disappointing results of e-book ventures so far suggest that few readers will choose to read books on-screen. Reading is a tactile as well as a visual and intellectual experience: given its low cost, convenience, and long familiarity, the traditional book form seems likely to survive its virtual challengers. Reference materials, which are out of date on the day they are published, however, will probably be sold on-line by subscription, as is the *Oxford English Dictionary*, for example, among a growing number of other standard references.

The new technologies I discuss here exist in workable form today and could be fully deployed tomorrow, but, unlike Gutenberg's invention, which threatened only a handful of monastic scribes and promised to further the interests of powerful elements within the Church, today's technologies imply the redundancy of a pivotal, if faltering, industry whose managers are understandably reluctant to welcome a radical alternative to the destructive system to which they are bound. New technologies, however, can exploit markets beyond the reach of today's Gutenberg system where institutional resistance is not a factor: for example, the potentially vast, underserved market in the developing world where various non-governmental organizations (NGOs) including UNICEF, the World Bank, and the World Health Organization now distribute millions of books at an average delivery cost per unit of $11.50. By placing book machines strategically in China, India, Central Asia, Russia, and Africa, for example, NGOs as well as commercial publishers may largely eliminate expenses and greatly extend their present reach. Eventually, readers in the most remote settlements might enjoy low cost access to vast virtual libraries in their native languages—libraries comparable to those that readers in New York, Paris, and Beijing currently enjoy. As Gutenberg showed, literacy spreads rapidly once the means become available. A further market largely inaccessible to today's Gutenberg technology consists of foreign-language communities living abroad—the great Hispanic, Hindi, Mandarin, and similar diasporas throughout the world whose members have scant access to books in their own tongues. Here, too, there are no institutional barriers to the distribution via these technologies of books in these and other languages to millions of potential readers.

By serving these and similarly underserved markets, the new technologies will demonstrate their utility and, like Gutenberg's invention, perhaps become the norm. Gutenberg's invention brought literacy to the darkest corners of fifteenth-century Europe and beyond. Before the century was over, presses were at work from Budapest and Cracow to London and Oxford, from Saõ Tome to Stockholm. As the Gutenberg era approaches its limits, today's new technologies will perform a comparable service for a worldwide marketplace. Given the use to which human beings have put all previous technologies, these developments should be welcomed with the now familiar two cheers.

"Only Copy Known": Random Reflections on Rarity

Bruce Whiteman

"Just what exactly *is* a rare book?" is a question casual visitors to book fairs or to rare book libraries often pose to booksellers and librarians. The waggish answer—a rare book is a book I want to buy, for stock or for my collection, but cannot find—is tempting but not really satisfactory. A bookseller friend of mine likes to say that he specializes in medium-rare books, although in fact the English word "rare," as applied to books and to filet mignon, actually represents two homophonous words with distinct etymologies. "Rare" as applied to cooking comes from an Anglo-Saxon word meaning uncooked or partially cooked, and was originally used only of eggs, not of meat. Through its Indo-European root it is related to the word "idiosyncrasy," a trait exhibited, of course, by many book collectors. "Rare" as applied to books has a different Indo-European root, and in a variant form is allied to the word "hermit," which some bibliophiles certainly are. ("Hermit" is in turn from a Greek word meaning desolate or empty, a feeling shared by many collectors when

---

An earlier version of this paper was given as the 2002 John Seltzer and Mark Seltzer Memorial Lecture at the Thomas Fisher Rare Book Library, University of Toronto. I am grateful to Richard Landon for inviting me to give this lecture.

the rare book they coveted is discovered already to have already been sold before their e-mail was sent or their phone call placed.) "Rarus" in Latin has the basic sense of thin, scanty, far apart, or infrequent, and my Latin dictionary also cites the rather uncommon verb "raresco," which apparently means either "to grow thin" or "to spread out." Bibliophily being the expensive and sedentary activity it is, these do seem like possible physiological destinies for the dedicated rare book collector. The *Oxford English Dictionary*, by the way, rather lamely can only cite an 1862 use of "rare book" (in Burton's *Book-Hunter*) as the earliest recorded, though, of course, there are many at a much earlier date in more obscure places.

In a certain quarter of the book business, rarity is not what it used to be. "Rarity," Nicholson Baker has said in a context that has nothing to do with books, "is an emotion as much as it is a statistical truth."[1] How often did one used to hear—as an emotional avowal rather than as a strictly statistical fact—that a bookseller had only seen two copies of X in twenty-five years, or had not handled a copy of Y since 1970, or had never seen Z in thirty-five years in the trade. This aspect of the book business has a cruder name, but more genteelly one might label it the empirical theorem—I, who am a dealer in a single city in a certain country during a particular period of time, can extrapolate my own experience to a universal truth. What has altered all of this, of course, is the Internet. Many booksellers who thought that certain books, which were rare because they seldom if ever showed up over twenty or thirty or forty years, now know to their grief that the Net lists multiple copies at quite various prices. It may be, of course, that a particular book, once thought rare, and now for sale by a dozen or more booksellers all across the continent, will relapse into genuine scarcity after those copies are absorbed, following the same pre-Internet principle, universally acknowledged by experienced bibliophiles, that genuinely rare books sometimes appear on the market in multiple copies in close temporal proximity.

1. Nicholson Baker, "Rarity," in *The Size of Thoughts: Essays and Other Lumber* (New York: Vintage Books, 1997), 19.

"Only Copy Known": Random Reflections on Rarity

Or, it may be that John Carter's principle of "localised rarity" no longer obtains in a market that has no remaining local aspect.[2] If ever there were copies of, say, the Canadian poet Irving Layton's rare first book, *Here and Now* (1945) that might have made their way to Mexico or France or South Africa, the chances of their subsequently finding their way onto the market are now increased exponentially, and the traditionally invoked rarity of that book might well have to be altered. Many collectors, I am sure, will remember a catalogue devoted to Henry Fielding issued by Ximenes Rare Books in the fall of 1991. It is the earliest bookseller's catalogue I can recall in which the availability of the *English Short Title Catalogue* (ESTC), published the year before, made an extraordinary difference to the number of recorded copies that were cited. In the pre-ESTC days a dealer might have said of a Fielding item that the *National Union Catalog* (NUC) recorded four copies, in addition to, let us say, the British Museum copy, the Rothschild copy, and the copies known to the bookseller to be at Toronto or the Beinecke Library, or in a private collection in Los Angeles.[3] With the ESTC, all of a sudden, the total number of seven or eight recorded copies swelled to twenty or thirty or forty, as copies in rural England and the Midwest and Göttingen and other locations turned up. What was rare before the ESTC went live was not necessarily so afterward. That worked both ways, however, as certain books one could not imagine being rare turned out, surprisingly, to be so. Charlotte Cowley's *Ladies History of England* (1780) is a good example. This is an imposing late-eighteenth-century illustrated folio that ought, instinctually, one thinks, to be everywhere. But the ESTC proves otherwise: it records only six copies in England and two—one at Kent State and one at Toronto—in North America. (A ninth, unrecorded copy, previously at the public library in Oakland, California, is now at the Clark Library.)

2. John Carter and Nicolas Barker, *ABC for Book-Collectors* (New Castle and London: Oak Knoll Press and the British Library, 2004), 182.

3. Ximenes Rare Books, Inc., *Occasional List No. 92* (New York: Ximenes Rare Books, Ltd., 1991).

We do not like to admit it, but rarity is to some extent a relative term and it can be twisted when the point is to turn something common and unattractive into something desirable. I have never forgotten the description of a copy of Edward FitzGerald's *Euphranor* (1851), a little platonic dialogue of eighty-four pages, which appeared in a Quaritch catalogue a dozen or so years ago. *Euphranor* is not a scarce book. When FitzGerald died in 1883, Quaritch purchased a batch of unsold copies, with the result that the book is found more often than not in perfect condition. The Quaritch copy, however, was "somewhat stained and faded, spine worn ... [and with an] owner's inscription." In other words, it was a ratty copy. But nothing daunted Quaritch, however, described the copy in this condition as "rare," precisely because it bore "evidence of contemporary readership"! Clever bookselling and outright gall often go hand in hand, but this is an especially impressive example.

I was recently moved to try to think more doggedly about rarity when I came across a passage in a book I was reviewing that commented on *Pauline*, Robert Browning's first book. The author called it "very rare" and then estimated that "only about a dozen copies of the original exist." Anyone engaged daily in the business of buying or selling old books sees this statement, or versions of it, all the time, and nothing about this particular example should have been striking. But, even I, as someone who has no specialized knowledge of Browning bibliography, realized that I could think of several copies of *Pauline* without even trying. My own library had one—and Mr. Clark did not specialize in the Victorians; there was certainly one in the Ashley Library at the British Library; there must surely be one at Texas among the Wrenn books, etc. And so I wondered how accurate that statement about *Pauline* really was.[4] I was wrong, incidentally, about the Wrenn library, although I was right about Texas.

4. The review was of Joseph Rosenblum's *Practice to Deceive: The Amazing Stories of Literary Forgery's Most Notorious Practitioners* (2000), and it was published in the *Papers of the Bibliographical Society of Canada* 39, no. 1 (Spring 2000): 109-11. To prove once again how error can be added to error where copies of rare books are concerned, I there stated that McGill also owned a copy of *Pauline*. This is not so. McGill owns only a copy of the 1886 Wise facsimile reprint.

"Only Copy Known": Random Reflections on Rarity

Thomas James Wise tried hard to secure a copy of *Pauline* for John Henry Wrenn, but he never managed it; and when Wrenn died in 1911, his library did not include the book. But a copy he had missed at Sotheby's was bought by Maggs Bros. Ltd. for £325 in June of 1904 and resold to the Chicago collector, John A. Spoor. Spoor's books were not sold until twelve years after his death, and at the sale, in spring 1939, Texas acquired *Pauline* for $3,900—a bargain, given the fact that the Jerome Kern copy had fetched $16,000 ten years earlier.

So how rare, exactly, is *Pauline*? In his Browning bibliography, issued in 1929, Wise called the book "one of the scarcest volumes in the list of modern poetical rarities."[5] As early as 1894, in his guide to collecting modern authors, J. H. Slater had stated that there were eight known copies.[6] In 1921, Seymour de Ricci detailed eighteen copies in his guide to collecting.[7] Fannie Ratchford, writing about the Texas copy in 1943, unaware perhaps of De Ricci's census, prefigured the book I began all of this with and stated that "approximately a dozen [copies] are recorded as extant."[8] The most recent census, published in 1984,[9] lists twenty-three copies, of which one, stolen in 1940, has not yet resurfaced. Not in that census are a copy at the University of South Carolina, which belonged to F. J. Furnivall, and a copy that may or may not be at Case Western Reserve University Library. That makes possibly twenty-four or twenty-five

---

5. Thomas James Wise, *A Browning Library: A Catalogue of Printed Books, Manuscripts, and Autograph Letters by Robert Browning and Elizabeth Barrett Browning* (London: Printed For Private Circulation Only, 1929), 4.

6. J. H. Slater, *Early Editions: A Bibliographical Survey of the Works of Some Popular Modern Authors* (London: Kegan Paul, Trench, Trübner, 1894), 46.

7. Seymour de Ricci, *The Book Collector's Guide: A Practical Handbook of British and American Bibliography* (Philadelphia and New York: The Rosenbach Company, 1921), 77.

8. Fannie Ratchford, "Browning's Pauline Comes to Texas," *Southwest Review* 28, no. 3 (Spring 1943): 282.

9. Philip Kelley and Betty A. Coley, *The Browning Collections: A Reconstruction with Other Memorabilia* (Winfield, KS.: Wedgestone Press, 1984), 215-18.

recorded copies, all but one of which are in institutional collections. The one privately owned copy, listed in the 1984 census as belonging then to H. Bradley Martin, is now in a private collection in North Dakota. It fetched $70,000 (to a bookseller) at the Martin sale in 1990. It is worth mentioning that even the wonders of online bibliographic databases and the Web do not necessarily make it easier to locate copies of rare books and to be precise about numbers. If you search *Pauline* in the Online Computer Library Center (OCLC) database, for example, you will find fifteen libraries reporting copies, including several not listed in the 1984 census. However, if you take the next step and check the various institutional online catalogues, you will find that at least three of these copies are surrogates—two photocopies and one microfiche—despite their being listed as books. One copy, recorded as being at the New Haven Free Public Library, is apparently listed in error.

So *Pauline*, like many books thought to be rare, really is not. A book that exists in more than two dozen copies cannot be considered rare in the strict sense, though "rare on the market" and expensive it obviously is. Many so-called rare books fall into this category, and many, clearly much less rare than *Pauline* and even more expensive, are really rather common.

Let me take an earlier book as a further example. Newton's *Principia*, published in 1687 and universally regarded as one of the most important scientific works ever written, is a stout quarto that, in its day, would have had a small audience. All the same, something over two hundred copies have survived, over sixty of which are in North American libraries. In the 1940s, John Carter commented on how the *Principia*, which had long been considered a "fairly common" book, now seemed to have become "scarcer."[10] A. N. L. Munby, in his essay on the distribution of the *Principia*, said in October 1952, it "can never be described as a *rare* book."[11] However valid these

10. John Carter, *Taste and Technique in Book-Collecting: A Study of Recent Developments in Great Britain and the United States* (New York: R. R. Bowker, 1948), 143.

11. A. N. L. Munby, "The Distribution of the First Edition of Newton's *Principia*," in *Essays and Papers*, ed. Nicolas Barker (London: The Scolar Press, 1977), 53.

impressions were then, the *Principia* today seems to have become common on the market again. In the fall of 2002, there were two copies for sale by booksellers in Los Angeles alone, not to mention others available in the English trade. One can quibble about these copies—from which issue do they come (there were two, and one is decidedly less common)? what condition are they in? and so on— and some of this sort of quibbling partially accounts for the variations in price that the copies now on the market exhibit, from a low of $175,000 to a high of over $310,000. A bookseller of my acquaintance believes that the day is not far off when a *Principia* will fetch half a million dollars. But, in any case, a book that you can buy in any month of the year, if you have the money, is not a rare book.

Of course, both collectors and booksellers have long played fast and loose with the word "rare," each for slightly different reasons. As early as the eighteenth century, a number of guides to books were published in Europe in which rarity was defined in greater or lesser detail, and many reasons adduced to explain why certain books are rare.[12] Most of the reasons then suggested still apply, as one might guess. An essay by Johann Georg Schelhorn, for example, which fills 115 pages of his book *Amoenitates literariae* (1725, new edition 1730), lists fourteen reasons for the rarity of books, including suppression by the authorities or by the author or publisher, export abroad, small physical size, etc.[13] As the eighteenth century progressed and collecting became less a scholar's and more a connoisseur's pursuit, *vade mecums* came to be more prevalent and the relationship between rarity and financial value was emphasized more. With that relationship solidly established, the language of description in auction, bookseller, and library catalogues became more fixed around the notions of rarity and uniqueness. This was so much the case that the bibliographer, Thomas Frognall Dibdin, whose own use of language is definitely not known for control or subtlety, warned the "sober and

12. M. S. Batts, "The 18th-Century Concept of the Rare Book," *The Book Collector* 24, no. 3 (Autumn 1975): 381-400.

13. Johann Georg Schelhorn, *Amoenitates literariae*, new and corrected ed. (Frankfort and Leipzig, 1730), II: 321-435.

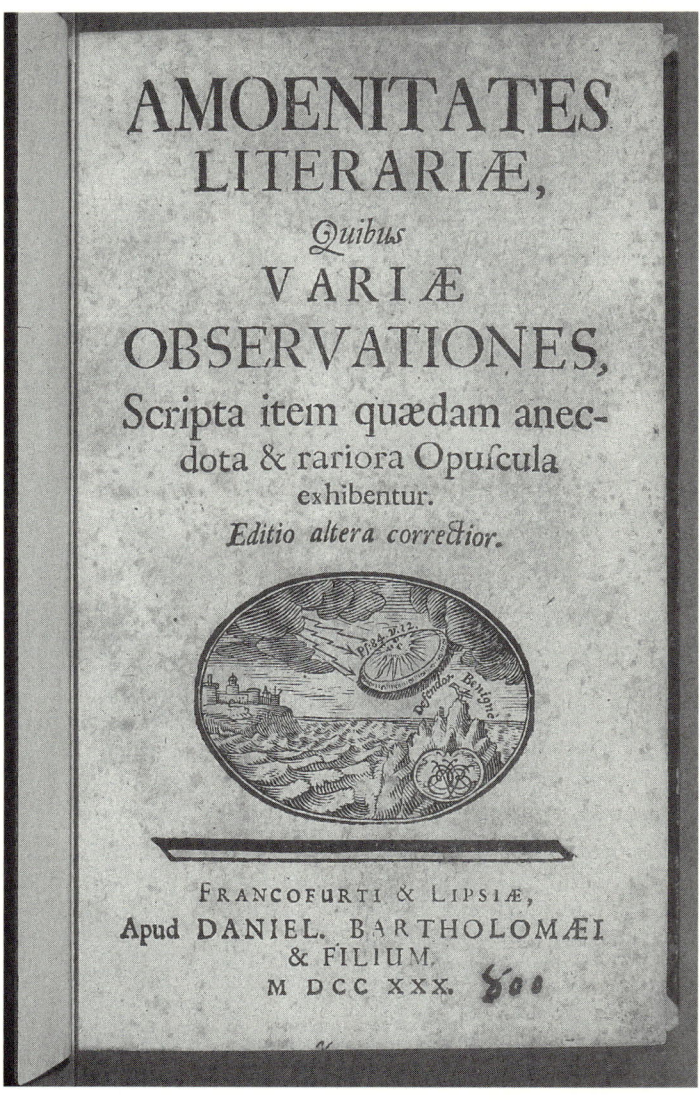

Johann Georg Schelhorn. *Amoenitates literariae*. New ed. Vol. 2. Frankfort and Leipzig: 1730. One of the early European guides to rare books. (Photo courtesy of the William Andrews Clark Memorial Library. UCLA.)

cautious collector" in his *Bibliomania* (1809) "not to be fascinated by the terms '*Matchless, and Unique;*' which ... are studiously introduced into Booksellers' catalogues to lead the unwary astray."[14]

A couple of examples—one a rather obscure auction sale catalogue from the early nineteenth century and one a rather famous private library catalogue from the late nineteenth century—bear out the ways in which words and phrases like "rare," "unique," or "only copy known" came later increasingly to dominate bibliophily. The sale in 1818 of the "library of an eminent collector, removed from the north of England" was typical for the period.[15] It took six days to put the 790 lots under the hammer, and the contents of the collection were largely what one would expect for the time: English poetry, topography, and illustrated books. The owner seems to have been James Midgley, Jr., of Rochdale, northeast of Manchester, although the sale also included books from the *Bibliotheca Anglo-Poetica*, a quite spectacular catalogue issued by Longman's in 1815 that had not at all done well. Midgley owned no Caxtons, indeed no fifteenth-century books at all; but he did have black letter books, and the catalogue singled these out. (The "black letter dogs of the present day," as Dibdin had called them,[16] were still very much a force in the book world.) Midgley had many extra-illustrated sets, and indeed the highest price realized at the sale—£262—was for one of these. Another, an extra-illustrated copy of Byron's *English Bards and Scotch Reviewers* (in 1818, a book that was less than a decade old), fetched

---

14. Thomas Frognall Dibdin, *The Bibliomania; or, Book-Madness* (London, 1809), 65.

15. *Bibliotheca Selecta: A Catalogue of the Library of an Eminent Collector, Removed From the North of England* (London: Robert Saunders, 1818). The Clark Library copy of this catalogue has the name Midgley added in pen on the title-page, and although De Ricci (*English Collectors of Books and Manuscripts, 1530-1930 and Their Marks of Ownership* [Cambridge: Cambridge University Press, 1930], 92) says only that the collector from the North of England, "was said at the time by gossips to be one 'Midgley,' about whom I have no further information, but he doubtless only possessed a portion of the books in the sale," Marc Vaulbert de Chantilly has made the identification with James Midgley, Jr.

16. Dibdin, *Bibliomania*, 56 n. 45.

the amazing price of £18.18.0. But the book in the catalogue one would most like to have a time machine at hand to pursue was Midgley's copy, apparently in an undisturbed seventeenth-century binding, of the Shakespeare First Folio, 1623, which was bought by Payne and Foss, the booksellers, for £121.16.0. (They sold it to Thomas Grenville and it passed from him to the British Museum in 1846—not, unfortunately, before Grenville had had it rebound.) That very substantial price, by the way, can be compared to a copy of the First Folio, which had been in the sale, five years earlier in 1813, of the library of Colonel Stanley, which, if less wonderful, was still respectable, and which had fetched only £37.16.0.[17]

But let us look at the auction house's annotations to the books. Here, we find a variety of phrases, variations of which are repeated any number of times: "so rare that one copy only is known besides the present" (lot 33, Richard Braithwayte's *Times Curtaine Drawne*, 1621, now known in ten copies); "of the most extreme rarity" (lot 415, Samuel Madden's *Memoirs of the Twentieth Century*, 1733, recorded now in fifteen copies); "of such extreme rarity that the present copy is probably unique" (lot 433, Arthur Newman's *Pleasure's Vision*, 1619, now known in six copies); "probably unique" (lot 379, Robert Holland's *Holie Historie of Our Lord and Saviour Jesus Christ*, 1594, now known in three copies); and just "unique" (lot 389, *The Husband, A Poem*, 1614, even today known in only two copies). There are, to be fair, at least two books in the sale which, described as unique, remain so today: the 1530 edition of Chaucer's *Parliament of Foules* (lot 108, today at the Huntington only) and An Collins's *Divine Songs and Meditacions*, 1653 (lot 176, today also only at the Huntington). These examples do not detract from my main point, however, that despite the validity sometimes of the vocabulary of rarity, many books described as rare simply were not.

At the end of the century, the published catalogue of a famous and influential collection provides an interesting example of the con-

---

17. Thomas Hartwell Horne, *An Introduction to the Study of Bibliography* (London: Cadell & Davies, 1814), 674. The First Folio was lot 426 in the Stanley sale.

tinuing use of the booksellers' vocabulary of rarity being assumed by an owner and his librarians and compilers. I am referring to the catalogue of the Rowfant Library, accumulated by Frederick Locker-Lampson and described in a one-volume catalogue in 1886 put together by A. W. Pollard and R. H. Lister, both librarians.[18] Locker-Lampson's approach to collecting was very persuasive to his generation. Instead of building an enormous library like most of his distinguished predecessors, he wanted only a small but choice collection of great English poets from Chaucer to Swinburne. The first section of the catalogue covers the period from 1480–1700 and contains just 529 books, not counting duplicates. Among these are twenty-three that are described as "unique," or "the only copy known," or "almost unique," or, in one case, "of the greatest rarity." Six of these twenty-three books are still, in fact, known only in the single copy that belonged to Locker-Lampson, and they are now in various institutional libraries. More typical are examples like Samuel Daniel's *Delia*, 1592, described in the Rowfant catalogue as "stated to be unique," but recorded now in ten copies,[19] or John Davies's *Microcosmos*, 1603, "according to Dr. Grosart [Alexander Balloch Grosart, 1827–1899, whose sale was at Sotheby, Wilkinson, Hodge on December 11, 1899] [...] almost unique," now recorded in the ESTC in more than ten copies.

Locker-Lampson, by the way, owned a copy of *Pauline*, indeed perhaps the most important copy of all. Browning used it to correct and revise the poem in 1868. He presented it to Locker-Lampson the following year and inscribed it warmly. Dodd, Mead, the booksellers, offered it for sale in a catalogue around 1905 for the amazing price of $2,500. The copy was bought by the poet Amy Lowell, who later gave it to Harvard. To demonstrate how comparative values change, I note that Dodd, Mead offered in the same catalogue Locker-Lampson's copy of Blake's *Songs of Innocence* (1789) for $750.

18. A. W. Pollard and R. H. Lister, *The Rowfant Library. A Catalogue of the Printed Books, Manuscripts, Autograph Letters, Drawings, and Pictures, Collected by Frederick Locker-Lampson* (London: Bernard Quaritch, 1886).

19. Locker-Lampson's copy is now at the Huntington Library (RB 58734).

Book Talk

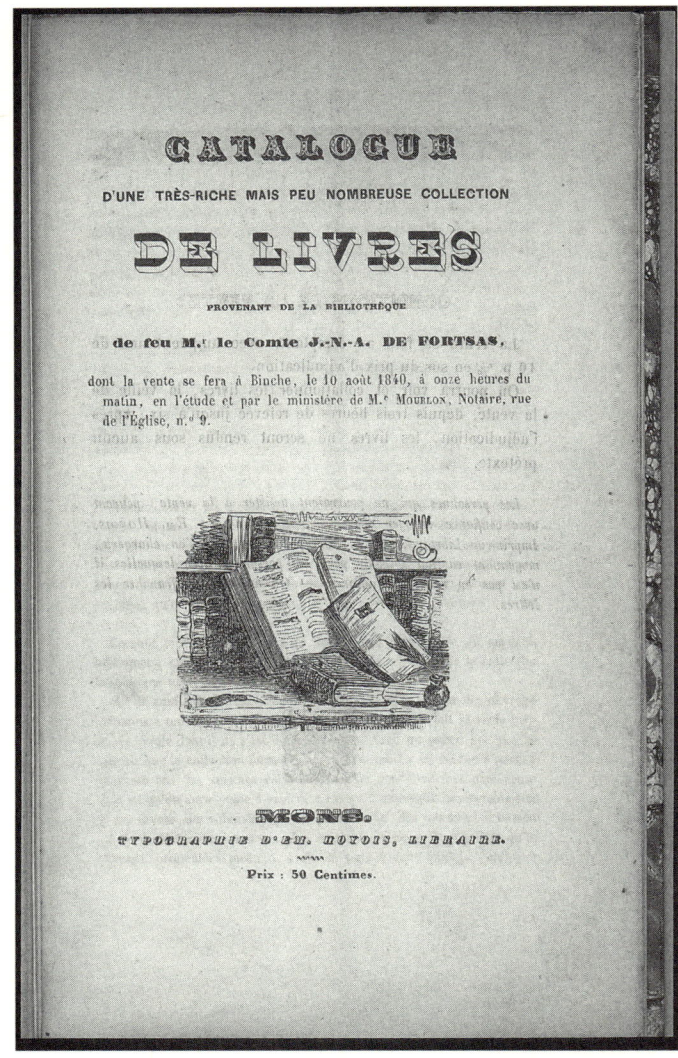

Catalogue d'une très-riche mais peu nombreuse collection de livres provenant de feu M.^r le comte J.N.-A. de Fortsas. Mons: 1840. This is the first edition of the catalogue for the Fortsas sale, a hoax perpetrated by the Brussels bookseller René Chalons.
(Photo courtesy of The Huntington Library, San Marino, California.)

"Only Copy Known": Random Reflections on Rarity

Today the Blake, of course, would bring many times the price of *Pauline*.

At a slightly earlier period, collectors' passion for the rarest of the rare led to the most famous bibliophilic leg-pull of the nineteenth century, the Fortsas hoax. The Brussels bookseller, René Chalons, printed an auction catalogue for the sale of the imaginary Count Fortsas's library, which was to take place in the small Belgian town of Binche on August 10, 1840. The count was said to have collected only books that were unique, discarding even great rarities when he learned of a second copy anywhere. No library so deserved the standard compliment of "small but choice." Chalons not only invented Fortsas, of course, but all the books in his imaginary library, as well, and some of which Chalons annotated amusingly. Lot 43, for example, is an anonymous work entitled *The Wages of Love, or, The Great King Uncomfortable in the Low Countries*, 1686, a duodecimo of 152 pages, illustrated, bound in black morocco, and so on. The annotation reads: "A libel of quite disgusting black humor concerning Louis XIV's fistula. One plate shows the royal behind in the form of a sun encircled with rays, with the famous motto: *nec pluribus impar*."[20] (A free translation of this might be "come one, come all.") A number of well-known bookmen made the trip to Binche for the sale, to the utter confusion of the citizenry who had never heard of Count Fortsas or his books.

Needless to say, despite this elaborate satire on the world of booksellers and collectors, the allure of the unique was in no way driven out by laughter. It was inevitable that a bookseller eventually would produce a catalogue devoted to genuinely unique books, and, in 1902, London dealer Wilfrid Michael Voynich did just that. Voynich was born in 1865 in Poland, and he moved to London in 1890. Millicent Sowerby, who began working for him in 1912, described him vividly in her memoirs, *Rare People and Rare Books*, where she

---

20. *Catalogue d'une très-riche mais peu nombreuse collection de livres provenant de feu M.^r le comte J.-N.-A. de Fortsas* (Mons: Typographie d'Em. Hoyois, Libraire, [1840]), lot 43. The translations are mine.

Wilfrid Michael Voynich. Reproduced from the frontispiece to
E. Millicent Sowerby, *Rare People and Rare Books*
(London: 1967.)

calls him "the greatest international rare book dealer of his time."[21] Voynich sold the British Museum more than 3,800 books during a thirty-year period; so unusual were many of them that the museum gave them a separate "Voynich" shelfmark.[22] His *An Eighth List of Books on Exhibition* contained only "unknown and lost books," although he was admirably circumspect about his claims. "It would be too much to hope," he wrote in the preface to the catalogue that no book in this list has ever been described by any specialist. We particularly wish to guard ourselves from asserting that no other copies exist. At the same time we must confess to believing that if the term could ever be applied to books not printed in one sole copy, most of those in the present catalog could be described as "unique." Voynich also took pains to assure his readers that "We have, of course, not searched works of recognized unreliability, such as sales catalogues and booksellers' lists."[23]

Voynich had warmed up in his *A First List of Books*, in which he cataloged twenty-five "unknown, lost, or undescribed books after 1525" in a separate subsection.[24] In his eighth list, however, there were 158 items, and they were offered first as a collection. Naturally, many of the books are no longer known only in the copy catalogued by Voynich. A 1572 London-printed piece entitled *Progymnasmata*, by fourth-century sophist Aphthonius, is now ESTC 700 and is known in three copies, while a Greek version of the *Catechesis tes Christianikes Pisteos* (London, 1655) is now Wing 1463A and is bountifully recorded in five copies. The first edition of a work on meteors by Thimon Judaeus (dated not after 1480), Voynich said, was "an entirely unknown book."[25] Ten copies are now recorded, including

---

21. E. Millicent Sowerby, *Rare People and Rare Books* (London: Constable, 1967), 8.

22. I am grateful to Nicolas Barker for this information.

23. Wilfrid Michael Voynich, *An Eighth List of Books on Exhibition* (London: 1902), 3.

24. Wilfrid Michael Voynich, *A First List of Books on Exhibition* (London: n.d.)

25. Wilfrid Michael Voynich, *A Second List of Books* (London, 1900), [65].

the British Library's (where Voynich's copy not surprisingly went[26]), bearing out his own skepticism in the preface to Catalogue 2 as to, "the existence of unique books . . . [W]hen one copy of a book has been recorded, other copies tend to appear from time to time; and the use of the word 'unique' appears to me unjustified and misleading."[27]

There is one other figure who needs to be mentioned in the context of emphasizing rarity and uniqueness as the heart and soul of book collecting, and that is Thomas James Wise. *The Ashley Library Catalogue*, the eleven-volume catalogue of his collection that Wise had printed between 1922 and 1936, is something of a monument to the centrality of rarity in the collecting enterprise. In the introduction to each volume, penned successively by Richard Curle, Edmund Gosse, Augustine Birrell, John Drinkwater, E. V. Lucas, and other writer-collectors, rarities in the Wise collection are marveled at. Curle, who was a collector, writer, and friend of Joseph Conrad, as well as of Wise, and who outlived Wise by over thirty years and doubtless therefore lived to regret some of his more innocently fawning compliments in his introduction to Volume 1, cites a score of books from Wise's collection of which he says variously that there is "only one other copy known," "only two or three copies known," or "the only other copy is in the British Museum." Most of these numbers do not stand anymore. Lyly's 1597 *Woman in the Moone*, for example, which Curle claimed to be one of only two or three known copies, is now known in nine; Pope's 1716 *God's Revenge against Punning*, called unique, is now recorded in fifteen copies spread among three editions; and likewise Gay's 1725 *To a Lady on Her Passion for Old China*, which Curle also claimed to be unique is now known in two editions for a total of nine copies.[28] I would emphasize that this

26. *Catalogue of Books Printed in the XVth Century Now in the British Museum*, (London: Trustees of the British Museum, 1908), 7: 977.

27. Voynich, *A Second List of Books*, [65].

28. Thomas James Wise, *The Ashley Library: A Catalogue of Printed Books, Manuscripts and Autograph Letters Collected by Thomas James Wise*, Vol. 1. (London: Printed for Private Circulation, 1922), xi-xii.

sort of numbers game, played by collectors and booksellers ever since the days of Dibdin, remains with us today, though the focus has shifted as collectors have begun to collect books, such as modern first editions, where true rarity or uniqueness is to all intents and purposes nonexistent.

The Clark Library recently acquired an uncommon little pamphlet from 1762, printed in Sweden, by Andreas Wallin, called *Dissertatio academica de bibliomania* (An Academic Thesis on Bibliomania). In it, Wallin says, "*Quot caelum stellas, tot habet Europa libellos*" ("Europe has as many books as there are stars in the sky").[29] Few of those books are unique, despite the fact that many fifteenth-century books, to cite just one group, survive in quite small numbers. Perhaps I can close with an example. The Clark Library has been collecting for some years translations into European languages of British books of the seventeenth and eighteenth centuries. This collection has reached the point where, if you need to read Locke in Swedish or Hume in German, the Clark is the place to do it. I recently acquired a number of editions of Samuel Richardson's novel *Pamela* and so-called Pamelaiana, which included a 1744 translation of the novel into Italian. I bought this book from an English bookseller who bought it at an auction in Rome, where the under bidder was the Biblioteca Nazionale. It is apparently unique. I cannot find it in any database or catalogue, and the only mid-eighteenth-century Italian translation of the book I can find is from a decade later, and that in only one copy too, at Harvard. All the same, it is hard to believe that this is a unique survivor. The publisher is a known one, the novel was famous almost instantly in England and in Europe, and the translator says in the preface that the translation was made, "with the consent of the author, who kindly passed on to me some additions and corrections."[30] Even if the edition was small, other copies must be "out there" that have simply escaped the usual

---

29. Andreas J. Wallin, *Dissertatio academica, de bibliomania, quam, venia incliti collegii philosophici, ad regium upsaliense lyceum* [etc.] (Uppsala: s.n., 1762), 11.

30. Samuel Richardson, *Pamela, ovvero la virtu' premiata* (Venice: Giuseppe Bettinelli, 1744), *4v: "Altro più non mi ramane a dire, se non che questa

databases and catalogues. The fact that the Catholic Church listed it on its Index of Prohibited Books makes it more, not less, likely that copies were read and kept. For the moment, the book is certainly rare, but unique? I doubt it very much.[31]

Traduzione è fatta col consenso dell'Autore ch'ebbe la bontà di somministrarmi alcune poche aggiunte e correzioni." I am grateful to Stefania Tutino for reading and translating the preface for me.

31. Since delivering this paper, and in apparent fulfillment of my prophecy, a copy of the Italian *Pamela*, complete in four volumes, turned up in the Bayerische Staatsbibliothek in Munich, Germany. I am grateful to the bookseller Peter Young for telling me of this copy.

Books That Everyone Has Forgotten: Some Preliminary Notes on Low Spots in Literature

Garrett Scott

I GOT MY START as a bookseller working for John Crichton at the Brick Row Book Shop in San Francisco. Due to a natural inclination toward the obscure (reinforced no doubt by a kind of indoctrination at the hands of an employer who had me cataloguing the likes of Daniel Ricketson and Annie Nelles Dumond[1]), I have found myself an advocate of the sort of book that might best be summed up by a broadside printed in (I believe) an edition of one by Alastair

1. See *Daniel Ricketson and His Friends: Letters, Poems, Sketches, etc.*, ed. Anna Ricketson and Walton Ricketson (Boston: Houghton, Mifflin, 1902) for more on this minor Transcendentalist and friend of Henry David Thoreau. Dumond is perhaps best remembered for her autobiographical account *Annie Nelles; or, The Life of a Book Agent. An Autobiography* (Cincinnati: the author, 1868), though her novels, such as *Christlike: Save the Fallen* (St. Louis: the author, 1896), are also engaging and make for more interesting reading than their rather forbidding titles might indicate. These two examples are chosen nearly at random and stand perhaps as emblematic rather than typical, since during my tenure at Brick Row one could also usually find books from Emerson, Hawthorne, Mark Twain, etc. But it was the willingness to stock books from peripheral figures, or from the once-esteemed whose reputations have since been eclipsed (George Pope Morris springs unbidden to mind), that obviously impressed itself upon my tender sensibilities.

Johnston of the Poltroon Press. Bearing the title "On a Distant Prospect of the Brick Row Book Shop," the sheet takes for its text a remark made by Lord Eccles on a rare visit to the shop: "You see so many books here that everyone has forgotten."[2]

That a book has been forgotten is not necessarily a measure of any intrinsic worth, but for my own rhetorical reasons I want to label neglected minor books as "low spots," in a kind of counterpoint to the high-spot approach to collecting. Much has been written on the nobility of building a collection of rare books, the party-line definition of a rare book generally being something akin to that offered by the Newberry Librarian Stanley Pargellis in a talk in 1954 on "The Rare Book and the Scholar," where he declared that there are "three factors which make a book rare, all of which must by present at any given moment: importance, demand, and scarcity."[3] This is fine as far as it goes, and I will not cavil with the thrills of owning a famous book in its first edition (or the occasional profitability of selling one), nor with the historical importance of many of these rare high-spot titles as laid out in notable catalogues.[4] Historically, however, collecting has benefited from those willing to pursue what has elsewhere been called "new paths" in book collecting; examples that come to mind are Michael Sadleir and Robert Wolff, collectors who revived a neglected field by the scope of their collections in Victorian English fiction,

---

2. Quoted with Mr. Crichton's permission.

3. *Book Collecting and Scholarship* (Minneapolis: University of Minnesota Press, 1954).

4. One could make an argument for *Printing and the Mind of Man: A Descriptive Catalogue Illustrating the Impact of Print on the Evolution of Western Civilization during Five Centuries* (London: Cassell, 1967) as the most elaborate example of both a high spot compendium and the skeletal framework upon which a number of well-heeled collectors have hung their collections. Since setting up shop in 1998, I have not handled a title from *PMM*—an indication perhaps of both the modest scope of my ambition as well as some fundamental personal unease in the face of doctrinaire pronouncements. Thus in the shadow of *PMM*'s cathedral have I erected the modest nonconformist meeting-house that is Garrett Scott, Bookseller.

collections which included the obscure as well as the renowned.[5]

This idea is not new and I am not the first bookseller to attempt to persuade others of the merits of those books most likely to be found on his or her shelves. How might I justify myself in light of the possible charges that I am simply making an attempt to pawn off on collectors otherwise unsaleable titles that deserve to be forgotten? I turn for my first case study to American fiction in that nominally barren period from about 1890 to 1920.

Aside from perhaps the dying strains of local color fiction and the occasional adventuresome foray into naturalism,[6] most people (when they think of this period at all) see it as marking time before the arrival of such later heavyweights as Ernest Hemingway, F. Scott Fitzgerald, and William Faulkner. Over these couple of decades, however—bookended by, say, *The Red Badge of Courage* (1895) and *In Our Time* (1925)—one can find shelves of interesting minor fiction. These novels and stories, even in the plentiful weaker examples of the day, can be read as entertaining cultural artifacts. I might even argue that the lesser works, often prone to idiosyncratic accretion of irrelevant narrative detail rather than deft dramatization, can do more to provide the receptive reader with evidence of period attitudes.

Consider George Horace Lorimer's 1906 novella *The False Gods*.[7]

---

5. Due in large part to their diligence, Sadleir and Wolff lived to see the Victorian three-decker turn highly collectible. With this in mind, both the 1934 collection of essays edited by John Carter, *New Paths in Book Collecting: Essays by Various Hands* (1934; reprint Freeport, NY: Books for Libraries Press, 1967) and the later *Collectible Books, Some New Paths* (New York: R. R Bowker, 1979), edited by Jean Peters, can be read as testimony to how once-innovative tastes become assimilated into the mainstream. To announce oneself, for instance, as a collector of detective fiction no longer carries about it the whiff of rebellion it may once have had.

6. Here I think of Frank Norris's *McTeague, a Story of San Francisco* (New York: Doubleday & McClure, 1899), which is considered by some a high spot of the period and by some less forgiving readers as an example of how far a critical reputation may be advanced in the face of weak contemporary competition.

7. George Horace Lorimer, *The False Gods* (New York: D. Appleton and Co., 1906).

Lorimer dictated a significant segment of commercial taste in literature from his position as editor of the *Saturday Evening Post*, and his story can safely be taken as typical of the period. The plot boasts a yellow journalist who under false pretenses works his way into the confidences of a lovely female Egyptologist whom he suspects of mummifying her husband in a bizarre love triangle plot. Aside from a rococo filigree of criminal detail, you also have in this slim volume discussion of peripheral issues of the time: press sensationalism and ethics, the drawbacks of celebrity, and exotic social threats like Theosophy and educated professional women. In short, a formulaic but entertaining tale that can be unpacked to give us hints about the foundations of modern American popular culture.[8]

With his ready access to the machinery of mainstream publishing, Lorimer represents what one might call the insider strand of low-spot literature. What of those authors of Lorimer's era against whom the doors of commercial publication remained stubbornly barred? Not surprisingly, there exists much in the way of self-published or locally published material from which one might extract sufficient thematic unity to build a satisfactory collection. Especially in the realm of marginal verse, this accretion of irrelevant detail—abhorrent to the judicious literary critic—is in especial evidence. One of my favorite examples of the compulsion to shoehorn the minutiae of daily life into literature is the sole collection of verse from O. A. Martin, *Sparks from a Farmer's Anvil* (Oskaloosa, IA, 1914). Martin explains in a prefatory note that he began to write verse on January 17, 1912 ("when I was in my 56th year") and he collects 200 of his poems on subjects ranging from meditations on fatherhood to his attitudes toward telephone calls. Despite his occasional opacity (which in fairness he explains by noting "I am a farmer with but very

---

8. Other examples of such fiction might include Henry Blake Fuller's *The Cliff Dwellers: A Novel* (New York: Harper's, 1893), a Chicago novel that was likely the first to be set in a skyscraper and which provides an early look a the social intricacies of modern urban life, or Oscar Graeve's *The Keys of the City* (New York: The Century Co., 1916), which traces a childhood in Brooklyn not unlike those later found in Henry Miller's novels (down to the inclusion of an adulterous affair that appears to have no lasting dire effects).

Books That Everyone Has Forgotten

Poet Richard Griffin, taken from the frontispiece of his collection *Bug House Poetry* (New York? 1917), an example of a neglected author who might be deemed collectible for purely aesthetic (as opposed to social or historical) reasons—though Griffin's aesthetic is perhaps something of an acquired taste.

David Mitchell Kinnear, taken from the frontispiece of his collection *Every Day Verses* (Albany 1904). Even a century after publication, Kinnear may very well remain the Hudson Valley's foremost versifier on the sport of curling.

Poet and occasional social critic Henry Johnson, author *Ballads of the Farm and Home* (Elkhart 1902). His poem "Only One Killed' may perhaps be read as an ironic commentary on economic class in America: "Only one among the hundreds,— / He was the only one to die:— / He was nothing but a brakeman,— / Hardly worth a tear or sigh."

little book learning"), he turns the material of daily life into emblematic tokens of larger truths: verses on safety pins, doorknobs, bucksaws, tractors, and the metaphorical implications of hot slop together present his brand of practical agrarian theology.

But this is not to say that homespun truth is necessarily the only ornament to grace the obscure or the forgotten author's work. One late nineteenth-century self-published American poet (whose identity I shall here obscure for reasons which will presently become clear) encompassed in the scope of his poetic work nuanced treatments of such topics as Darwinism, paleontology, Spiritualism, the verses of Walt Whitman, and the possibility that future technology would replace the consumption of food with the periodic inhalation of nutritive gases through flexible tubes. What might appear to the casual reader as an occasional lapse in lucidity or a lurching bit of prosody might best be explained by the lingering effects of the hard fighting seen by the author's regiment during the Civil War. (The author's service is described in some detail in his semifictional autobiography, which presents the diligent reader with a wealth of historical information—despite the rather prominent narrative role given throughout to a garrulous spirit from the astral plane.)

But this author also illustrates a hazard peculiar to the pursuit of the neglected low-spot author. So enthusiastic had I become for his writings that I began a haphazard accumulation of his (not inconsiderable) output with an eye toward offering his work in bulk to a discerning institution. I had made some small steps in this direction when I received a note from a bookseller who had earlier sold me one of this author's works. The bookseller offered a duplicate copy of the original title at a reasonable price and, when pressed, admitted that he had purchased from a descendant of this author all that remained of the author's writings. The bookseller now possessed multiple copies (as many as fifty) of practically every title from the pen of this author.

I related this wrinkle in the market to another colleague who shared my enthusiasm for this marginal poet; he suggested that in an ideal world the output of eccentric minor authors would share the fate of "[*Citizen Kane's*] Rosebud ... pages curling and gilt evaporating in the white heat of some basement inferno, with just enough randomly dispersed copies left behind to fuel a small cult." Rarity (in the sense of absolute scarcity) can be a precarious proposition when dealing with an author whose works remained largely unsold and untouched in his lifetime.

With all of my talk of reclaiming forgotten authors, I do not wish the unwary reader to suspect me of being a ranting leveler who would claim that all books are equally collectible.[9] I have seen

---

9. I am fortunate that my personal (and economic) interest in overlooked or eccentric authors has been in line with the general scholarly drift over the past several decades away from the study of grand political histories to the examination of the lives and ideas of those who had previously found themselves living lives outside the scope of the historian. For a succinct summary of this movement away from political history to social history, see Edmund S. Morgan, "The Other Founders," *New York Review of Books*, September 22, 2005. One excellent specimen of this trend is David Reynolds's study of nineteenth-century American literature in the context of popular culture, *Beneath the American Renaissance: The Subversive Imagination in the Age of Emerson and Melville* (Cambridge: Harvard University Press, 1988).

enough late nineteenth-century cheap reprints of *The Song of Hiawatha* to last me a lifetime. I would instead suggest that the standards of importance and demand, as outlined by Pargellis, may with some careful reading and a little ingenuity be fitted to many neglected texts.[10] With pleasing frequency, low-spot authors treat the traditionally major personal themes of literature—social responsibility, personal identity, the ties of family and the tenacity of grief—while also addressing the social questions of the day. And though a low-spot author's handling of these themes may at times produce risible results, the best examples of these marginal works offer deeply personal voices with a poignant immediacy.[11]

10. I have seen the works of eccentric poet Richard Griffin enjoy a moderate surge in popularity over the past five years, in part because he makes a compelling figure and in part because several booksellers have chosen to advocate repeatedly and at length for the self-published poet's work. I first encountered Griffin, the author of such collections as *The Lobster's Gizzard and Other Poems* (New York: the author, 1916) and *Bug House Poetry* (New York: the author, 1917, et seq.), in a squib bookseller Eric Korn had written for the *TLS* that was subsequently collected in Korn's *Remainders from the Times Literary Supplement 1980-1989* (Manchester: Carcanet, 1989). Korn characterizes Griffin as a "lobster Laureate and lunatic of major importance." Despite boasting a poetical range that encompasses such topics as yaks, 19th-century street gangs, lepers, and the bastinado, Griffin is not necessarily the foremost lunatic poet (cf. Griffin's contemporary John Armstrong Chaloner, *né* Chanler, who built a corpus of work peppered with the catch-phrase "Who's looney now?"). But even with the market for Griffin having been somewhat pumped up of late (prices for his works have increased nearly ten-fold, and the twenty-dollar volume of Griffin is but a fleeting memory), one might still put together an extensive collection of his work for an investment substantially less than the cost of a single Hemingway first edition. (The collection might also be assembled with even greater satisfaction in the hunt, since only a fraction of Griffin's work is easily obtained at any given moment.)

11. For instance, I await the labor historian's critical gloss on the links between William Henry Taylor Shade's *Buckeyeland and Bohemia* (Hillsboro, OH: Lyle Printing Co., 1895), Henry H. Johnson's *Ballads of Farm and Home* (Elkhart, IN: Mennonite Publishing Co., 1902), and Elden Small's *Songs at Twilight* (Detroit: P. G. Munro, 1919). Each collection includes an indignant poem inspired by a cavalier newspaper account of the death of a railroad brakeman;

I could evangelize at length on kindred authors and subjects, but realize that further examples of neglected books must necessarily continue to be anecdotal and idiosyncratic. Nothing I have suggested here precludes many of the other received truths about collecting (i.e., focus on a manageable interest, familiarize yourself with your subject, and worry about the condition of your books). But I would also suggest that the traditional standards of rarity and importance have shifted somewhat, especially in the current market where the Internet seems to render many high-spot collectible titles nearly ubiquitous. Perhaps the scarcity of a given individual book becomes less important than the context in which one places the work. A collection's worth might grow in proportion to its value as an example of social significance of once-popular genres, or as it demonstrates historical contexts in the connections among different texts. These are a few of the reasons, I would argue, why one might wish to seek out those books that everyone has forgotten.

---

an extract from Small's "Only a Brakeman Killed" may be taken as representative: "'Was there nobody hurt?' the question came, / 'Not a soul!' another said. / 'Twas a wonderful piece of luck, indeed— / 'There's only a brakeman dead.'"

Herakleitos binding

The Pre-Socratic Project and Remarks on the Philosophical Side of Fine Printing

Peter Rutledge Koch

I HAVE ALWAYS worked in the vineyard of the text. I began, as we all do, a reader and a writer. In my earliest chrysalis-like beginnings, a text was fluid and plastic, much like a monologue that runs continuously in one's head. My association with the text as physical and fixed flowered only after I became a reader. Finally, as a designer and publisher I came to the whole book, the book as text and as an object of art. Studying book design and soon thereafter learning to print, both for pleasure and the control it gave me over the physical beauty of the book, I quickly sprouted those tendrils that take root in the rich soil of bibliophilia. Concerning the harvest, my two greatest intellectual loves being poetry and ancient Greek philosophy, I never doubted what I would publish and the more poetic the philosophy (and vice versa) the more I desire to print the text.

The pre-Socratic project began in 1986 just after I had completed *Point Lobos*, a collaboration with the photographer Wolf von dem Bussche to publish a collection of Robinson Jeffers's poems and von dem Bussche's photographs in a monumental portfolio edition that explored the typographic limits of Jeffers's poetry in single sheet or broadside form. Jeffers, a strong classicist, had whetted my appetite for an exploration of the typographic form of archaic Greek thought and I asked Jack Shoemaker, then editor-in-chief at North Point Press, to suggest a contemporary writer capable of translating classical Greek poetry with both precision and literary style. Jack immediately suggested Guy Davenport and his translation of the pre-Socratic philosopher Herakleitos of Ephesus, previously published in a very modest paperback edition by Grey Fox Press in Bolinas, California. I was delighted by the suggestion and immediately set about the task of studying the history of Greek printing. I discovered, during my subsequent researches various nineteenth-century and twentieth-century editions of Herakleitos, none that were distinguished or presented in a fashion that I considered worth emulating. W. K. C. Guthrie, in his famous work *The Greek Philosophers from Thales to Aristotle* had referred to the Ionian poet-philosopher as 'enigmatic' and his method of communication as 'disjointed, dark, and oracular.'[1] I was searching for the form that would embody the "Heraklitean book." Herakleitos strikes out against peaceful mystics and the Pythagorean ideal of a harmonious world declaring that they idealize death. Instead he asserts that "War is the father of all," and that "Strife is justice." Where earlier philosophers sought permanence and stability, he claimed there was no such thing and that one should not desire a stagnant world. Where was I to turn? Fine editions of Greek classics were common enough but where was the new Heraklitean model? I was feeling for a shift in the paradigm of the fine book and seeking the paradoxical cutting edge of a traditional craft.

Scholars searching for the original Herakleitos discovered that a book entitled *On Nature* was attributed to him but no copy of it survived. What we do have are *doxographi*, fragments and opinions attributed to him and quoted in later writers and compilers. Thinking about what form *my* Herakleitos would take, I wondered what I would see if I visited the great library of Alexandria and asked for his book. During this early period of thinking on form I dreamt that

---

1. W.K.C. Guthrie, *The Greek Philosophers From Thales to Aristotle*, (New York: Harper & Row, 1975), 43.

Remarks on the Philosophical Side of Fine Printing

I found myself in a Mediterranean library seated in a small and enclosed courtyard at a large oak table under the open sky. Around the courtyard were many small doorways leading to darkened rooms. A man brought me a codex written on papyrus and bound into plain wooden boards. The shape was that of a Michelin guide, twice as tall as it was wide, and as thick as *Webster's College Dictionary*. The text, written in a Greek script, was in a single narrow column on each page. I began reading the text and discovered it to be the lost book of Herakleitos and was so excited by my discovery that I awoke with only the shapes and colors remaining in my mind.

About the same time that I was puzzling over the ideal form of the Heraklitean codex, the conservation bookbinder and scholar, Gary Frost, was teaching Coptic sewing structures to book artists and conservation binders around the country in his now famous workshops. My former wife, Shelley Hoyt, had taken his workshop and had made a model book structure with hand-painted *faux bois* boards that resembled the codex I had seen in my dream and I adapted her design to my book.

Seeking a typographic form as well as the book structure, I searched the current type catalogues for an appropriate Greek typeface that would resemble written Greek of the fourth century BCE or even earlier. I was drawn to Gill Sans Greek Light capitals with its allusion to the simplicity of a handwritten archaic letterform. I was satisfied that I had the right typeface for the Greek but it took me nearly two years to find a typefounder with the matrices and to get the sorts cast for hand-setting. Dan Carr and Julia Ferrari at their Golgoonoza Type Foundry in Ashuelot, New Hampshire cast the type.

I was working across two millennia to create an entirely "new" *codex Heraklietos* utilizing the tools and thoughts of contemporary scholars and craftsmen to support the new, critically acclaimed and most eloquent translation of a Greek pre-Socratic in the English language. The design was essentially from a "retrieved dream object" and not a copy of an existing book. I was working with an imagined archaeology of form and seeking the simplicity of the unadorned text.

Herakleitos prefigured *Diogenes*, my next philosophical project. While working on the typographic form of Greek thought I ran across a brilliant article by Thomas McEvilley in an *Artforum* magazine on Diogenes of Sinope.[2] In this article, McEvilley retells the anecdotes that surround the life and teachings of Diogenes, the arch-cynic, and characterizes him as a "performance philosopher," not unlike our local unsavory beggars on Telegraph Avenue in Berkeley making life uncomfortable for fellow citizens by confrontations and charades.

The source of our knowledge of Diogenes and his life is from *The Cynic Epistles*, later texts that arose in and around the Cynic tradition a few hundred years after Diogenes died. It is likely that Diogenes himself did not leave any written texts and none are attributed to him. He was reputed to live in a jug in the city dump at Corinth and display himself daily in the public forum. A typical anecdote is: "A rich man took Diogenes into his house and warned him not to spit on the expensive rugs or furnishings, whereupon he spat in the man's face, saying that he could find nothing else there cheap enough to spit on." The man is reputed to have been Plato. And, most famously: When he was sunning himself in the square, Alexander came and stood over him and said, "Ask of me any boon you like." To which Diogenes replied, "Get out of my light."

I was so intrigued by the archeology of Greek texts that the idea of discovering a text written in Diogenes' own hand had begun to form. I began to imagine digging around in the dump of Corinth and unearthing a box inside of which there were hasty and unkempt scratchings of a vitriolic nature. At first I imagined a cigar box with papyrus leaves inside, but when I had a look at the world papyrus supply I was disappointed in the effect and began to look further. It was my good fortune that while looking for examples of Greek epigraphy I stumbled across a copy of *The Inscriptions of Kourion* by T. B. Mitford, published by the American Philosophical Society in 1971. Among the excavated fragments of this Greek colony on Cyprus, there were a number of *defictiones* or lead curse tablets covered with

---

2. *Artforum* magazine, March 1983.

rustic scratched or incised letterforms that were exactly what I was looking for. These *defictiones* were small lead sheets or tablets that were addressed to someone with whom the curser was in litigation. The client would go to a magus and commission a curse which the magus would then write out on a sheet of lead and the tablet would be buried in the house of the cursed, or thrown in the drinking well, or even in the grave of a child who it was believed would have a restless spirit up for some serious mischief. I could imagine Diogenes himself writing such curses and burying them in the dump where he lived. I commissioned the stonecutter and lettering artist Christopher Stinehour to write out McEvilley's anecdotal retelling of the exploits of Diogenes in a rustic letter form that resembled the Kourion curse tablets. Then I sent my assistant, John von Zelowitz, on a mission to find blank lead tablets on which I could print the texts. The final piece fell into place when I commissioned the sculptor Stephen Braun to hand build fifty raku-fired clay caskets with instructions to make them each unique but all to look as if they had been freshly cleaned off after being buried for two thousand years. The result is a collaboration that produced an object that has historical precedents and yet is an original form. I prefer to call this work a "text transmission object" thereby circumventing the fruitless issue of whether it is a book or a sculpture. In my mind it can be classified as a book if you are exhibiting it as an artist book, or it can be classified as sculpture with letterpress printing on a lead surface. In either sense it commands a place in the library as readily as a box full of papyrus fragment from crocodile mummy wrappings or a collection of sheet music from a *Scuola* in Venice.

My third foray into the form of Greek poetry and thought is in every way more classical and traditional in its concept and form. With *The Fragments of Parmenides*, I set out to make a book in the grand tradition of classic fine printing, incorporating the canonical principles of textual, typographic, and artistic integrity while following to the edge my own concept and design. This was to be a masterwork, embodying my mature thoughts on printing and publishing, philosophy and art, design and composition.

I knew when Robert Bringhurst agreed in 1994 to translate Parmenides for me that I was embarking on a major publishing adventure. Robert's translation is the best of its kind, treating Parmenides' poem as poetry and as philosophy. Parmenides' Greek descended from the oral style of Homeric epic on the one hand and from the philosophical tradition of Orphic and Pythagorean prehistory on the other. Now, for the first time, Parmenides' poem reads in English as elegant poetry and at the same time uncluttered and authentic archaic philosophy.

My earliest thoughts about the typographic form of Parmenides were that I should commission a Greek typeface for the original fragments, one that would originate in the world of the pre-Socratics themselves. I invited Christopher Stinehour to design a digital font based on our earlier explorations of letterforms for the Diogenes project. Christopher was enthusiastic and after he had worked up his alpha version of Diogenes based on archaic Greek letterforms, I asked Dan Carr in the fall of 1997 if he would cut steel punches by hand and cast the type in hard foundry metal for hand composition. This invitation came after a conversation with Dan and Julia about their recent visit and studies with Christian Paput and Nelly Gable, punch-cutters at the now imperiled Imprimerie Nationale in Paris. Dan was confident that it could be done and as he began to work on the drawings he added his own special touch based on fresh research into earlier Ionic Greek letterforms. Although it took Dan over four years to complete his work, we in the meantime secured the name Parmenides for the new typeface and began the page design and selection of an accompanying Roman typeface for Robert's translation. I chose Giovanni Mardersteig's monotype Dante both for its stately beauty and for how it held up to but did not dominate the Greek majuscules on the facing page. I was also, in my fashion, showing my admiration for Mardersteig's great press, the Officina Bodoni.

With typographic and page design questions resolved I was finally free to begin concentrating on the task of commissioning suitable illustrations. From the beginning I had it in mind to

Remarks on the Philosophical Side of Fine Printing

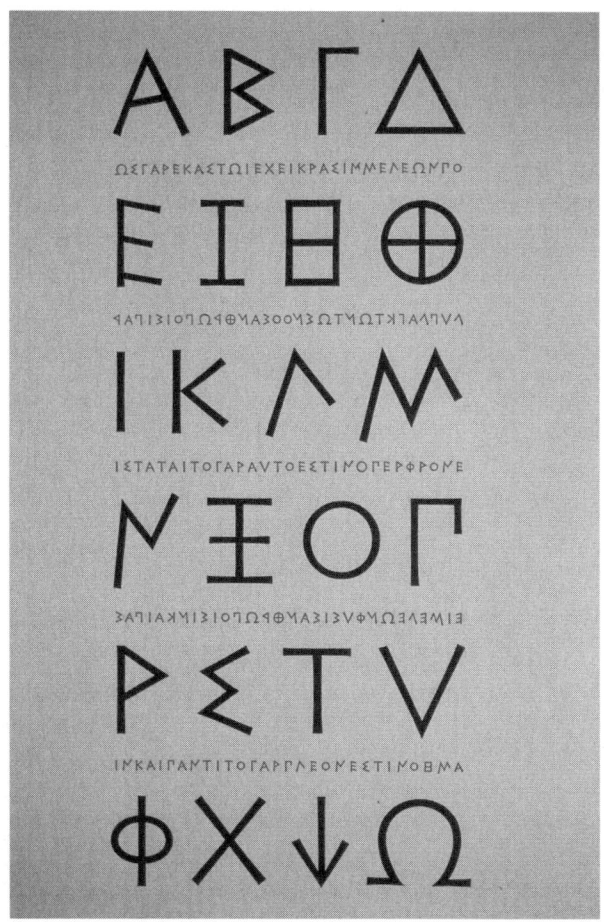

The Fragments of Parmenides
(cover art, Diogenes Greek by Christopher Stinehour)

incorporate prints with the text and had had my eye out for the right artist for years. I knew that I wanted nonfigurative work to accompany Parmenides' intense dialectical thinking. In the summer of 2002, I saw Richard Wagener's recent wood engravings—brilliantly colored abstractions—and was deeply impressed. I had recently completed a seven-year-long project with Richard entitled *Zebra Noise with Flatted Seventh*, an abcdarium and bestiary with more than forty exquisitely detailed wood engravings and original accompanying texts by the artist. I knew that it would be a real pleasure to collaborate with him once again.

The decisions that I had left to the very end depended upon the printing requirements of the illustrations and about the materials and binding designs that would follow. After extensive experimentation, Richard and I agreed on a heavy white paper from the Zerkall mill in Germany for printing both his colored wood engravings and the type. For the binding, I relied first of all on the warm red and orange palette of the engravings and moved on to choosing harmonizing Japanese silks and Hahnemuhle Bugra papers.

The binding designs came last and were executed in close collaboration with my favorite colleagues, Peggy Gotthold and Daniel Kelm. Peggy bound the numbered edition and devised the strong yet elegant enclosures for both editions and Daniel Kelm was responsible for the thin and flexible full leather treatment of the lettered edition.

Ten years had passed and *The Fragments of Parmenides* was finally at the bindery. Robert Bringhurst had in the meantime completed editing and designing the companion book, *Carving the Elements*, a compilation of essays and photographs documenting the whole process from idea to execution including philosophical essays from each of the collaborators.

In April 2004, we celebrated our decade long collaboration with a publication party at The Grolier Club and have since been planning volumes two and three of the trilogy, *The Fragments of Empedocles*, to be followed finally by a new edition of *The Fragments of Herakleitos* in the same format.

Remarks on the Philosophical Side of Fine Printing

Diogenes Defictions, lead and ceramic edition

I have described some aspects of the making of the Herakleitos, Diogenes, and the Parmenides as a preamble to essaying on the nature of fine printing. My thoughts are fragmentary and unsystematic, much like the texts I have been discussing and printing.

In an orderly and peaceful world, more suited to metaphysical contemplation, we might have no deep needs to make and then defend what we think. We could contemplate rather than create. However, Herakleitos is right and we could never thrive in such a world for it would be static, frozen, and, even if some small sign of life were to be seen wriggling about, it would soon bore us to death. Consequently, the making of fine books dwells in the world of things and of craftsmanship and of thoughts on the nature of art and the human condition.

Fine printing brings the dimensions of long exposure, study, discipline, talent, and craft knowledge to the book. Yet you can have the entire realm of craft and all the two-thousand-year-old traditions of books at your fingertips and still not be working with texts or art that challenge the mind of the reader. Books that look and feel expensive but fall far short of an exemplary fine book are not uncommon. The ingredients for the exemplar are exacting. The aesthetic of fine printing must necessarily take into account the luminosity of text and image, and the meaning that subsists in the structure and the details of the book as object.

From my own observations, I have come to understand that the fine book of the twenty-first century, in order to be outstanding, must bridge two worlds successfully. First it must fully realize the classical qualities of all fine books: clear and excellent typography; fine materials and masterful craftsmanship conjoining to create a durable object; a suitable design to present the contents of the book with respect for the reader in mind; and finally, that it not be overwhelmed by luxury or beauty for its own sake.

Second, it must, in some sense, lead beyond tradition. What enables a book to transcend its content and the craft of its making is the idea of the book. The idea resides within the context of the history of printing and publishing. Does the book remain safely within or with some aspect of risk extend beyond the historical tradition? Does the book considered as designed object bring something exceptional to the form of the book: a new typeface, an innovative binding structure, or fresh method of illustration? And, including its design, does the book bring fresh material to the intellectual ferment of our time? Simply reprinting a chestnut in an expensive edition with name-brand reproductions does not constitute fine printing.

Succeeding at both the above criteria implies mastery at all levels from concept to content and by definition is difficult to achieve. It is necessary, but not sufficient, to study and master traditional knowledge, it is also necessary to live, think, and create at the cutting edge of our time.

In 2002, the Association Typographique Internationale, sponsored the international type design competition "bukva-raz!" in Rome and published a four-hundred-page catalogue entitled *Language Culture Type*. The title has no commas dividing the words. This deliberate lack of punctuation symbolizes in a limited way an ideal book where there are no divisions between form, context, and content. The occasion of this competition was to celebrate the "United Nations Year of Dialogue among Civilizations." Parmenides, the archaic Greek typeface that I had recently commissioned from Dan Carr won an award of merit. The exhibition eventually traveled from Rome to Moscow, St. Petersburg, and the United Nations in New York City. This is one small example of how I understand the practice of fine printing to fit into the greater world of print and culture . . . as exemplary and as a bridge between communication supertechnologies and the human scale of the hand and the eye working together to create a work of art.

The story of my press and my philosophy begins when I bought my first press. I decided that I would master only one craft. I never tried to make my own paper or mine and cast my own lead or sew my own bindings. I saw the infinity of goat leather tanning, punch-cutting, flax spinning, and needlework stretching out before me and decided instead to collaborate with experts in those fields while I concentrated on the editing, the design, and the presswork. I was instantly relieved of years of apprenticeships and craftwork and began to think about who and what I wanted to work with to make the books that I really wanted to add to my library.

So much depends upon the text. I have spent my lifetime reading the poets and the philosophers and I have come to the conclusion that the text is absolutely primary. A book to me is a container and a reading machine designed for the transmission of meaning. Some are of elegant design and some are clumsy.

I have in my book collections close to a thousand volumes on lettering, typography, papermaking, bookbinding, the history of the book, and examples of books that I admire purely for their physical characteristics, that is, for their beauty. Because I believe that a book is a text transmission object I have a special category in my library that I have designated "the visible aspects of language" and include therein the books on book design, typography, and lettering. These books live with me in very close proximity: in my home library and in the studio. They live where I live.

I have studied each one with a critical eye for the qualities, proportions, and weights that feel good, look true and, excepting a few didactic binding examples, when read, please and exercise the mind. This collection has been acquired one book at a time and has developed as my *aesthetic* has matured. What greater way to learn what the fine book really means?

To borrow a phrase from Sandra Kirshenbaum, I have been a privisher not a publisher. My little editions, seemingly never destined to sell out, are neglected once made and sit handsomely on the shelf. I still have a few unsold copies of a book I published in 1976. On the brighter side, the American Philosophical Society still has unsold pamphlets from 1807 on *their* shelves.

The sales business is of a completely different order than the making. Social skills and an ability to build and sustain interest in an arcane and difficult subject are but a few of the required qualifications for the task. Rational sales incentives, a fondness for travel, and a good public relations staff would be helpful. Instead, I rely on my own personal relations with librarians and collectors and hope along the way to make new friends for the press. When asked recently how I sell a book like *Parmenides* by someone who was clearly in shock at the price, I found myself replying, "One book at a time."

Conventional wisdom will tell you that only a fool would attempt to make a living from printing and publishing fine books without a considerable stable of patrons all lined up and ready to pay what seems to most booklovers an immodest amount for a book they can read for free at the library. However, since I have always been willing and able to design and print for others, I have benefited greatly from my associations with noted bookmen and institutional patrons of fine printing. I was fortunate early on to be discovered by the unforgettable Jesuit bibliophile and librarian Fr. William Monahan, who kept me in chevre and pinot noir for years. His prodigious commissioning of keepsakes and wonderful and elaborate programs and announcements slowly dwindled as he did but I was by then accepting commissions from the Book Club of California and Stanford University Library. All this is to say that I have afforded myself the luxury of publishing finely printed books around my more pressing business needs and commitments. No time was wasted in these commercial enterprises for I have, as a result, kept abreast of technological change, as well as design principles and good production management techniques. I can honestly say that my professional design work for hire has informed my private press work to great

Koch Studio (1995)

advantage. I have necessarily worked slowly and deliberately and with great circumspection and delicacy on my books because I could go no faster.

Concerning the audience and the patronage for the contemporary fine book, I see that the going is getting steeper and steeper. The old-school bibliophile is aging gracefully but few replace them when they go. Whereas the successful businessman of the 1920s and 1930s was often enough a member of the Grolier, Roxburghe, or Caxton club and sponsored, both directly and indirectly, magnificent books by patronizing printers who published books to their taste, today's equivalent is likely neither a book collector nor a patron of a printer. Their leisure is not spent in their private libraries writing poems, essays, and memoirs, but rather in less intellectually demanding but perhaps more immediately pleasurable pursuits such as travel, wine, fine food, and antique furniture. There are certainly reasons for this, the decline of intellectually rigorous educational standards, the ease of travel today, the better food and wine that is available in most cosmopolitan cities and, directly related to the decline in patronage, a real scarcity of fine books being published and offered for sale.

The meaning of fine printing has not changed since the advent of digital printing, recalling Marshall McLuhan can be no more current or modern than quoting John Ruskin or William Morris. McLuhan had the advantage of a hundred years of lightning swift change but the dialectic of change that turned Morris and company to their arts and crafts was more catastrophic than the change that the personal computer has brought over the past twenty-five years. In 1890, Utopian Socialists in England and elsewhere, in revolt against the brutal pace of mechanical production turned to the handpress and to the crafts of hand-bookbinding and paper-making that were the outdated and impractical technologies of the preindustrial revolution. Since Morris, manufacture has only accelerated, the mechanical augmented by the digital, creating even more distance between the handmade and the robotic industrial goal of totally effortless and instantaneous cheap production—no real change, no real difference except in speed and scale.

The major and unavoidable factor in the scarcity of fine books is the escalating expense of making them and hence the expense of acquiring them. As the technologies of the digital and mechanical world increase the ease and speed of manufacture, thereby increasing the availability of durable and intellectual goods, all the while tending to bring the price downwards, the hourly rate charge by a craftsman (who repairs or creates objects slowly and carefully by hand, one at a time) is forced to rise according to the escalating factors of economic viability such as medical care and housing. In the world of fine books this means that the paper-maker, punch-cutter, typefounder, leather tanner, letterpress printer, and bookbinder, must each charge the same hourly rate as the plumber or the electrician and, if they expect to dine at good restaurants and drink good wine, the same wage as the lawyer, surgeon, or dentist. A classic example is that today you can buy a newly published first printing of a trade novel for $35 (for which the publisher paid $6 from the manufacturer) and you must pay $150 to have your old copy of a much beloved cookbook rebound by hand in a modest but serviceable binding and $300 and up to have a good leather binding replaced. This reversal in value is the absolute norm in the post-industrial world. When you add up the hours that go into each book you not only account for handmade paper, typefounding, printing, and binding, you must also include the editorial, design, and production management time, as well as the capital outlay of the publisher, including the sales costs of travel and advertising. Factor all that into fifty or a hundred copies of a book that takes years to produce and you can readily gauge the sanity of a publisher of fine editions. As the divide will only widen between trade publishing and fine printing, real art in typographically distinguished editions will become ever more inaccessible. Only the *very* fewest, the bibliographically intrepid and sophisticated souls with tangible wealth and their counterpart, the passionate collector who will readily sacrifice in the service of their daemon, will seek out for purchase and thereby support the publication of new fine press books.

Remarks on the Philosophical Side of Fine Printing

I must leave you with a problem to solve: now that the market has dried up and the cost of manufacture has escalated out of sight and it was a difficult sell in the first place, what are we to do if we wish to preserve the values of the hand-printed book in the electro-robotic future?

Missale secundum ordinem carthusiensium.
Ferrara: [Lorenzo di Rossi] for Carthusian Monastery, 1503.

The Woodcut in Ferrara in the Late Fifteenth Century

Daniel De Simone

THE THEME of this essay is the development of the woodcut in Ferrara from 1479 to 1503. My work is based on preliminary research on the subject that I hope will blossom into a larger study documenting in greater detail the stylistic influences that forged the Ferrarese style at the end of the fifteenth century. My concluding observations, reflections on the evolution of this style, are based on my instincts, which are way ahead of my scholarship at this point in time.

To begin, a brief chronology: The first book printed in Italy, Cicero's *De oratore*, was produced by Sweynheim and Pannartz in Subiaco in 1465. In 1467, Ulrich Han printed his edition of Torquemada's *Meditationes*, which was illustrated with thirty-four half-page woodcuts. The *Meditationes* is the first book printed in Italy to contain a series of images. Also in 1467, Sweynheim and Pannartz moved their press to Rome where they printed their edition of Saint Augustine's *City of God*.

The first book to be printed in Venice was Johannes de Spira's edition of the *Epistolae* of Cicero, which appeared in 1469, and the first book printed in Florence was the first volume of Servius's *Commentaries* on Virgil, which appeared in November 1471. The first printer to work in Ferrara was Andreas Belfortis and his first book, Augstino Dati's *Elegantiae minores*, appeared on 12 March 1471.

Between 1471 and 1493, Belfortis printed fifty-five titles. By 1475, there were four more printers working in Ferrara besides Belfortis. By the end of the century, a total of 121 titles that we know of had been produced in that city. The first illustrated book appeared in Ferrara in 1479 and was printed by Augustino Canerio. There are three known copies of this title, one of which is at the Huntington Library in San Marino. The book, the *Constitutiones* of Pope Clement V, contains one small rectangular image cut in thin outlines of various thicknesses. It shows a seated Pope Clement in the center of the cut facing forward. His hand is raised, perhaps offering a blessing. He is flanked by two cardinals, also seated, set in profile, with the cardinal on the left gesturing to the pontiff. All three hold books in their laps.

The simple outline was cut with a lightness of hand evident in the thin lines that define the drapery in the background and the fold of the garments, the headdresses, and the hands of all three figures. An attempt is made to give each figure distinctive facial characteristics, with emphasis on the eyes, especially in the case of Clement V, where the lines are delicately cut and turned to produce a unique facial construction. To date, I have not found a source for this image,

Clement V. *Constitutiones*. Ferrara: Agostino Canerio, 1479.

but I suspect that a closer study of illuminated books produced in Ferrara will yield an answer.

Ten years would pass before the next illustrated book appeared from a press in Ferrara. This book, printed by Lorenzo di Rossi in 1489, was an anonymous text entitled *Legenda di San Maurellio*. Saint Maurellio was a bishop of Ferrara, a martyr, and one of the city's patron saints. This book also is known in only three copies, none of which are in the United States. The book is illustrated with two woodcuts, one of Saint George slaying the dragon, and one of Saint Maurellio, which concerns us here.

Lorenzo di Rossi, the printer whose books we will be focusing on for the rest of this essay, began his career in Ferrara in 1482 and worked continuously until 1522 when his last imprint is recorded. In a short biography of di Rossi which appears in Gustave Gruyer's essay "Les livres à gravures sur bois publiés à Ferrare," published in the *Gazette des Beaux Arts* in four parts in 1888–1889, the printer is variously called Lorenzo di Rossi, Laurentius de Rubeis, and Lorenzo Rossi di Valenga. He is apparently the son of Antonio de Rubeis, a papermaker who was registered in Ferrara in the 1470s. Gruyer was not able to establish whether di Rossi was of French or Italian origins. His surname appeared in Parisian, Venetian, and Ferrarese imprints, but no link has been established connecting these various printers to one another. By 1501, di Rossi had printed about thirty titles, including the two most important illustrated books produced in Ferrara, folio editions of *De claris mulieribus* by Johannes Phillipus di Bergomensis and the *Epistolae* of Saint Jerome, both of which appeared in 1497.

Returning to di Rossi's first illustrated book, the *Legenda* of 1489, we encounter a much more elaborate and detailed woodcut than that found in its predecessor from Augustino Canerio's *Constitutiones* of 1479. Di Rossi's woodcut contains elements suggesting that the image may have been based on local sources and indeed, perhaps, on the paintings of Cosimo Tura, the most important painter working in Ferrara during the period.

Legenda de Sancto Maurellio. Ferrara: Lorenzo di Rossi, 1489.

The Woodcut in Ferrara in the Late Fifteenth Century

The woodcut illustrated, reproduced from a copy in the Biblioteca Comunale Ariostae in Ferrara, depicts Saint Maurellio in a monumental pose, set within the confines of an elaborately decorated architectural element of columns and an arch, holding the Church in his left hand and his bishop's mitre in his right. He is flanked by two monks, each holding a book, and two angels are perched above on either side of the arch. A wash has been applied to this image, making it a bit more decorative but partially obscuring the shading of the garments.

The lines of the image are thinly cut, and the extensive use of parallel lines to shade the design provides a level of detail that both contributes perspective to the woodcut and accentuates the natural physicality of the saint's body beneath his robes. The facial features of Saint Maurellio are quite distinctive, with well-defined eyes, nose, and mouth, and with the suggestion of a beard above the collar of the robes. The ceiling of the arch behind the saint is clearly defined with what appears to be a repeated pattern of rosettes and leaves, set within a pattern of squares that recede, giving the image a sense of perspective but with limited success.

The most well-defined aspect of the woodcut is the manner in which the artist rendered the robes of the saint. The cutter has used a slightly thicker outline to detail the outer edges and the rough folds of the sleeves and to delineate the core of the saint's lower body. Angled cuts and "V" cuts suggest the presence of his legs, and a series of parallel lines, all similar in pattern and thickness, although varied in length, shade the garment, giving it a billowy, natural fall. The effect of rendering the robe in this way, and the slightly forward position of the right foot of the saint, give the woodcut image a quality that suggests momentary movement, an action that connects the viewer with the image in the present time.

This focus on robes is one of the hallmarks of paintings by Cosimo Tura, the celebrated artist who was court painter to the Estense dynasty in Ferrara from 1458 to 1485. Tura's style has been described by various art historians as anxious, nervous, tormented, and for some, pathological. The accentuation of the garments in this woodcut resembles Tura's style as seen in his painting of Saint Maurellio, which hangs in the Pinoteca Nationale in Ferrara. Tura did many paintings for the local churches as well as for the Estense palace during this period, including a series of portraits of saints, like Saint Francis and Saint Louis of Toulouse, and his energetic style would have been well known in Ferrara during the last decades of the fifteenth century.

Monica Molteni, an art historian who published a monograph entitled *Comsé Tura* in 1999, studied the woodcut of Saint Maurellio and suggested a close association between the ceiling of the arch that appears in the cut and the arch that Tura painted for his *Annunciation*, part of a four-panel painting for the organ doors in the Cathedral of Saint George in Ferrara. A quick comparison of the two ceilings shows very similar patterns, including the decoration of the roundel within the square, which also appears in the colored woodcut in the *Legenda* from the Biblioteca Centrale Ariostae. Molteni also discusses two works by Gentile Bellini, the Venetian artist active in the second half of the fifteenth century. In her book, Molteni illustrates two of Bellini's portraits, San Mateo and San Teodoro, both set in similar architectural environments and possibly another link connecting Venice with Ferrara.

The style of the saint's garments and the architectural elements just pointed out can be found in a number of sources both from paintings and from the highly stylized manuscripts traditional in Ferrara at the time, but I hope that these two examples will be sufficient to suggest local sources for the early woodcuts produced in Ferrara. More familiarity with the paintings of Tura, Francesco de Cossa, and Ercole di Roberti, and the miniature paintings of Taddeo Crivelli, Franco dei Rossi, and Giorgio d'Alemagna, all of whom worked in Ferrara, will, I hope, help identify other characteristics of the Ferrarese tradition that appear in the early woodcuts.

As already noted, Lorenzo di Rossi printed his two most famous books in 1497. On April 29 of that year he completed his edition of *De claris mulieribus*, which contains biographies of celebrated women from mythology, ancient history, the Old and New

Testaments, and some who lived in the later part of the fifteenth century. This edition is illustrated with three leaves with full-page borders and woodcuts, 173 woodcut portraits, many of which are repeated throughout the volume, elegant initial letters, and a printer's mark. The work is very well known and there are many copies of it in both American and European libraries.

On 12 October 1497, di Rossi issued his *Epistles* of Saint Jerome. The text includes a life of the saint, his letters, and commentaries on Saint Jerome by Fra Matteo de Ferrara. The book is illustrated with two full-page woodcuts enclosed by decorative borders and 180 small cuts set throughout the text, resembling in manner and format to the 1490 edition of the Malermi *Bible* published in Venice by LucAntonio Giunta and the 1491 edition of Dante's *Divine Comedy*, also printed in Venice, but by Benalius and Capcasa. These two books are notable in that they contain artistic elements from Venetian, Florentine, and Ferrarese styles and are excellent sources for studying how these influences informed a local style which appears in the *Missale secundum*, printed for the Carthusian Monastery in Ferrara in 1503, which will be discussed later.

It is clear to most who examine the *Epistles* of Saint Jerome that the woodcuts that illustrate it are of the Venetian style of the 1490s. This tradition has been documented over the years by numerous bibliographers and print historians, one of the most notable being Lilian Armstrong of Wellesley College. Documenting the work of four Venetian illuminators, the Putti Master, the Pico Master, the Master of the Rimini Ovid, and Benedetto Bordon, Armstrong has forged a clearer understanding of the transition from the manuscript tradition to the woodcut tradition in Venice from the 1470s to the first years of the sixteenth century.

In the two books being discussed here, some pages are adorned with monumental woodcut borders characteristic of the style of the Pico Master, who was so influential in Venice in the 1490s. Cut in outline, these architectural borders contain the elements of the Pico Master's designs that Armstrong has identified, including putti playing musical instruments, angels and cherubs, griffins, sphinxes, dragons, and soldiers on horses. These same borders appear in both books with minor variations. They echo designs from the Pico Master's miniatures that decorate both manuscripts and early printed books produced in Venice in the late 1480s and early 1490s. To use Professor Armstrong's terms, the "boneless bodies" of the putti, the "accentuated eyes" of the figures, and the playful manner in which the figures are presented are characteristics that distinguish designs created by the Pico Master.

These stylistic elements are repeated in the 180 cuts that illustrate the text of the Saint Jerome, and follow closely the harmony of text and image that appear in Venetian books from earlier in the decade, like the Dante and the Malermi Bible already noted. For Armstrong, the migration of this distinctive Venetian style to Ferrara can be documented if one examines the early and late career of the Pico Master. In two entries written by Armstrong for the exhibition catalogue *La miniatura a Ferrara*, edited by Federica Toniolo and published in 1998, Armstrong identifies two Ferrarese manuscripts that contain miniatures by the Pico Master. One was produced around 1480 and the other in the first years of the sixteenth century. In her descriptions, Armstrong suggests that elements that appear in the 1480s manuscript reflect mid-century Ferrarese miniature style and that the Pico Master may have trained in Ferrara in the early 1470s before moving on to Venice. Looking at the sixteenth-century manuscript, she notices many of the design elements that appear in borders similar to the ones just examined and she proposes that the Pico Master, whose work in Venice ended in 1495, may have come to Ferrara, perhaps returning home, to begin making the designs that appear in the books printed in Ferrara after 1496. This hypothesis may explain the blossoming of the woodcut in Ferrara during the last years of the fifteenth century.

As we turn our attention to the cuts in the *De claris mulieribus*, we find a greater variety of influences in the images that decorate the text. The historians Gustave Gruyer, Friederich Lippmann, and Arthur Hind all agree that this work contains images that carry with them elements from Venetian, Florentine, and Ferrarese design. The approximately 3-inch-by-3-inch blocks depicting celebrated women from all eras of history, include eight portraits of Italian women from the fifteenth century.

One of the portraits is of Marcella, a saint from the early Christian period. This block's black sky produced in the dotted manner and the white-on-black effect of the striated lines in the background provide the image with a dramatic setting for the figure depicted in three-quarters' with a slight tilt of the head, a well-proportioned body, slender hands, an elegantly defined head with well-designed headdress and hair, has a slightly dreamy expression on her face. It has been suggested that this image is very modern in its compositional format and that the architectural element in the background and the tufts of grass in the foreground may indicate a Paduan influence and elements of Montagna's style. Others have suggested that the style is linked to the Florentine school as the charm of Marcella's facial features, the costume, and the evocative personal characteristics would suggest.

The second portrait to examine is of Ginevra Sforza, wife of Giovanni II, Bentivoglio. Her portrait in profile presents her in old age, and although not as flattering as that of Marcella, this woodcut depicts a woman of fading beauty with strong features, who exudes a resolute personality. As dreamily as Marcella is rendered, Ginevra is straightforward in manner, with a focused gaze and a firm chin. The white-on-black striated line of the background, accentuated by an architectural element, and the blank shield hanging from a leafless tree, reinforce the idea of Ginevra's age and provide the composition with balance.

This woodcut can be compared with a painted portrait of Ginevra Bentivoglio painted by the Ferrarese artist Ercole de Roberti. Roberti worked in Bologna and Ferrara during the last quarter of the fifteenth century, and he, along with Francesco del Cossa and Cosimo Tura are considered the most important painters to work in Ferrara during this period. His portrait of Ginevra, also in profile, is from the collections of the National Gallery of Art in Washington, D.C.. It was painted in the 1480s and depicts an

Johannes Phillipus di Bergomensis. *De claris mulieribus*.
Ferrara: Lorenzo di Rossi, 1497.

equally focused subject that could be the source of the image that was cut for the *De claris mulieribus*. The knotted headdress, the tight, simply designed costume, the background that hints of the world beyond, all provide a clue that perhaps Roberti's portrait, or others he painted in this style, could have been used as a guide. A close examination of all the portraits that appear in this work could reveal numerous other influences, including those from Florentine and Milanese traditions.

Now, I would like to turn to the two woodcuts that inspired my interest in the stylistic development of the woodcut in Ferrara. They appear in the 1503 *Missale secundum* printed for the Carthusian Monestary in Ferrara. Although his name does not appear in the colophon, most agree that this work was printed by Lorenzo di Rossi. An examination of the type fonts used to print this book are all associated with his press and it seems very unlikely that the monastery would produce one book of this magnitude without the help of the Ferrara's most important printer.

The first image is *Saint Christopher Crossing the River with the*

Christ Child. The figure of Saint Christopher is set front and center in the design and it dominates the composition of the woodcut. He is dressed in a modest costume in the classical style and his face is well defined with expressive eyes and an aquiline nose. The saint's body is modeled by a few well-chosen lines and the shapeliness of his bare leg, partially submerged in the river, demonstrates that the artist was interested in detailing the physical form. The Christ Child and the background are less well defined, but the striated lines representing the flowing river are cut in a wave pattern and effectively rendered. Hind suggests that the image was inspired by the popular style of the Venetian woodcut, perhaps by the Pico Master himself. But other sources may be at work here.

The next image, *Saint Christopher and the Christ Child* by the Florentine artist Domenico Ghirlandaio (1448–1494), hangs in the Metropolitan Museum of Art in New York. It is strikingly similar to the composition of the woodcut, but in reverse. The pose of Saint Christopher with his head turned toward the Child, his focused gaze, his right arm holding the palm branch, his left arm cocked with hand on his hip, his stance leaning against the flow of the river, and the well-delineated leg muscles appear in both the painting and the woodcut. These similarities may come from another sources but thus far, I have located no Ferrarese or Venetian artist who handled the composition of Saint Christopher and the Christ Child in just this manner. But I will keep looking.

The final image I want to examine also comes from the *Missale secundum* of 1503. It is a stunning Crucifixion scene set with an elaborate four-part border and it was chosen to be the frontispiece of the exhibition catalogue. The central cut is similar to one found in the 1498 Venetian *Missale* printed by Johannes Emericus for Johannes Paep. The two differ in background, and in the fact that the Venetian image was cut in outline while much of the Ferrarese block is cut in a white-on-black technique that appears in the *De claris mulieribus*. The border is also cut with faint striated lines, embellished by the series of dots used as background in the corner cuts of the Evangelists.

What drew me to this image was its highly sculpted background with its striated white-on-black lines, and the emotional power that comes from the facial expression and posture of Mary Magdalene. There is a unique quality to the cut that reflects an individual creativity. The more images created in Ferrara that I examine, including paintings, miniatures, and woodcuts, the more I am beginning to think that it is not necessarily only the designs that distinguish the Ferrarese woodcut, but it is the choices made by the cutter who renders these designs into art. The manner in which the background is defined, how the hair, the eyes, and the facial expressions are represented, the mingling of Venetian border formats with Florentine compositional forms all seem to me to be part of the unique style that came together and contributed to the formation of the Ferrarese woodcut style at the turn of the sixteenth century.

REFERENCES

Lilian Armstrong. *Renaissance Miniature Painters and Classical Imagery: The Master of the Putti and his Venetian Workshop*. London: Harvey Miller Publishers, 1981.

Lilian Armstrong. "Woodcuts from Liturgical Books Published by LucAntonio Giunta in Venice, 1499-1501," *Word and Image*, 17, nos. 1-2 (January - June 2001).

Lilian Armstrong. *Studies of Renaissance Miniaturists in Venice*. 2 vols. London: The Pindar Press, 2003.

Daniel De Simone, ed. *A Heavenly Craft: The Woodcut in Early Printed Books*. New York and Washington: George Braziller and The Library of Congress, 2004.

Gustave Gruyer. "Les livres a gravures sur bois publiés a Ferrara." *Gazette des Beaux-Arts*. Paris: Published in four parts, 1888-1889.

Arthur M. Hind. *An Introduction to a History of Woodcut*. 2 vols. London: Constable and Company, 1935.

Friedrich Lippmann. *The Art of the Wood-Engraving in Italy in the Fifteenth Century*. London: Bernard Quaritch, 1888.

Aurora Australis (1908), Edited By Ernest H. Shackleton: A New Description of the First State of the First Book Published on the Antarctic Continent

Martin L. Greene*

MOST READERS of adventure books recognize Sir Ernest H. Shackleton as the heroic leader of the Imperial Transantarctic (*Endurance*) Expedition of 1914–1917. Collectors of books on polar exploration, however, celebrate Shackleton as the editor and publisher of *Aurora Australis*, the first book actually written, printed, and bound on the Antarctic continent. *Aurora Australis*[1] is a centerpiece for a serious collection of books on Antarctic exploration. The book was the product of an earlier Shackleton-led expedition, the British Antarctic (*Nimrod*) Expedition of 1907–1909. Shackleton brought paper, ink, type, and a small hand-printing press to Antarctica. During winter 1908, *Aurora Australis* was written, engraved, printed,

---

* I wish to thank Larry Conrad and Michael Rosove for their very helpful reviews and comments. Their combined knowledge of Antarctic book matters kept me from falling into several crevasses.

1. Ernest H. Shackleton, ed., *Aurora Australis* ([Antarctica]: Winter quarters of the British Antarctic Expedition, 1908).

and assembled by the men of the expedition in their cramped, frozen hut. The extreme difficulties of producing the book in very cold temperatures is a story by itself; its details are graphically described by Shackleton[2] and by James Murray and George Marston[3] in their well-written books about the expedition. In the Antarctic summer of 1908-1909 that followed the printing of *Aurora Australis*, Shackleton and his men reached the furthest south point then achieved, ninety-seven nautical miles from the South Pole.

Aurora Australis is made up of ten chapters written on site by various members of the expedition. Some chapters are based on personal experiences and some are fantasy; some are written as poems and others as narratives. The production of this epic was Shackleton's solution to the problem of maintaining the mental health of his expedition members during the long, dark winter months.

Each copy of *Aurora Australis* consists of ninety-five leaves bound by hand in wooden boards made from packing crates. Spines were made from harness leather, and stout cord bound the perforated pages. Perhaps one hundred copies of each leaf were originally printed on a handpress by expedition members Frank Wild and Ernest Joyce, but only about sixty-five complete copies of the book are now believed to exist.[4] Individual copies of complete books are now affectionately referred to by the stenciled names still visible on their wooden covers: e.g., BUTTER, (Bottled F)RUIT, (Ir)ISH STEW, BR(itish)/ANT(arctic)/EX(pedition).

There is no published inventory of locations of copies of *Aurora Australis*, but many are in institutional collections. In recent years, the occasional copy sold on the open market has brought auction prices in the range of $50,000 to $75,000. The sale catalogue listings

---

2. Ernest H. Shackleton, *The Heart of the Antarctic: Being the Story of the British Antarctic Expedition, 1907-1909* (London: Heinemann, 1909).

3. James Murray and George Marston. *Antarctic Days. Sketches of the Homely Side of Polar Life, by Two of Shackleton's Men.* (London: Melrose, 1913).

4. Michael H. Rosove, *Antarctica, 1772-1922. Freestanding Publications through 1999* (Santa Monica, CA: Adélie Books, 2001).

and other descriptions of *Aurora Australis* describe two major variants of the book. One variant has ten printed plates, and another has eleven printed plates. Before now, book dealers and collectors have generally shared conventional opinions that the eleven-plate variant is more "complete" (and therefore more valuable) than the ten-plate variant. However, I could find no prior discussions of why the book has these two major variants.

I asked, "Why are there these two states of *Aurora Australis?*" Certainly, it was difficult enough to produce a single state of the book. What would prompt Shackleton and his men to print two different versions? It had to be a very good reason to justify this extra work. In general, when a book exists in two states, there is an obvious reason why a change was made from the first state to the second state. Added text may correct a serious omission, a misspelled name may be corrected, or facts may be added or clarified.

These two *Aurora Australis* variants differ in only a single leaf. In the very rare variant, the leaf contains text on both of its sides and is included in a book with a total of ten engraved plates. The other variant of the book (most existing copies) has a leaf similarly placed but with text on one side and an engraved illustration on the other side, yielding a book with a total of eleven plates.

The mystery of why there are two states to this rare book is solved by doing what Shackleton originally intended—*read the book*. Comparing the text of the two variants, it seemed plausible to me, and indeed probable, that Shackleton's men printed a first version that was so offensive that Shackleton ordered an entire leaf to be revised, removing and rewriting the text and filling the empty space with a new illustration, resulting in a first and second state of this famous book.

My hypothesis is that the rarer *Aurora Australis* variant with ten plates is actually the first state of this book. I believe that the second state with eleven plates arose when Shackleton reprinted one leaf to get rid of certain offending text. The removed text was replaced by adding a new plate on the verso of this leaf. If this plate had not been added, there would be a blank page in the middle of a chapter, or the entire chapter with multiple leaves would have to be reset and reprinted by hand. Considering the primitive equipment available to the men in Antarctica, this latter option was most unattractive.

The leaf that differs in the first and second states of *Aurora Australis* is the fourth in the chapter entitled "An Ancient Manuscript" written by Frank Wild. The chapter, written in biblical language, describes Shackleton's difficulties in conceiving, organizing, funding, and launching his attempt to be the first to reach the South Pole.

Both versions of the leaf, which exist in recent facsimile publications, are shown in juxtaposition in Table 1.[5] I believe that careful reading of the textual difference supports my hypothesis.

Six paragraphs of text present in the first state are omitted from the second state. These paragraphs describe five wealthy men who were approached by Shackleton to help fund his British Antarctic Expedition. Since this chapter is a factual narrative, we must believe that the text describes real encounters with real potential financiers who turned down Shackleton's requests for money. Shackleton, with his background as an Irish commoner, had already been turned down by the prestigious Royal Geographical Society in his request for support, and perhaps his friend Frank Wild vents here with some bitterness toward the British establishment. Or perhaps Wild is just poking fun at men who had little vision, were stingy, or just plain uninterested in the worthy pursuits of polar exploration.

The paragraphs clearly identify the five who refused Shackleton's request:

A major landowner and cattle breeder
A wealthy cigarette manufacturer
A major publisher (or dealer or collector) of books
A profiteer only interested in making more money
A hard-hearted broker/businessman/gambler

5. Ernest H. Shackleton, *Aurora Australis*, facsimile, preface by Lord Shackleton, introduction by John Millard (Alburgh, Harleston, Norfolk, England: Bluntisham – Paradigm, 1986); and Ernest H. Shackleton, *Aurora Australis*, facsimile (English issue), introduction by Mary Goodwin (Shrewsbury: England: SeTo Publishing Ltd and Airlife Publishing Ltd., 1988).

Table 1: Text of First and Second States of *Aurora Australis* (1908), Fourth Leaf of Chapter "An Ancient Manuscript"

First State (Original) Text	Second State (Revised) Text
therein.	therein.
And another who did own vast tracts of land and many herds of cattle, answered him thus; Owing to possible territorial changes in the laws of the land do I stand in fear of losing all my possessions, therefore must I say thee nay.	And it came to pass that though many of the rich men gave unto him of their gold, yet had he still need of many more shekels before he could say, Now can I buy and furnish me a ship for my journey.
Yet another did speak long and loudly of the many pieces of gold which he did give to the poor, and to the sick and needy, and then did press into the hand of the man who would go exploring, three rolled pieces of dried leaves, which the people of the land do burn in their mouths, in order that they may be comforted.	ℂ And the heart of Shackleton was heavy, and was sunk even unto his shoes, when there arose a great and mighty man who did build ships for the Great King; And who wrought cunningly in iron, with which he made the ships so strong that they could not be broken, and he did speak in this wise saying;
ℂ And it came to pass that the shoes of Shackleton did wear thin on his feet with his wanderings, when he did come to one who had of his stores of wealth given unto the people of the land many thousands of books of great price, so that the people who did receive them became sadly in want by spending their money in keeping them in order, and to him he did say;	My son, though my house in which I do dwell, lieth a long journey to the north of the chief city of the Great King, even the city of London, yet hath it come to my ears of the work which ye would perform, and it seemeth good in mine eyes.
Give unto me I pray thee, a little of thy gold that I may fulfil my labours. But the rich man answered him saying, Nay, for in this thing have I no interest.	It hath also been told unto me that because thy purse is not too heavy, thy way is not clear before thee.
And one there was who scoffed saying, Go to, [page break]	Behold! I have here great stores of gold and of silver and because thy design hath found favour with me, take of my wealth sufficient for thy needs.
	ℂ Then indeed was Shackleton a happy man, and he straightway cast about him for a ship which should [page break]

Table 1. Text of First and Second States of *Aurora Australis* (1908), with illustration.

what is there in this thing in the which I can make
more gold.

And one who was called a broker, which being interpreted meaneth gambler, answered, A business man cannot afford to be sentimental; for which saying no interpretation can be found.

⁋ And the heart of Shackleton was heavy, and was sunk even unto his shoes, when there arose a great and mighty man who did build ships for the Great King, and who wrought cunningly in iron, with which he made the ships so strong that they could not be broken, and he did speak in this wise saying;

My son, though my house in which I do dwell,
lieth a long journey to the north of the chief city of
the Great King, even the city of London, yet hath it come to my ears of the work which ye would perform, and it seemeth good in mine eyes.

It hath also been told unto me that because thy
purse is not too heavy, thy way is not clear before
thee.

Behold! I have here great stores of gold and of silver and because thy design hath found favour with me, take of my wealth sufficient for thy needs.

⁋ Then indeed was Shackleton a happy man, and
he straightway cast about him for a ship which should

MANY SHEKELS WERE NEEDED FOR THE SHIP TO GO FORTH.

I propose that the after Frank Wild's original text was set up and printed, Shackleton realized that the five prominent, wealthy (and now, in retrospect, short-sighted) citizens who declined to share their riches with him could be easily identified. If any of them read the book, they certainly could have identified themselves. Other knowledgeable readers in the rarified British society might also recognize them. The negative word-of-mouth fallout from the unflattering descriptions of these men could doom fund-raising for any future expedition led by Shackleton. I believe that Shackleton could not take this risk. The offending text had to be removed.

Simple deletion of this text, however, would cause an important printing difficulty. Seven leaves of the chapter (14 pages, up to 1400 printed sheets) would have to be reset and printed. This unpopular alternative would take "printers" Frank Wild and Ernest Joyce a week or more of work, based on their reported best production of two pages per day.[6] However, a simpler solution would involve reprinting only a single leaf (two pages, two hundred printed sheets). I propose that Shackleton asked George Marston, who served as engraver and lithographer, to fill the space left from deleting the offending text by creating another (the eleventh) plate. One side of the new leaf would have the revised shortened text, and the other side the new engraved plate. This new plate, entitled "Many shekels were needed for the ship to go forth," shows the *Nimrod*, the expedition ship, readily identifiable from photographs of the ship in *The Heart of the Antarctic*.[7]

Shackleton had to accept the compromise that his new cancel leaf departed from the style set for *Aurora Australis*. All other ten plates in the book had been printed on individual leaves with blank reverse sides. But his newly added eleventh plate, of necessity, had printed text on its reverse side.

Replacement of the first state text with the cancel leaf was done for most copies of *Aurora Australis*. However, I believe a few copies of the book with the original leaf (and only ten plates) escaped

6. Shackleton, *The Heart of the Antarctic*, 217.
7. Ibid., 42.

correction and exist today as a first state of this famous publication. Did the chapter's author, Frank Wild, secretly object to Shackleton's editorial pruning of Wild's text and hide away a few copies in their original state? One can only guess.

Earlier scholars have described the two variants of *Aurora Australis* but reached no conclusions about their relationship. In his 1985 introduction to the first published facsimile of *Aurora Australis*, John Millard of Toronto comments on his survey of fifty-six copies of the rare book.[8]

> Some interesting differences between the copies have come to light as a result of the survey. A major difference appears in the article "An Ancient Manuscript" by Shellback (Frank Wild) which was printed in two versions. An American owner, comparing his copy with several others, discovered that in most copies this article has an illustration on the verso of one of the leaves, part way into the article. The illustration—entitled "Many shekels were needed for the ship to go forth"—is a line drawing of a three masted sailing ship, with all sails furled, tied up at a wharf. The illustration did not appear in his copy, and its place was taken by additional text. For identification purposes the version with the illustration is designated Format 'A' and appears in nearly all of the copies located in the survey. The version without the illustration, Format 'B', appears to be very rare. So far there is no information on why this particular article was printed in two versions. This is the only major variant so far discovered.

The 1988 second published facsimile of *Aurora Australis*, reproduced the *"ULIENNE SOUP"* copy in the Alexander Turnbull Library (Wellington, New Zealand).[9] This copy is actually one of the rare first state copies in existence. A 1979 article by Mary Goodwin of Los Angeles was used as a preface to this facsimile. The irony is that

8. Shackleton, *Aurora Australis* (1986 facsimile), xv–xvi.
9. Shackleton, *Aurora Australis* (1988 facsimile), xi–xxiii.

Goodwin says in her article and preface that *Aurora Australis* has eleven full-page illustrations, but the facsimile photographs that follow her introduction were made from a rare first state edition with only ten illustrations. Neither the publisher nor Goodwin seems to have picked up on this discrepancy. The net result, however, is that with the Bluntisham and SeTo facsimiles now available at low cost to libraries and scholars, both states of *Aurora Australis* are readily available.

The 1994 Gaston Renard catalogue *Fine and Rare Books, Antarctica*, a standard reference for bibliographers, book dealers, and collectors, includes sale copies of both the second state (Renard 1435) of the first state (Renard 1436).[10] Renard describes the latter as "THE FIRST BOOK PRINTED IN THE ANTARCTIC—WITH VARIANT TEXT" and states, "This copy has the variant text for the article An Ancient Manuscript so that it has 10 illustrations rather than 11, but as usual does not contain the final title leaf found in a few copies. We believe this variation to be much rarer than the version with 11 illustrations. In other respects, it collates identically with other copies we have handled."[11]

The excellent 2001 publication by Rosove, an authoritative and detailed bibliography of Antarctic books from the "heroic age," lists the first state variant as number 304.A1c.[12] However, in regard to this variant, Rosove incorrectly notes, "The illustration 'Many Shekels Were Needed for the Ship To Go Forth' (leaf 63 verso) is replaced by duplicate text (that of leaf 63 recto); ... Rare variant ...." There actually is no "duplicate text" as Rosove states. Rosove has indicated to me in private communication that he will clarify this distinction in a future Addenda and Corrections supplement to his publication. Neither bibliographies by Spence or Conrad nor *The Taurus*

10. Julien Renard, *Fine and Rare Books. Antarctica. To Be Sold at Auction by Leonard Joel, 15th, 16th, and 17th November, 1994* (Melbourne: Gaston Renard Fine and Rare Books, 1994).

11. Ibid., 199.

12. Rosove, *Antarctica, 1772-1922*, 377.

Collection comment on variants or different states for *Aurora Australis*.[13] By assigning letters or numbers to the two variants, Millard (Format A vs. Format B), Renard (1435 vs. 1436) (7) and Rosove (304.A1a vs. 304.A1c) imply that the *Aurora Australis* version with eleven plates is superior to or has priority over the variant with ten plates. Book collectors and dealers have also assumed that the eleven-plate version is more desirable than the ten-plate version. Evidence presented here challenges those assumptions.

The existence of only a few copies of the first state compared to many copies of the second state supports my hypothesis that Shackleton wanted to keep the potentially damaging text from surfacing in Great Britain after the expedition's return. Also, the fact that the "new" eleventh plate differs from the other ten by being the only one printed with text on its reverse side further supports the hypothesis.

I base my hypothesis on what I consider a "best-fit" analysis of the actual text differences between the two states of *Aurora Australis*. The hypothesis cannot be proved or disproved, since none of the existing sources that describe the production of *Aurora Australis* speak to the point. There are also no manuscripts or other personal testimonials that refute or support the hypothesis.

---

13. Sydney A. Spence (compiler), and J. J. H. Simper and J. I. Simper, eds., *Antarctic Miscellany. Books, Periodicals & Maps Relating to the Discovery and Exploration of Antarctica*. 2nd ed. (London: J. J. H. and J. I. Simper, 1980); L. J. Conrad, *Bibliography of Antarctic Exploration. Expedition Accounts from 1768 to 1960* (Washougal, WA: L. J. Conrad, 1999); and Julian Mackenzie, *The Taurus Collection. 150 Collectable Books on the Antarctic. A Bibliography* (London: The Travellers' Bookshop, 2001).

BOOKSELLERS

The Messiah Factor in Bookselling

Tom Congalton

MY FIRST REAL entry into the antiquarian book world, was in the early 1970s, standing in line for library sales, where treasures could be purchased for a quarter or less. It was during the tedious hours of waiting where I had my first encounter with the "messiah factor" in bookselling. Granted, gasoline was expensive and difficult to obtain, inflation was moving full steam ahead, and the mood in the country was generally surly. But the assembled booksellers huddled in the cold outside a small municipal library were the picture of optimism, and with good reason. The influx of oil money to the Middle East was going to transform the Arab nations into a hotbed of rare book collecting. What could be a more appropriate and suitably extravagant use of the petroleum bounty than the purchase of rare and exotic books? Rumors that various Arab sheiks, and even the Sultan of Brunei (the world's richest man), were collecting books en masse, warmed the cockles of our greedy hearts. Although only a beginner, I was sure this tectonic shift would enhance the value of my small stock. We had heard the Good News. The world might be going to hell, but the Arabs were going to save us.

When I became a full-time bookseller in the early 1980s things had changed. Gasoline prices had stabilized, and the new messiah had already arisen, this time even further to the East. As I idled away my time, talking with other booksellers on the phone, awaiting orders from our catalogues, we were uniformly optimistic. We had all heard rumors of Japanese collectors and institutions snapping up Shakespeare folios, Books of Hours (whatever they were), and every available copy of Chagall's *Jerusalem Windows*. Who cared that virtually no booksellers of my acquaintance owned any Shakespeare folios, Books of Hours, or the like? What matter if those who might turn up the occasional copy of *Jerusalem Windows* had no direct contact with the Japanese market?

We had all heard rumors of American dealers who carefully and profitably cultivated the Japanese market and trade. While few of us believed in the freshly posited trickle-down theory, we were all perfectly willing to benefit from it. Presumably, our colleagues, flush with profits from the Japanese trade, were going to convert the gains from their Shakespeare folios into the hypermodern first editions I offered for twenty or thirty dollars each in my first few catalogues. We had seen the light—the Japanese were going to save us. (It is perhaps only a bitter footnote to remark that in the 1980s my total dividend from the Japanese economic miracle was $680, which I received when I sold an inscribed photograph of the grumpy-looking Japanese author, Junichiro Tanazaki, to a Japanese dealer at the ABAA's Boston Book Fair.)

By the late 1980s, we had found a "new" (or at least recycled) deity: the book fair. As rents increased and urban centers changed, many booksellers found it more convenient to close shop and hit the expanding book fair circuit. What could be better? Book fairs had previously been confined to a handful of regional events and the few fairs run by the Antiquarian Booksellers' Association of America (ABAA), which had pioneered them in this country in the early 1960s. Now, in the mid- to late 1980s, a bookseller had his or her pick of regional fairs. On the East Coast at least, one could attend as many as three fairs on a single weekend. Freed from the shop, dealers could meet new collectors and vice versa, as well as benefit from the efficiencies of scale a book fair might provide. Scouting a fair with a hundred dealers was like going to a hundred bookstores. The conventional wisdom among dealers on the book fair circuit was that if you could not sell your way out of a book fair, you could always buy your way out. One wise man in the book trade once remarked to me that the way to judge the success of a book fair was not by one's sales, but by adding one's sales to one's purchases—advice that has always struck me as true. Perhaps most important about the book fairs was easy proximity to colleagues. In the event of a total meltdown, one could always meet friends and rivals afterward and commiserate over cocktails. On one such occasion fifteen years ago, a couple of my colleagues and I, with the collective courage born of several post-bookfair libations, determined to buy a book from another colleague for $18,000. I am chagrined to admit that we still own it.

In the late 1980s, I joined the ABAA, and in short order a new savior arose: Hollywood and the entertainment community. Unlike previous messiahs, visible evidence indicated that we might be on to something. The tedium between sales at West Coast book fairs was leavened by occasional celebrity sightings: Brad Pitt, Lana Turner, Johnny Depp, Whoopi Goldberg, Jay Leno, and many others, not only attended but occasionally purchased books, sometimes expensive ones. We had all heard the legends that the Heritage Book Shop and other strategically placed West Coast dealers had successfully cultivated the Hollywood carriage trade. Now we too, while not perhaps having had our brush with fame, had at least had our brush with the famous. Booksellers could casually mention in the company of their fellows that they were going out for a drink with Johnny, had Jay's home phone number, or had spent an amusing half-hour trading quips with Whoopi. Probably some of it was true.

Perhaps a single anecdote will help to elucidate those heady days. One afternoon I received a call from a woman obviously filled with misgivings. She identified herself as the accountant for A Major Hollywood Star, someone everyone has heard of. After some preliminary pleasantries, she stated the purpose for her call. Her client had a $14,000 credit card charge with our firm, apparently filed under "research." Was this correct?

"Yes, it is," I replied.

"Could I ask you a personal question?" she asked, apparently more than a little afraid of the answer.

"Yes."

"What do you sell at Between the Covers?"

"Rare books," I answered.

"Oh, thank God," she said, breathing a sigh of relief.

While such interludes made for amusing cocktail chatter and the income was certainly welcome, objective scrutiny made it clear that for the vast majority of booksellers Hollywood had not saved us. No matter, because by the mid-1990s we put all false gods behind us and accepted the one, true messiah: the Internet.

Books were (and still are) the perfect commodity to sell on the Internet: alike enough that they could be entered and stored in a well-ordered database, but different enough that their individual characteristics would be easily distinguished and searchable. At first, fledgling Internet search services were a boon to savvy dealers and collectors. Collectors who had spent decades looking for a specific title, might with a few keystrokes have a choice of copies in a variety of conditions and price ranges. Dealers who received multiple orders for a book from their catalogues could often provide equivalent copies on short notice. Most online services provided some capacity for maintaining want lists, with automatic notification when a copy of a desired item was put into the system. Dealers learned to be wary when they received a half-dozen or more orders for a book the day after they had listed it; books that quickly elicited multiple orders had been under priced.

Such phenomena required adaptable bookseller behavior. For example, one New Year's morning I stopped into the shop to feed our cats. Checking my e-mail, I saw that one of my "wants" had come up: a nice copy of Tom Graham's *Hike and the Aeroplane* offered for $35. Experience dictated that I was not alone in my search for this book, and ordering it outright was bound to result in disappointment. In my machinations to acquire the book, I opted for a new and ingenious book-buying technique: telling the truth. I immediately both e-mailed and called, leaving a message on the seller's answering machine. They were offering Sinclair Lewis's pseudonymous and very scarce first book for a fraction of its retail value. I would pay something in the mid–four figures for the book depending on further details of condition. The bookseller was happy to oblige, sending me the book on approval and receiving a check back in short order for the eventually agreed upon price. After we completed the transaction, he told me: "You know, I got over forty orders for that book, and no one else offered me a penny more than $35." Let me stress that my behavior in this incident was in no way altruistic or motivated by my love for either fair play or my fellow booksellers; rather, it was a new strategy to cope with a changing environment. I had left myself plenty of room for profit, and unlike the forty other prospective buyers, I had the book.

Like all good messiahs, the Internet had its apostles as well—some high-tech millionaires and even billionaires looking to acquire the trappings of wealth and taste saw rare books as part and parcel of the cultured and sophisticated life they could now afford. Bill Gates bought the Codex Hammar in a much-celebrated auction, and rumors that Gates, Paul Allen, and other high-tech moguls were amassing huge libraries were rife in the trade. Dealers flocked to the new Seattle book fair, expecting to exchange their stock for trunks full of money from new collectors flush with dot com wealth. On opening night at an ABAA New York fair I overheard one dealer excitedly telling another that not only had two billionaires been in his booth, but that they had been there *at the same time.* Apparently, billionaires travel in packs. For my part, I was woefully unfamiliar with the more important identifying characteristics of the species. I have recently taken up bird-watching, hoping that the lessons inherent are transferable to this more lucrative pastime.

Talk at book fairs had ceased to be of rare books, but was now almost exclusively devoted to the Internet. Increasing numbers of dealers listed their stock on the Net, and collectors were eager to embrace this new method for finding books. However, for dealers in very modern first editions this new messiah quickly showed signs of being a wrathful Old Testament–style deity, unforgiving and quick to disperse our traditional marketing base—those collectors who bought almost exclusively from our catalogues. For example, search engines began to list in profusion books that had been moderately uncommon books between the 1970s and 1990s, books for which there might have existed regional disparities of supply, but copies of which an active dealer could usually find in his or her daily rounds and make available through a print source. Where before one might reasonably expect to make continuous and repeated sales of specific titles in the $50 to $500 range, now one could only be confident of selling them if one had the cheapest copy for its condition on the net.

If the ABAA's proprietary Internet discussion group was any indication, a few dealers in antiquarian, or "brown books," found this fitting revenge for the brisk commerce they had been forced to observe at modern first edition booths in the past decades of book fairs, as well as for the assumed inferiority of the product modern dealers purveyed. Even if the market for esoteric antiquarian books remained relatively small, at least they were confident in the knowledge that because of the limited supply, there would be only modest price competition on the Net. The feeling among at least some of these dealers was that the Internet had finally revealed the egregious depredations and practices of the modern first edition dealer. One listed example of these outrageous practices was that some first editions of recent vintage, such as John Grisham's *A Time to Kill*, were then selling for $2000.

In one exchange about this topic on the ABAA discussion group a vocal member of this small group of dealers had in his most recent catalogue a single volume identical in price to *A Time to Kill*— a second edition of an eighteenth-century Swedish book on meat carving. While one might be hard pressed to defend a John Grisham novel as the pinnacle of Western culture, I am quite sure it is in no way exceeded by an eighteenth-century how-to manual on slicing Swedish rump roast.

Another unforgiving factor of the Internet was that we were selling too many books. Books we had previously devoted little or no time to selling, as they were not worth including in a printed catalogue, became available for sale to a large and not necessarily discriminating audience by virtue of being in one's database and thus available through a simple search. Many dealers complained to me that they were spending, as was I, the greater part of their time processing orders for relatively inexpensive books. At Between the Covers, it became increasingly apparent that if we continued to experience this large volume of Internet sales of cheap books, we would be increasingly less able to devote our time to the more expensive books that made up the largest part of our income. We were rapidly going to go bankrupt; again, we needed a new strategy to address this.

In our case, we sought out a local bookseller with a different problem but the same cause. The walk-in traffic in his shop had dissipated, apparently because his regular customers were spending their book-buying budgets on the Internet. We formed a company, bought a large but inexpensive building, contributed our less expensive stock to the venture, and hired relatively low-wage employees to list large quantities of books on the Net. The resulting company, named Alottabooks, now has nearly two hundred thousand books listed online for sale, and, mercifully, I can go about buying and selling the more expensive and to me more interesting nineteenth- and twentieth-century first editions.

Every self-respecting new messiah wants to destroy or discourage the vestiges and symbols of its predecessors. What former icons of the rare-book world has the Internet displaced or weakened? For one, there remain only a few open shops, as booksellers have increasingly discovered the benefits of selling books in the comfort of their homes, unencumbered by the expenses of running a shop, and undistracted by the occasional idiosyncrasies of those likely to be found haunting rare-book stores or, as they are known in the trade, the collectors.

Book fairs are another fading icon of the past. Two of the best regional book fairs, the Florida Antiquarian Book Fair in St. Petersburg, and the Long Island Book Fair, both of which have had long-time waiting lists of over a hundred dealers, reportedly now have a short waiting list, if they have one at all. Other fairs have folded completely. Many of the lower-level dealers who attended these fairs and who had previously hoarded books to bring there, had already sold the better ones through the search services or online auction sites, and now saw no reason to go to the trouble and expense of exhibiting at these events.

Another casualty of the Internet is likely to be price guides. These have always been something of a hit-or-miss affair, often obsolete as soon as they are published. When the first edition of Allen and Pat Ahearn's general price guide *Collected Books: A Guide to Values* was published, the date of publication was timed to coincide with opening day of the 1991 New York Antiquarian Book Fair, then held at the Sheraton Hotel. A few minutes before the fair opened, another first edition dealer, Jeffrey Marks, and I encountered Allen Ahearn in the elevator carrying a beautiful copy of *The Sound and the Fury*. Jeff and I expressed our interest in the book. Allen said the selling price was $17,500, but pointed out that availing ourselves of the reciprocal 20 percent discount would bring the final price down to $14,000. Our efforts to convince him that the book was worth $7500, according to his new price guide, issued on that very day, fell on deaf ears. Allen was smart enough to write and publish his price guide, but not dumb enough to follow it when his instincts told him otherwise. I expect some price guides, including the Ahearns', will survive, but many more seem destined for oblivion with more current and reliable information available free on the Internet.

Bibliography too may soon go the way of the price guide. In the past, the mark of a serious collector or dealer would be a reference library numbering from the hundreds into the thousands of volumes. Bibliography was the foundation on which most booksellers built their careers, and on which most collectors built their collections. According to California bookseller Mark Hime, attempting to challenge accepted bibliographical knowledge was akin to dating outside one's own species: rarely satisfying, and mortally embarrassing if caught. Now with millions of books listed on the search services, each accompanied by a more or less competent description, a bookseller with no reference library can appropriate the research and descriptions of their more, or occasionally less, competent fellows. On the ABAA Internet discussion group much time seems devoted to the proper form of "cease-and-desist" letters aimed at those who have lifted painstakingly crafted and researched book descriptions from member dealers for use with their own books listed online.

I recently shared a booth at a book fair with Boston dealer Peter Stern. During the first night of the fair, Peter and I left our booth in the care of one of his employees. We had to decide where he should leave the key to the glass case that contained perhaps a half million dollars worth of books, for us to retrieve the next day. The choice was clear: beneath the massive Gibson and Greene bibliography of Arthur Conan Doyle that Peter had recently had reprinted, prominently displayed on a table for all to examine. There was obviously no safer place to hide the key, especially in a crowd of a hundred or so booksellers, than under a bibliography. On another occasion, a young cataloguer at our shop misinterpreted some penciled notes in a book and listed a common title as being in the "scarce first state dust jacket." As far as I know this book had no second state dust jacket. Over the course of the next few weeks, we were inundated with e-mail from various booksellers not of our acquaintance, demanding to be enlightened as to the point of issue on the jacket. Motivated equally by science and malicious curiosity we declined to change the description or to respond to any of these e-mails. Within months, dozens of copies of this title were listed online, confidently described as being in the "scarce first state dust jacket." Most of these dealers were probably correct, they just did not know why.

This reliance on the Net as the final arbiter of all bibliographical knowledge and of scarcity has led to a couple of my favorite new bits of bookseller jargon: "Not on the Net," or "Not on eBay."

But what about eBay and other online auction sites? Used judiciously by the experienced, such sites can be beneficial to one's collection or stock. Nothing is so disconcerting or amusing, however, as an experienced dealer or collector browsing among the offerings of an online auction site. Buried beneath the mass of misdescribed books and inferior copies of desirable titles, there might lie an occasional gem or modest bargain—but to me, it hardly seems worth the effort. In applying myself with a certain degree of attention to the online auctions, I have found that I average buying about one book a month.

Another phenomenon is the bookseller or collector who deals exclusively, or almost so, online. I was recently treated to the first book fair appearance of a dealer—I'll call him Dealer X—who had purchased most of his stock online. About half of the more expensive books X was offering for sale as authentic were sporting photocopied or otherwise reproduced dust jackets. The jacket on one F. Scott Fitzgerald first edition that he offered me for $24,000, turned out on closer inspection to be a color copy of a First Edition Library facsimile jacket, the original of which had had the facsimile notice sanded off. X had bought this jacket for $7,000 on a popular online auction site from Dealer Y who also dealt almost exclusively online. Eventually, I became involved in X's effort to return the jacket to Y, who told me that he had bought the jacket from Dealer Z for $4,000 on the same auction site. This is an example of what is known in the rare book trade as provenance.

My observation, and one that I have also heard from others, is that collectors have reaped the benefits of a one-time windfall. Most of the professional dealers willing to list their stock on the Internet have done so. Although increasingly larger numbers of books will be listed online, and surprises are bound to be among them, the vast majority will be of the used, not rare, variety. I have already noticed that the market has begun absorbing relatively uncommon books, which were for a time available in profusion, restoring some equilibrium between dealers and collectors. The Internet seems to have greatly broadened the market for rare books, but not necessarily to have deepened it. Through this window, many more people have been exposed to the rare book world, and some of them, happily, have been attracted to it. This phenomenon is most immediately evident in two fields that seem to function as entry-level genres for book collectors: modern literary first editions and children's books. Not surprisingly, few new collectors begin by collecting incunables.

Many new collectors are members of the baby boom generation at the peak of their earning capacity. Like many affluent collectors, they want to start at the top. Thus, the past few years have seen a remarkable rise in the prices of prime condition high spots in those two fields in response to a great increase in demand. At a recent Christie's East auction of the collection of Henrik Falktoft, a Danish collector of both modern first editions and children's books who paid close attention to condition, the prices realized were generally adjudged stunning: *The Sound and the Fury* brought $58,750, *To Kill a Mockingbird* and *The Catcher in the Rye* brought $32,900 a piece, and *The Lord of the Rings* brought $56,400. On the children's side, *The Wizard of Oz* brought $64,625, *Where the Wild Things Are* nearly $20,000, and *The Cat in the Hat* over $10,000. What is remarkable is that dealers purchased most, and maybe all, of these books. The Christie's sale was strategically held the day before the opening of the New York Antiquarian Book Fair and successful bidders exhibited two of the books they had bought. As is custom in the trade, the dealers duly raised the prices, and both copies sold at the fair.

How have such high prices affected collectors? They have set a discouragingly high bar for new collectors who want to accumulate recognized high spots. Conversely, high prices have worked to the advantage of veteran collectors who assembled their collections in a more forgiving era, and have seen the value of their collections grow exponentially. Dealers of high spots now must compete with collectors for the best available copies of the best books. Inflated prices have also encouraged dealers to do what they have always done—when the available supply of high spots dwindles or disappears, we look for new candidates to promote to that status. The collector who once accused me of being criminally avaricious when I catalogued a nice first edition of *To Kill a Mockingbird* for $275 a dozen years ago, is probably still waiting accusatorily in the wings to denounce me for the price of the next future high spot that will appear in my catalogues.

Perhaps the Internet is not really the new messiah, just a very large and unexpected bump on the rare book selling landscape. The theory that I cling to now in my apostasy, is that the new messiah is really the old messiah, he or she who will save us has been there all along—the determined and resourceful collector. The smartest 1 percent of rare book collectors and librarians set the agenda for all of the others in the trade. They determine the subject and scope of their collections and set out with all their tenacity and a good portion of their resources to construct them. Following close on the footsteps of this charmed rank of collectors, are the smartest 1 percent of booksellers, who take their cues from the collectors, faithfully and industriously fulfilling their wants, and by use of their wiles and imagination, attempting to, and often succeeding in, forcing the boundaries of these collections ever outward. (I should here mention that this last observation is offered as a generally crowd-pleasing remark, as I have never yet met either a collector, a librarian, or a bookseller who did not consider himself or herself to be among the smartest 1 percent of their respective breeds.)

The Internet is neither the new messiah, nor the ultimate bookselling weapon, but just another arrow in the quiver of the working bookseller and collector. Some may be able to survive exclusively on Internet sales. However, the booksellers most serious about their trade and collectors most serious about their collections will continue to use the Internet to their advantage, while scanning catalogues, attending book fairs and auctions, and doing pretty much everything else they can think of to advance their agendas. The contract between collector and bookseller is still very much in force. We can frustrate or enlighten, delight or infuriate one another, but we cannot survive or thrive without each other. In other words, the collectors are going to save us.

The American Antiquarian Book Trade: Yesterday, Today, and Tomorrow

John Crichton

THE FOLLOWING observations, first presented in an address before the Antiquarian Booksellers' Association of Japan in Tokyo in January 2005, are based on my dual role as president of the Antiquarian Booksellers' Association of America (ABAA) and as the proprietor of an antiquarian book business, the Brick Row Book Shop. The shop has been through three generations and has witnessed and survived many changes in the American antiquarian book trade. From these combined perspectives, I want to examine the current state of the American antiquarian book trade and some of the trends and developments that have affected it in the past twenty-five years, followed by some speculation as to where we might be going in the future.

In looking at the past seventy-five years of the American antiquarian book trade, I can safely say that the Brick Row Book Shop is a good example of a successful, medium-size, American rare book firm, which has continued to function as it was originally designed to do while also adjusting to change. The Brick Row Book Shop is even, at least by American standards, antiquarian itself. It was founded in 1915 in New Haven, Connecticut, on the Yale University campus. The first motto of the business was "Books for libraries, scholars and collectors," and through three owners and ninety years of doing business, the motto still fits. The Brick Row Book Shop is a classic example of how our trade has fundamentally changed very little over the years, and I use it as an example, obviously, because it is close to me, but Ed Maggs of London or Michael Dawson of Los Angeles could easily be telling the same story. The Brick Row Book Shop is also a classic example of an American antiquarian book business that established itself, grew, and has continued to survive on business with American, Canadian, and English libraries.

In the first fifty years of the Brick Row Book Shop (1915–1965), virtually every sale was to a library. Hundreds of libraries across America, Canada, and England ordered almost every book from every catalogue we issued. These libraries had a nearly unquenchable thirst to build collections, and the Brick Row Book Shop, as did many American antiquarian booksellers, benefited by recognizing and responding to this demand. Another part of our business from those years was an occasional sale to a collector and, less frequently, to another dealer. During these early years, dealers did not trade amongst themselves as they do today.

Our primary tools for selling books were then, as they are today, the printed catalogue, direct contact, and the presence of an open shop in a major metropolitan area. The American book trade was once dominated by large open shops with familiar names, such as Dawson (Los Angeles), John Howell (San Francisco), Goodspeed (Boston), H. P. Kraus (New York), or Hamill and Barker (Chicago), or districts, such as Fourth Avenue in New York or 4th Street in Los Angeles, where city blocks were filled with large antiquarian bookshops to which you could walk from the center of town, as you can in the Kanda book district in Tokyo. In the early 1960s, the book fair began to emerge in the American antiquarian book trade as an important instrument for promotion and sales, and many American antiquarian booksellers added book fairs to the list of catalogues, direct contact, and open shops as one of their means of selling. The first book fairs were organized and sponsored by the ABAA, which itself was founded in 1949 to fill a need for a trade association that would promote and set standards for the growing numbers of booksellers. The ABAA was founded with about ninety members, and twenty-five years later it had grown to over 250 members.

The overall conditions of the marketplace for rare books and manuscripts during these years were very favorable to the bookseller, and its major components were strong institutional business; an influx of well-educated and affluent young collectors; and a trade that was still controlled by the dealers. The institutions and the collectors were dependent on the dealers for material—material that was becoming increasingly scarce. It was the classic scenario of increasing demand and tightening supply, which prices began to reflect. The auction houses, particularly Sotheby's and Christie's, had yet to try to take advantage of this market by directly appealing to collectors, and they were, through the 1970s, still primarily wholesale distributors to the trade—a trade that still controlled the flow of goods. It was difficult not to succeed as an antiquarian bookseller in this business climate. All of the economic and cultural currents were moving in directions favorable to the bookseller. As a consequence, the numbers of booksellers, collectors, and book fairs increased, and a strong seller's market emerged.

Approaching the middle 1980s, the business environment for antiquarian booksellers slowly began to change. The Brick Row Book Shop, as an example, still primarily supplied libraries, collectors, and, increasingly, other dealers with antiquarian books and manuscripts, but, unlike the early years when virtually all our books and gross sales went to institutions, now the majority of our gross sales were from collectors and other dealers. The once enormous American institutional market was contracting. In 1960, the Brick Row Book Shop had approximately eighty libraries per year ordering from our catalogues, and institutional business represented 85 percent of our annual sales. In 1985, it was down to forty libraries per year, representing 50 percent of our annual sales. Catalogues that once sold 70–80 percent were now considered successful if they sold 40–50 percent. But the decrease in these traditional sales was more

The Brick Row Book Shop in 1916.

The Brick Row Book Shop in 2005.

than been made up for by a young generation of eager collectors, the expansion in the numbers of young booksellers who needed inventory, countless book fairs, and an important influx of business from foreign countries, notably Japan. Beginning in the late 1960s, Japan gradually emerged as an important new market for American and English antiquarian booksellers, and by the early 1980s, in the minds of many American and English booksellers, Japan had replaced American institutions as the destination for rare books. While business with Japan did not replace the American institutional market, it certainly played a very important role in the economy of the American antiquarian book trade in the 1980s and early 1990s. During these years, "Japan" became a major buzzword in the book trade, which a decade later would be replaced by the word "Internet."

Two other important changes took place slowly during this time: the developing role of the auction house and the gradual disappearance of open, walk-in bookshops. As the scarcity of high-quality material drove up prices, the major auction houses, now owned by shopping mall magnates and financiers, wanted a greater part of the action. They accomplished this by appealing directly to collectors, thus circumventing the traditional retail trade. Before long, the control of the flow of goods was no longer the exclusive domain of the dealers. Auction houses encouraged collectors, who were increasingly focusing their attention on high spot material, to bid directly by catering to them with flashy color catalogues, telephone bidding, guides to prices that they called "estimates," and customer services designed for the wealthy. Soon it was not uncommon to see collectors bidding for themselves at auction or having a dealer do their bidding on small commissions. This had been virtually unheard of twenty years before and it had a direct impact on dealers purchasing books at auction. Sotheby's and Christie's were no longer interested in book sales that would not bring at least $1,000 per book, and this left a lot of material destined for auction with no place to go. The result was an expansion of the smaller auction houses—several of which specialized in books only—that were willing to take on this less expensive material. Several of these small book auction houses do very well today on the books Sotheby's and Christie's turn down.

At about the same time the major auction houses transformed themselves from wholesalers to retailers, another important change was taking place: the disappearance from American cities of the large, general antiquarian bookshop. It is ironic that membership in the ABAA continued to grow while the numbers of general antiquarian bookshops decreased, but that is what has happened. Between 1975 and 2000, the ABAA grew to over 450 members, but there were fewer bookshops to visit, and increasingly young booksellers entered the trade as specialists—a bookseller who only sold books on a specific subject: wine and food, modern poetry, early printed books, applied arts and architecture, music, science and medicine, and so on. The American trade that had once been dominated by generalist antiquarian booksellers was now being dominated by specialists, who worked out of their homes or in small offices with hours by appointment only. To add to this irony of more antiquarian booksellers but fewer antiquarian bookshops, there are now fewer and fewer antiquarian book businesses that have employees; they do not service large open shops and consequently do not need as many, if any, employees. With fewer employees and apprentices there are fewer mentors, and it is unlikely that businesses such as these will be carried on into the next generation. Of equal significance is the lack of establishments where young booksellers and collectors can learn about, see, touch, and feel the world of rare books. This was one of the great roles of the large general antiquarian book firms, and it is a role not being filled today.

With these changes also came changes in how we purchase material. In the early years of my business, we bought our inventory in three ways: travel to England, private collections in America, and at auction. Purchasing collections of early printed books and English literature in England from 1930 to 1960 was very advantageous for American dealers. The vast majority of the institutional customers were in America, there was a glut of good material on the market, and currency exchange rates were in our favor. It was not unusual for an employee of the Brick Row Book Shop to make a two-month buying trip to England, which would produce crate loads of books headed to America, which would fill several catalogues. This began to slow in the 1960s, as the English postwar trade emerged economically and the British pound began to strengthen. It slowed even more with decreasing American institutional demand. But travel to other regions of America, to England, Ireland, and Australia to purchase books directly from other booksellers, and at book fairs, is still a very important source for the Brick Row Book Shop in maintaining our inventory. Approximately 50 percent of our inventory is acquired this way; 30 percent of it is bought privately; and only 20 percent today is acquired at auction. We also get duplicates from university libraries. American libraries are not releasing duplicates as they used to, but I think that is going to change, and in the future this will increase as a source of inventory.

By the mid- to late 1990s, the antiquarian book marketplace had changed: there was a seriously contracted institutional trade; there was a narrowing focus by collectors on high spot material, which is in short supply; the major auction houses were functioning as retailers; traditional antiquarian bookshops were closing and being replaced by specialists; and the trade was no longer in control of the flow of goods in the marketplace. And then the Internet came along.

The Internet and the new technological age has brought the book trade great advantages, as it has to all businesses, and at the same time it has challenged and changed a number of the ways we have been accustomed to doing business. I think that for the antiquarian bookseller—as opposed to the general second-hand bookseller—the Internet has really only been a great benefit. We have used it like any other positive business innovation. It has not fundamentally changed what we do, but aided how we do it.

The Internet has provided us with a wealth of information in two areas of research. The first is bibliographical and scholarly research; the second is market research—searching to see who has had and who currently has a book, what the price is, its provenance, and the like. In the first category of scholarly research, this flood of information has been enormously helpful and has provided booksellers instantly with research that once took hours, days, or even weeks to obtain and sometimes involved travel. The change that has been more controversial and even threatening to traditional ways of doing business is instant access to millions of antiquarian, used, and rare books and modern first editions in online databases. This readily accessible information about the quantities and prices of books in the marketplace has permanently changed our traditional sense of scarcity and rarity of the books we deal with, and it certainly has affected some booksellers much more than others. For general scholarly books, references works, many standard literary first editions, histories, and the like, these online databases have created a "Wal-Mart" effect on supply and demand, driving prices both down and up and taking the market-making ability out of individual bookseller's hands, thus further separating the bookseller from the control over the market. For the most part, when and where these booksellers have survived, they have become smaller parts of a larger machine. Many simply went out of business. For the antiquarian bookseller the change has not been as dramatic, but it has been felt, particularly in the way we acquire books, the type of books we acquire, and how we price them once they are acquired.

The Brick Row Book Shop confronted these changes by ceasing to purchase the kinds of books that were suddenly readily available through online databases. For example, I rarely buy the everyday literary first edition that I once eagerly sought, and I almost never purchase for inventory books about books or bibliography. I do not entirely regret this because it comes from the perspective of a bookseller who is always looking for something he has never seen before or better yet something that he did not previously know existed, and consequently this "Wal-Mart" effect on our book economy has actually helped me turn my attention away from ordinary first editions to more unusual rare and antiquarian books. This has made me more disciplined and a better bookseller, but at the same time many of my colleagues and my traditional sources of supply have suffered. For example, it is no longer as easy to travel across America,

England, or Australia to replenish inventory by visiting bookshops and booksellers. Many of the shops have closed, and many of the booksellers no longer depend as they once did on visiting booksellers as an important source of their sales. But I still find that "scouting" books—as it is called in America—is a profitable and rewarding way to acquire inventory. I often will purchase books that a bookseller—sometimes a very prominent bookseller—has had on the Internet for over a year, put the book in my next catalogue, and get multiple orders for it. This is a good example of how we all make our own markets, and how customers will choose to look to us for material they would not necessarily purchase elsewhere.

The "Wal-Mart" effect has forced the book trade to democratize, to change how it sells books. It is now possible for those booksellers I once visited in the countryside, in small towns, and in distant cities to advertise and sell their inventory in the same venue, directly next to the internationally known dealers from Tokyo, London, and New York, at essentially the same price. The public can compare copies, and if the bookseller from the countryside is a savvy businessperson, they will offer their copy for a somewhat lower price than that of the Tokyo, New York, or London dealer. This does not give country booksellers more knowledge or expertise; it does not give them professional equality or standing; but it does gives them a platform that previously was available only to the more prominent booksellers through expensive catalogues, open shops, book fairs, and travel.

A negative aspect of this democratization is that now anyone with a few books in the attic can advertise themselves next to those of us who have spent years acquiring knowledge, professional standing, and expertise; they can even plagiarize our readily available catalogue descriptions and give the appearance of expertise. There are many complaints about this from established dealers, and to some extent they are justified, but I think of greater importance is the effect this openness has had on the trade: it has allowed literally thousands of unknown newcomers into our ranks who will use these new, open venues of selling material for fraudulent purposes, such as forgeries, color Xeroxes of dust jackets, misdescribed books, stolen materials, and so on. This is a serious situation, particularly with self-regulated online auction businesses like eBay. The ABAA, together with International League of Antiquarian Booksellers (ILAB), is devoting more resources and time to monitoring fraud and theft. As booksellers, our warning to the book-collecting public should be always to work through a trusted, reputable, dealer (preferably a member of the ABAA or ILAB), where if you do not get satisfaction or have a misunderstanding, you are guaranteed recourse.

Overall, the financial viability of the antiquarian trade has undoubtedly been helped by the Internet, which has assisted in spreading the word about the accessibility of rare books and manuscripts in ways that were incomprehensible just a few years ago. The Internet has made the materials that once seemed available only to a small, refined community suddenly obtainable for anyone, anywhere who has access to a computer. But for the second-hand book trade, as I have pointed out, it has been a mixed blessing, and the technological age may soon be making this difficult adjustment even more difficult. Google, the American mega-database—the most talked about company in America today—announced recently that it is beginning a working relationship with the New York Public Library, Harvard University, Stanford University, the University of Michigan, and Oxford University in England, to digitize millions of books in their libraries in order to make them accessible in the Google database. And this is obviously just the beginning of a digital revolution as many other mega-databases attempt to follow Google's lead. Michael Keller, librarian of Stanford University, said that within two decades most of the world's knowledge will be digitized and freely available on the Internet, just as there is free reading in libraries today. Some have even suggested that the Google project and others like it will have as revolutionary affect on the world of books as did Gutenberg, and it is difficult to argue with that.

Digitization is never going to replace the printed book, and its full impact is not going to be felt for some years, but this will be a challenge for booksellers in the future. Two hundred years ago, booksellers and publishers were suspicious of public libraries and free access to books. They thought free access to books in libraries would undermine their trade, and they were wrong, but it is difficult to see a silver lining for second-hand booksellers in this recent development. I do not think the antiquarian bookseller is threatened by digitization the way the second-hand bookseller will be, but all booksellers will find that they are going to have less and less control over the flow of goods—and information—in the marketplace.

This may all seem somewhat ominous, but looking at it through the eyes of my third-generation business, the Brick Row Book Shop, I see that the fundamentals of the antiquarian book trade have remained remarkably constant. Despite all the changes, my business is doing well in a complicated marketplace and in a manner not altogether inconsistent with how we did it seventy-five years ago. A catalogue we issued in December, received orders from twenty-three libraries, nineteen collectors, and ten dealers. At the end of 2004, our sales were slightly up over the previous year, with approximately 40 percent to libraries, 40 percent to collectors, and 20 percent to other members of the trade, which is fairly representative of our business over the past decade. Catalogues and direct sales are still responsible for the majority of our gross sales, at approximately 85 percent, with Internet sales at around 15 percent. And, as president of the ABAA, I can say that in general the state of the trade is healthy, and in some cases it is very strong. We have more members of our association than ever before, almost 460, and gross sales overall appear to be steady, if not on the rise. Almost all of our members use online databases to their advantage, and have websites for their businesses, which are inexpensive to set up and essential advertising and promotional tools. Regardless of negative comments you hear about the influences of the Internet on the book trade in general, I know of no bookseller who worked hard to adjust to this new age and failed because of it, and in fact many have prospered where they once struggled, if they applied themselves to the challenge.

The distribution of income in the trade concerns me. Although the overall gross sales are steady, if not on the rise, I do not think they are as equally distributed among our membership as in the past. In part, this is because of the split, two-tiered market for our goods—that is, an ever-increasing focus on high spots to the exclusion of other antiquarian material, resulting in a market where 20 percent of the goods are highly desirable and 80 percent are much less saleable, and for which there is continually less and less demand. This has happened in large part because of the enormous infusion of recently made capital—the billions of dollars made in America between 1990 and 1999—that dictates the conditions of the market. This second market of goods is decreasing in appeal for two reasons: the institutional trade had a strong influence on the demand for secondary material that it no longer exercises. Libraries once purchased large quantities of general antiquarian material to fill gaps in collections. Booksellers with want lists once eagerly sought out this material for their library clients, thus creating a general climate of demand. This type of purchasing by libraries has seriously contracted, and the loss of business has been felt in the marketplace. There are also cultural reasons for these two tiers: over time the focus on the past narrows, there is a weeding and filtering, which is beyond our control to regulate, and thus the interest in and demand for certain commodities slackens, creating a situation with antiquarian books where the supply of certain types of books is increasing because the demand for them and interest in them has diminished. Consequently, the majority of gross sales are confined to a smaller number of the important high spots changing hands and income produced is being shared among fewer upper-level dealers, thus making it more difficult for the other, second-tier dealers, to make a living in this profession. There has always been some element of the two-tiered system in the rare book business, but it now appears to be more one-sided than in the past.

Another concern I have is for businesses like the Brick Row Book Shop—the typical medium-size American antiquarian book firm: will they be thriving in the next generation? There is no doubt there will always be a demand for second-hand books of all kinds and for rare and antiquarian books and first editions, but the field is going to tighten and the focus will continue to narrow towards the high spots, as it has done noticeably over the past decade. Those booksellers who exist outside of the high-end market will be increasingly looking for niches, for specialties, in which to survive. Second-hand bookshops are going to have to find carefully thought-out locations, with captive markets in university districts or major pedestrian thoroughfares, like the Kanda district, as well as an Internet presence. Those who are not willing to recognize this will struggle against change.

As we look to the immediate future, the Internet world is obviously replacing the platform from which we have traditionally done business, and we must adjust with it, just as we have adjusted with other innovations in the past. In fact, we have already begun these adjustments. The advent of the specialist was a reaction to the difficulties of the general antiquarian, and increasingly the antiquarian booksellers of the future are going to have to understand their niches and focuses, using the tools of the technological world to their advantage while not completely abandoning the tools of the past. Many of our customers, as an example, still want and order from printed catalogues, to the exclusion of other methods, but there is also a large and growing body of customers who rely solely on the Internet. We attempt to appeal to both with printed and digital catalogues. We have our catalogued stock on five online databases: ILAB, ABAA, ABE, ALIBRIS, and BIBLIOPOLY, in addition to our own website, which is searched by Google and others. By doing this, we are guaranteed a broad cross-section of the potential market. But we also seek to preserve our own markets, and we have increasingly narrowed our focus to those areas in which we have the most knowledge and expertise and for which we are known and respected. Knowledge and respect together are the most powerful tools in the rare book business, and they will never be replaced by technology.

There will be noticeably fewer participants in this profession in the next generation, but the current generation is safe, if somewhat diminished. Antiquarian booksellers are an enormously resilient, self-reliant group, in which individual members almost to a person write their own paychecks, call their own shots, and admirably live by their intellect and wits. As a group, booksellers have adjusted to some threatening changes in the market in recent years, and they have come through intact because the fundamental aspects of what we do have a foundation that simple trends and market changes cannot easily undo. Though some of my more cynical colleagues may disagree, I believe there is a sense of professionalism that binds and assists booksellers who genuinely participate in their trade. Over fifty years ago, nearly seventy-five American antiquarian booksellers came together to establish an association to foster friendly relations among themselves, to promote professionalism and ethics in the trade, and to join the International League of Antiquarian Booksellers. Those goals are just as important to a healthy antiquarian book trade today as they were in the formative years of the ABAA. I have no doubt the same will be true in the future.

Adventures of a Bookseller

Priscilla Juvelis

I HAVE BEEN a rare book dealer since 1980. Before that, I worked in New York for Harcourt Brace Jovanovich—as it was then known—and later at a book club. For the former I sold subsidiary rights, for the latter I bought them. I then spent one year working for the late John F. Fleming, perhaps the foremost bookseller of his generation.

John was the successor to Dr. A. S. W. Rosenbach, who was generally considered to be the greatest antiquarian bookseller ever. Although John liked rather facetiously to say that Corning Glass heir and noted bibliophile, Arthur Houghton, was the most successful bookseller he ever knew because of his purchase and subsequent very lucrative sale of what is now known as the Houghton Sha Na Ma. John often talked about his experiences with "the Doctor." And he had some wonderful stories, starting with how he came to be employed at Rosenbach's straight out of high school. He had seen a notice on the bulletin board at the YMCA and applied for the job. I think it was at a stationery supply store. At the end of the summer, he was told his services were no longer needed as it was a summer post. He was furious and went back to the Y and demanded another job (this time without a finder's fee) and was sent over to the

Rosenbach premises on East 51st Street. And the rest, as they say, is history. But just how did a boy whose first duties were limited to opening the door and announcing visitors come to succeed Dr. R? John told me more than once, "This," waving his arm about the great book room at East 57th Street, "was not supposed to be mine."

John gradually took on more responsibilities, but he told me that early on he had opened the door one morning to an older lady

Vincent FitzGerald & Co. *Epiphanies* by James Joyce. Interpreted by Susan Weil and Marjorie Van Dyke. New York: Vincent FitzGerald & Co., 1988. One of 52 copies.

who was poorly dressed and carrying a paper bag. She gave her name, which meant nothing to the young Fleming, and asked to see Dr. R. John informed her that he was with someone and invited her to have a seat. He got her a cup of coffee and made her comfortable and, after about an hour, summoned up the nerve to interrupt Dr. R. He told me how he timidly went into Rosenbach's presence and said there was a lady who had been waiting to see him for an hour. John then mentioned the name she had given, Mrs. Rebecca Harkness, and Dr. R. went running out to her, as John tells it, almost knocking him over. She was one of the Doctor's best customers, a shy woman, but a wealthy and important client. The moral of that story was not lost on John—anyone could buy anything—an interesting corollary to Larry McMurtry's bit of dialogue from his hilarious novel of an antique picker, *Cadillac Jack*, in which Jack proclaims, "Anything could be anywhere."[1]

I met John when I was a bit older than seventeen. It was in 1979 and I had been working in publishing for nine years buying and selling subsidiary rights, but wanted to go into business for myself. A friend of my father's, who was director of Old Master pictures at the Knoedler Gallery, said, "Well you're into books and I know this man who's also into books—Knoedler's has always done business with him—I'll introduce you." So, a week later I found myself at 322 East 57th Street for lunch, John's premises, which had been Dr. Rosenbach's premises. They have been described as having "baronial splendor," which is not an exaggeration. Several months later we agreed that I would work for him for a year before returning to Boston to start my own business. I had the idea of specializing in modern first editions as that had been the aspect of publishing in which I was involved. I never quite followed that idea through. After starting on my own, I had the opportunity, through another art dealer friend, to bid on a collection of livres d'artistes in wonderful bindings by Legrain, Bonet, Creuzevault, and other twentieth-century artists. I

---

1. Larry McMurtry. *Cadillac Jack*. With a New Preface. New York: Touchstone Book Simon & Schuster, 1987, 23.

Unique binding by Donald Glaister on *The Côte D'Azur Triangle* by Harry Kondoleon. Etchings and lithographs by Mark Beard. New York: Vincent FitzGerald & Co., 1985.

went to Buenos Aires, where the collector and his collection resided. I made my bid. There were two other dealers, both Parisian, bidding. I was successful. I got the collection to Boston. I will not bore you with the sordid details of that exercise, suffice it to say that Argentine customs, as a group, seemed to me to function in the manner of medieval secret societies.

After shelving the books in my apartment, I called John to tell him about the collection. I asked if he wanted to be partners with me on it. He was on the afternoon shuttle to Boston that very day. Like all great bibliophiles, one of the wonderful things about John was his willingness to go anyplace at the drop of a hat for a chance at a great book.

When John sat down to view the collection, I picked out what I thought was the best book: a splendid copy of Bonnard's *Parallèlement*, which was the artist's first book, the art-dealer-turned-publisher Ambroise Vollard's first book, and generally considered to be the first modern livre d'artiste. It was published in 1900. This copy was the very rare first issue with the unchanged title page and half-title litho and was especially strong in its images. The lithos were printed in rose and black, not the single rose that is the norm. (I've seen no other such copies.) In addition, it was in a marvelous binding by the greatest of the modern masters, Paul Bonet. And, it was Bonet's first attempt at using material other than leather in his bindings: in this case hand-carved ivory onlays. John looked at it and said nothing. I then took out what I thought to be the next great book, a splendid copy of Pablo Picasso's great Cubist book, *Le Siege De Jerusalem*, published in 1914 by another art dealer turned publisher, Henry Kahnweiler, in a beautiful binding by Semet and Plumelle after one of Picasso's drypoints from the book. Again, no reaction. I showed him the rare Giorgio De Chirico *Calligrammes*, with De Chirico's shaped black lithographic images surrounding, intersecting, and generally enhancing Guillaume Apollinaire's revolutionary shaped poetry. It was in a stunning Bonet binding. And then I pulled out Bonet's miraculous pierced screen binding on Raoul Dufy's charming *Tartarin De Tarascon*. Still no response from John. And I was beginning to panic. What if the collection was not as great as I had thought? The silence was deafening and then John said, "It is very clear that the English can't hold a candle to the French when it comes to making beautiful books!" "Now dear, how much did you say you paid for this collection?" I told him and he said, "Right, dear, we'll be partners on this and on any business we get as a result of it." And so began a very special time in my life.

    John had been known as a specialist in English literature. But he was truly a generalist—of very great books and autographs. Years with Dr. R had prepared him for nothing less. There were those who, on learning of my partnership with John on this livres d'artiste's collection, said John was out of his depth. Not true!

    On quiet days at Fleming's when just the two of us were around (I was there Wednesday through Friday nearly every week), I would pull out one of the old Rosenbach stock books to peruse and to elicit stories from John about the books and collectors detailed in them. Rosenbach's stock books were created when the U.S. government changed the tax laws in the early 1930s and required written inventories from antiquarian booksellers for their tax returns. To John fell the task of noting every book on the shelves, all the prints, drawings, and autographs—everything that made up Rosenbach's—and he always maintained the experience was one of the secrets of his success. John told me that Dr. R. had purchased at least eleven major libraries en bloc in the 'teens and 'twenties and by 1935, he, John, knew the almost overwhelming stock better than anyone except Dr. R. and would assist the Doctor by always being able to put his hands on whatever item was needed to tempt the prospective purchaser.

Two of the en bloc collections purchased by Rosenbach were from France, both made up of the greatest illustrated books: one was the Schumann Library and the other the Roederer—the so-called million-dollar library—at that time a very high sum. Where the Schumann collection was strong in bindings, the Roederer was strong in original art. Roederer, known as 'the champagne king,' had amassed as spectacular a collection of French illustrated books, often with the original drawings and extra suites, as well as proofs of the etchings. It was John who sold a great many of the items in the Roederer collection and a number of the choicest items went to Chicago bibliophile and Sears, Roebuck heir, Lessing Rosenwald. Among those treasures going to Rosenwald was a very desirable set of the *Fables of La Fontaine*, with etchings by Jean-Baptiste Oudry, generally considered to be the most beautiful French book of the eighteenth century. This copy had many of the original drawings. Another rarity that was part of the Roederer stash: 276 original drawings by Jean-Honoré Fragonard for an unpublished *Orlando Furioso*. Fragonard's fabulous drawings were never published as they were deemed to be too free, too loose, to be translated into etchings. And it was the perspicacious Rosenwald who got a number of those splendid drawings. He was probably Rosenbach's closest friend among his customers, and, by the late 1940s, the firm's biggest client. In 1943, at the Crowninshield auction, record prices for modern

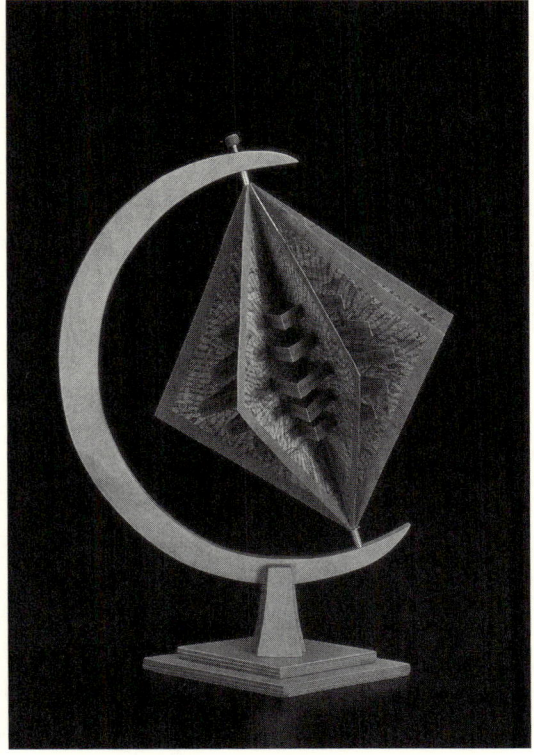

Flying Fish Press. *World Without End* by Julie Chen. Berkeley, CA: 1999.

books (many of the very same titles that were in the Argentine collection) were established by John, bidding for Rosenwald. It was John, from the mid-1930s on, who executed the Doctor's bids at auction as Philip Rosenbach, Abe's brother and business partner, feared the passionate bibliophile in the Doctor would get the better of the businessman, and pay too much for an item.

Over the years, Rosenwald amassed one of the greatest private collections of illustrated books ever, including great block books, English illustrated and finely printed books (yes, Caxtons and Blakes enough for anyone), and Italian and French incunables, as well as Henri Matisse's *Jazz*. This great connoisseur donated his prints and drawings collection to the National Gallery of Art and his books to the Library of Congress, where it now forms the Lessing Rosenwald Collection of Printing and Graphic Arts, has its own curator, and has been added to since the initial gift. The collection is certainly one of this nation's treasures.

John's 57th street co-op was full of treasures, not all of them books and manuscripts. Others were souvenirs of special days. I remember one day looking for something that John had asked me to find in one of the closets in the back of apartment near the room that was "my" bedroom (it had been Dr. R's and therefore John would not use it). The bath in the bedroom had an old steam bath machine belonging to Dr. R (it was the size of small car) and it was hard indeed not to feel the presence of those bibliophiles who had been there before me, especially in the middle of the night when I was there alone (John at home in Larchmont) and the old co-op's creaks were somehow more noticeable. I rooted unsuccessfully through the closet (nothing it seemed had ever been thrown out or changed from the time the Rosenbachs had moved there in 1947). John came back to help me and pulled out an auction catalogue and exclaimed, "Oh, this is really important! This is the marked copy when I bought Poe's *Tamerlane* for Mrs. Joseph Regenstein." She presented it to the University of Chicago's Rare Book Library, thus completing their collection of first editions of Poe. That library was under the direction of John's very good friend, the incomparable bookman Bob Rosenthal.

Louis Silver was a most important collector from 1952 until his death—first to the firm of Rosenbach and then to John Fleming. In fact, it was Silver who loaned John the money needed to purchase the Rosenbach inventory and premises from the Rosenbach Foundation after the deaths of Dr. R and his brother Philip. In return for the loan, Silver did, of course, have an opportunity to buy from the inventory that John purchased from the foundation.

John's love and enthusiasm for books was contagious. He caught the disease from Dr. R and I am sure I caught it from him. But the truth is I did not understand the true nature of the illness until fairly recently. John had often told the story of his questioning the importance (and subsequent high price) of a Kilmarnock Burns that Dr. R. had just purchased. "Hell, John," the Doctor said, "This book changed a country." It had, contended Dr. R, restored to Scotland its national consciousness. Just as John had not "gotten" the mysterious allure, the "fantasy" as he often called it, of the Kilmarnock Burns, I, quite frankly, never really got the "fantasy" of those books with more intangible charms, as opposed to the obvious allure of, say, a *Hypnerotomachia Poliphili* or a Naples *Aesop* or a Jasper Johns *Fizzles*, or a great binding, or a book with Matisse lithographs.

This all changed some years ago when I finally obtained a rare volume in American literature, Margaret Fuller's *Woman in the Nineteenth Century*, published in wrappers in 1845 in an edition of 1,500. You might expect it to be a common book but this is decidedly not so. Shortly thereafter (the old saw about things coming in threes must have been in operation), I purchased two other remarkable

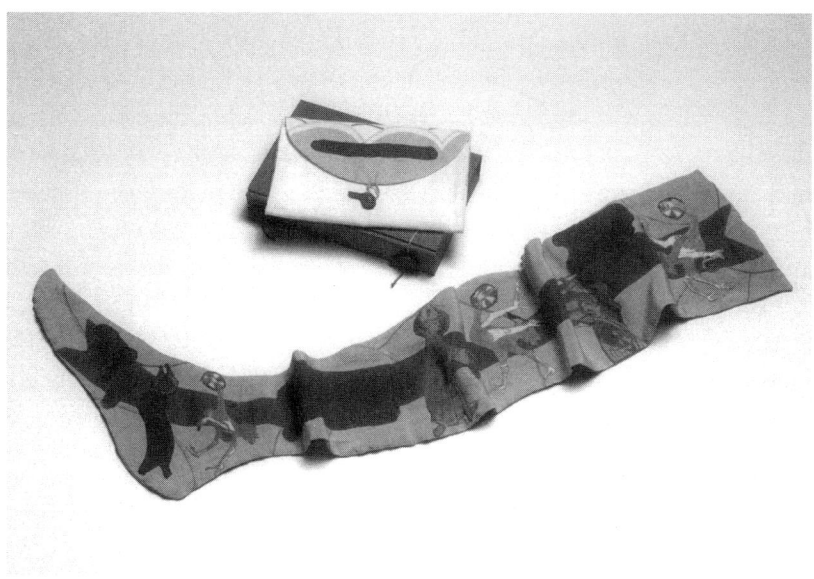

Lois Morrison, Ste. *Ostrich & St. Valentine*. Leonia, NJ 2002.

Fuller items—an eyewitness account of her tragic, premature death by drowning off the coast of Long Island, and Fuller's own beloved signed copy of Johann Wolfgang von Goethe's *Faust*. Fuller had always fascinated me (and many others) and she has been called "one of America's genuine heroines." She was accepted as an intellectual equal by Ralph Waldo Emerson and other Transcendentalists. As I plunged into my Fuller readings, I was astounded at the scope of her influence. She was, along with Edgar Allen Poe, this country's first major literary critic and, of course, her mysterious death equals the stories about his. She was one of this country's first international correspondent's (for Horace Greeley's New York *Tribune*). In fact, she was returning to the United States after covering the Italian Risorgimento when she died. It was she who translated much of Goethe's poetry for her fellow Transcendentalists, infusing that group with her own views on German Romanticism.

But—and this is the key point—she was the first American to write a book advocating women's rights, *Woman in the Nineteenth Century*. It was her masterpiece. Among other things, the book attacked the hypocrisy of men who campaigned for the abolition of slavery while supporting laws that prohibited women from owning property or having rights over their children. She bitterly pointed out that men educated women, "more as a servant than a daughter," and that as a result of being thus educated women were fit only for domestic roles. Fuller urged women to see themselves as more than appendages and to seek wider, more self-reliant lives. The book became a cornerstone of American feminism, mightily influencing those of her own generation. The fact that Lucretia Mott, Elizabeth Cady Stanton, and others organized the world's first conference on women's rights just three years after its publication (in Seneca Falls, New York, in 1848) surely was not a coincidence.[2] In fact, at the first National Convention for Women's Rights (held in Worcester, Massachusetts, on October 23 and 24, 1850), the main organizer, Paulina

---

2. Elizabeth Cady Stanton, Susan B. Anthony, and Matilda Joslyn Gage, *The History of Woman Suffrage*, Volume I. (New York: Fowler & Wells, Publishers, 1881), 51.

Wright Davis, wrote in the official minutes of this significant meeting, "One great disappointment fell upon us. Margaret Fuller, toward whom many eyes were turned as the future leader in this movement, was not with us. The 'hungry, ravening sea' had swallowed her up, and we were left to mourn her guiding hand—her royal [yes, Paulina Wright Davis actually said and wrote "royal"] presence. To her, I, at least had hoped to confide the leadership of this movement. It can never be known if she would have accepted it; the desire had been expressed to her by letter; but be that as it may, she was, and still is, a leader of thought; a position far more desirable than a leader of numbers."[3]

Further, in the Appendix of Volume I of *The History of Woman Suffrage*, edited by Elizabeth Cady Stanton, Susan B. Anthony and Mathilda Joslyn Gage, the authors devote two pages to an essay on Fuller's primary importance, stating, "Margaret Fuller possessed more influence upon the thought of America, than any woman previous to her time. Men of diverse interests and habits of thought alike recognized her power and acknowledged the quickening influence of her mind upon their own. . . ." Later in the essay, they state, "In calling for the opinions of her sex upon Life, Literature, Mythology, Art, Culture, and Religion, Miss Fuller was the precursor of the Woman's Rights agitation of the last thirty-three years."[4] Stanton, Anthony, and Gage could not have been more clear in their assessment of Fuller, allowing her pride of place in the struggle for women's rights to which these women devoted their lives.

When I offered my first edition of *Woman in the Nineteenth Century* for sale in a catalogue I was stunned to have orders from three major American institutions that did not own the book. Imagine if, say, the Pierpont Morgan Library or Yale's fabled Beinecke did not have a first edition of *Walden* or Emerson's *Essays*. I had to wonder, how could such a well-respected classic be missing from at least three great rare book libraries in this country. Somehow, although

---

3. Ibid., 51-52. See also the minutes of the Worcester meeting which were printed by Prentiss & Sawyer of Boston in 1851.

4. Ibid., Appendix, 217.

her peers valued Fuller, posterity seemed almost to have forgotten her. Her *Woman in the Nineteenth Century* was the first great expression of American feminist thought, and its shadow is still long. It is to the women's rights movement what *Walden* is to the environmental movement and its influence on twentieth and twenty-first century life has not yet been felt to the fullest extent.

As I began to read more and more, I discovered the Grimke sisters. In 1838, when criticized by male abolitionists and clergy for speaking in public against slavery, both Sarah and Angelina wrote pamphlets articulating their moral right—indeed, their *moral obligation*—to speak. In 1870, at age seventy-eight, Sarah Grimke, then living in Malden, Massachusetts, led a suffrage demonstration of fifty-eight women through a snowstorm, a fitting cap to a career that defined the burgeoning women's movement and propelled it into the public sphere.

What captured my imagination—yes, John, I finally got the "fantasy" of a book—was how these women refused to be deterred. If an obstacle was placed before them, they went over it, around it, or simply through it. And these women were important figures in their own day. For example, in 1898, Congress authorized a photograph postcard of Susan B. Anthony's home: they would not let her vote, but there was an official postcard of her house.

In the passing from generation to generation of this country's history and culture, the women who changed their world and ours seemed to have gotten short shrift. Of course, I had heard of Stanton and Anthony, but not of Fuller *as a feminist* and certainly not Charlotte Perkins Gilman, author of *Women and Economics*, the 1898 book that had the audacity to call for equal pay for equal work and which is now considered a cornerstone of feminist thought. And, I got As in American history in high school and college.

Further illumination came in the literary field. I had always loved the fiction of Edith Wharton and Sarah Orne Jewett and was determined to keep both writers in stock from the day I started my book business. I remember in 1982 or so, buying a copy of *Ethan Frome* in dust jacket—a splendid copy—and taking a big gulp and putting what I thought to be the very steep price of $800 on it. My Wharton collector also took a big gulp, and bought it. Now, of course, you could add a zero to that number and still not reach the retail price for that copy. I was grateful to my customer, but for more reasons than her purchase. She urged me to explore the other works of women writers. Years later her enthusiasm for works by American women led to the landmark exhibition and catalogue, *Emerging Voices*, organized for The Grolier Club in 1998. I discovered Gilman's classic, *The Yellow Wallpaper*, published in 1892, which is a fictionalized account of her mental breakdown, brought on by postpartum depression—the first mention of this in fiction. I also discovered Kate Chopin's *The Awakening*, published in Chicago in 1899 by Herbert S. Stone. Both are now taught in almost every high school American literature course, but that was not the case in the 1960s when I was in high school. *New York Times* reporter Margo Shapero recently explained the century in which this major literary work was ignored by citing an early review of Chopin's novel of female lust and infidelity. "Faced with those distasteful subjects the critic simply pulled back and announced in a perfect union of arrogance and ignorance, 'A fact which we have all agreed not to acknowledge is as good as no fact at all.'"

What I have found in buying books and letters by Anthony and Stanton and Lucretia Mott, Lydia Maria Child, the Grimkes, Gilman, Rachel Carson, Jane Addams, Sophonisba Breckinridge, Julia Lathrop, Carrie Chapman Catt, Alice Howard Shaw, Lucy Stone, Alice Stone Blackwell, Julia Ward Howe, Alice Hamilton, Myra Breckenridge, Mary Livermore, and a host of other significant Americans is that there is still great material out there as these women have largely been ignored by institutions and collectors of the past.

John would have been proud of me—finally getting the mystery of the written word and its power over my imagination—although he might not share my passion for the subject. I cannot be sure of that, though. He always did say his favorite customers were women and I know he thought them the equal of any male bibliophile.

Book Talk

Let me go back to the beginning of John's and my partnership, the Argentine collection. He instructed me to prepare a catalogue worthy of the books in the collection and I did, although it took me nine months. When the catalogue was nearly ready, I brought the books to John's and we installed them in the big bookroom on 57th Street—which was no mean task as we had to pack up the existing inventory and store it on the second floor. It is hard for me to describe the thrill I felt at seeing this collection that I had bought in this place of prominence in a room where so many other great books had been shown. In fact, it was the greatest of thrills. John had invited one of his customers to lunch soon thereafter and, on the appointed day, I flew in from Boston with an advance copy of the catalogue hastily bound up. The color plates had not yet been tipped in and I was in the kitchen gluing them in when John's customer turned up early. I continued my task but after about five minutes John came into the kitchen and said, "Don't bother dear, come out and join us; he's just bought the collection en bloc." I don't much remember the lunch—I was too much in shock. But later, when it was just the two of us, with all sorts of thoughts swirling around in my head (and the overwhelming emotion of relief at the thought of being able to pay off the enormous debt I had incurred to purchase the collection), I remembered John had once given me some advice on how to be a successful dealer. "The great thing," he said, "was to catch a trend at the beginning." So, I reminded him of his dictum about the great thing of catching a trend at the beginning, hoping the day's sale was such an example. John was silent for a bit, then he smiled slightly, and I noticed a distinctly Irish twinkle in his blue eyes as he said, "I may have to amend that, dear. The *really* great thing is to start a trend."

Roxburghe to eBay: A Brief Survey of the Way Books Change Hands

Peter Kraus

Almost two hundred years ago on June 7, 1812 a group of bibliophiles assembled in London to form The Roxburghe Club, the world's first, and still, after all this time, the preeminent club for book collectors. The fact that America could now have not just one, but many book-collecting clubs, is only one example of the vast changes that have taken place in the world of book collecting in the past two centuries. To those first Roxburghe members, the world of book collecting today would seem like science fiction. As it happens, 2003 was the fortieth anniversary of my entering the antiquarian book trade. Although forty years is only a small fraction of the time elapsed since the founding of The Roxburghe Club, I believe the founding members would have felt completely at home in 1963, and quite bemused in 2003. The early Roxburghe members collected in what I would call the area of classic bibliophily: manuscripts, early printed books, fine bindings, and the classics. In addition, they would have tended to subscribe to the important new books as they came out. This was a time when most of the elaborate publications were published for subscribers, as the lists of eminent people in the front of many surviving books attests. While classic bibliophily was still active forty years ago, the intervening period has largely

Hans P. Kraus, leading bookseller of his generation, and my mentor.

witnessed its demise. In this essay, I address the changes in the world of book collecting and bookselling, and try to offer some clues as to where one should look for signs of hope for the future.

Among my earliest memories are the continual lamentations of my elders and betters concerning the disappearance of good books. It was the classic situation of "the good old days." In those days, I took most things my elders and betters said at face value, and I duly accepted these dire utterances without questioning them, even though things seemed pretty good to me. I was working in a shop surrounded by unimaginable treasures, such as a complete copy of the Gutenberg Bible and a folio Audubon *Birds of America*. With the benefit of hindsight, I do not think the situation was actually that bad. In my opinion, the reality was that there were still good books in abundance but the quality and nature of what was available had changed. The booksellers who were active when I began my career had lived through a time of seemingly endless supplies of great books, for which, believe it or not, there had not always been a corresponding endless supply of clients. Forty years later, we face a landscape that none of those booksellers could have imagined in their wildest dreams. It is not that the good books have reappeared, or that every last book has vanished, but that vast quantities of books have disappeared from dealers' shelves, and sadder still, many of the bookshops, especially in the United States, from which these booksellers operated, have gone the way of the dodo, and even the ones that are left no longer boast the sagging shelves of former times.

This simple fact of life, more than any other, is altering the nature of the world of which The Roxburghe Club, and the clubs that belong to Fellowship of American Bibliophilic Societies (FABS), forms such an important part. Before examining the ramifications of this, I would like to put the current situation in historical perspective. From the time of the sale of John Ker, the Duke of Roxburghe's books, books were sold, for the most part, by booksellers operating out of traditional shops, mainly, but not wholly at street level. These shops tended to be in large urban centers, but England and the United States both had a healthy supply of "country booksellers." Many, but far from all, booksellers issued catalogues as a means of reaching customers who did not have the time or opportunity to visit them. Apart from their not insignificant scholarly value, these catalogues are now a unique archaeological guide to the vast migrations of books over the centuries, and a testimony to the key role the book trade has played in the history of book collecting. Alas, these migrations have largely ended, due to the books having reached their final resting places on the shelves of the world's institutional libraries.

These bookshops were often large establishments with a substantial staff occupying many floors; as often as not they dealt in a vast range of subjects and new books as well as old. The American versions have all gone—Howell and Zeitlin on the West Coast and Goodspeeds and Sessler's in the East being probably the best known. In England things are somewhat different. All the great London firms of forty years ago survive in name, but not always in the same location, or even in London. But at least Quaritch, Maggs, Francis Edwards, Thorpe, Sotheran, Pickering and Chatto, Foyles, Dawson's, and Sawyer still exist, and the concept of the shop has not been entirely extinguished, although none of them possess anything remotely like the kind of stock they had on their shelves forty years ago. Of course there has always been more to the trade than the grandees. And on both sides of the Atlantic there was an abundance of such distinguished booksellers as Bernard Breslauer and E. P. Goldschmidt who either had small shops, office-type premises, or simply operated from home. The fact is that the number of booksellers in both London and New York always seemed to make visiting them all a full-time occupation.

It goes without saying that the bookshop was the first port of call for any serious book collector. In America, New York had the lion's share of shops. In the early 1960s, there was still "Booksellers Row" on Fourth Avenue; later, in the 1970s, I was lucky enough to have my shop at 667 Madison Avenue along with no fewer than ten other booksellers, of whom the most distinguished was the fabled Margie Cohn of the House of Books. In my rosy (and doubtless exaggerated) memory, every day seemed like a book fair, with a seemingly endless stream of visitors coming through the door. Beyond New York, Boston, Los Angeles, and San Francisco had the major concentrations of shops. And one could also find shops of varying importance in Chicago, Philadelphia, Washington, and Cleveland. The rest of the country was home to countless book barns, and shops of varying size and importance.

In Europe, England led the way, with London having the heaviest concentration, but there were important establishments as far north as Edinburgh, and most provincial cities boasted at least one significant bookshop. Across the Channel, the French had concentrated almost all their shops in Paris, with very few outposts in the provinces. The Dutch, Germans, Scandinavians, Italians, and Swiss also boasted a lively supply of bookshops in almost any city of significance. The rest of the world paled to insignificance with the exception of Japan, where Tokyo had, and for that matter still has, a whole district devoted to the book trade.

The question then has to be, what, Tokyo notwithstanding, caused the bookshops to go the way of the dinosaur?

A Brief Survey of the Way Books Change Hands

Until 1963—the year I entered the trade—book collecting was largely the pursuit of individuals. This resulted in a steady cycle, in which collections largely assembled during one person's lifetime, would for the most part be sold after their owner's death. Some families, especially the grander ones, might hang on to a library, and only very occasionally were books donated to an institution. However, starting in the late 1950s, a tiny snowball grew into an avalanche, and this snowball was the institutional library. Institutional libraries had been around forever, but they were few in number, and generally lacked the means to add significantly to their collections. All this changed dramatically in the early 1960s as the world, led by America, moved out of the postwar doldrums, and into an era of seemingly ever-increasing prosperity. The growth of institutional libraries began as an American phenomenon, but the phenomenon gradually became global. Europe, Japan, and then Australia all developed a ravenous hoard of libraries. These were mostly to be found in the new universities, which were springing up everywhere like mushrooms, but some libraries were self-supporting, and some like the local celebrity were attached to museums. These libraries were falling over themselves to compete for books and manuscripts. The result is that the cycle has ended. Most books left the bookseller with a one-way ticket. In a bizarre twist, selling books to institutions, which has proved a huge boon to the book trade, can now be seen as a form of suicide, for it has altered the cycle, changing a natural ebb and flow that had occurred over centuries into a one-way street. I must admit that when I started my own business it was with the hope that, even though it would take time to develop a private clientele, I could hope for the support of the many librarians I already knew (which, in fact, they very generously gave me). As booksellers' stocks diminished, urban rents began to rise, and inflation forced salaries up, with inevitable results. Many firms closed, some switched to a by-appointment situation, some moved to the country, and only a handful have stayed the course. There were some sixty rare bookshops in New York in the early 1960s and now there are just a few.

In 1967, I was given the full-time job of visiting the English and Continental trade on a regular basis. This formed a key part of my apprenticeship. Being able to browse the shelves and pick the brains of grizzled veterans was a priceless experience, and it is still difficult for me to grasp the fact that this is largely no longer possible. For those of you who were not fortunate enough to have been around then, I will give a brief picture of what things were like.

The larger shops generally were split into numerous specialist departments, and when visiting Maggs, Quaritch, or Edwards, which were all in their own townhouses in those days, once you found what you wanted, it was like visiting a shop within a shop. Many of the people in charge were world-renowned experts, like Mr. Tooley at Edwards, and I mean real experts, not experts in the way that word is so loosely bandied about by the auction houses. These establishments acquired a steady supply of books, mostly in the form of libraries, but also as books purchased at auction, or from colleagues, or even, in the case of the London trade, from that uniquely British individual, the runner, who, if he ever actually ran, would almost certainly drop dead of a heart attack. I remember thinking that I had arrived when I received my first visit from a runner. Unfortunately, the New York versions were not only fewer in number than their London counterparts, but their offerings were next to useless.

An article in the issue of *The Book Collector* published to celebrate the centenary of Quaritch perfectly illustrates the way books used to circulate. Entire libraries would arrive in a seemingly endless stream. (Believe it or not, the day I started work in 1963, the first thing I did was help unload an entire boxcar of books. The Kraus outpost where I worked backed onto a rail siding. These libraries would first be unpacked and sorted. Then the books would be collated and catalogued, priced, and sold either from the shelf or via catalogue.) This was also a time of endless auctions, the majority in London and Paris, but this was still the era of the fabled "country auction," and the notorious rings. I attended my first auction alone in 1967. Although short by comparison with the forty-two days of

A Brief Survey of the Way Books Change Hands

Philip Hofer, legendary collector, librarian, and connoisseur.

the Roxburghe sale, the auction in Utrecht was still an endurance test forever etched in my memory because of two incidents. The first was a result of my employer having told me to bid under the assumed name "Mr. Smith." I duly purchased one of the first lots (these sales always started with illuminated manuscripts), and to my horror and embarrassment, when "Mr. Smith" was called out by the auctioneer, the entire room burst into a mixture of applause and laughter (I was not as incognito as had been hoped). For some years until the joke wore thin, colleagues greeted me as "Mr. Smith." Later in the sale, having taken a break, I came back and purchased a set of the magazine *Signature*. A minute or two later the entire room turned the page except for me. I was one hundred lots out, and was not even supposed to bid on *Signature*. By the grace of God I had not missed anything, but it was a sobering experience. With the exception of the semi-annual German auctions, these marathon sales are mostly a thing of the past.

As alluded to earlier, if there was a shortage of anything at this time, it was clients not books. In this world, the relationship of book collector to bookseller was key. A good relationship was the only way a collector could possibly keep up with the mass of material flowing onto the market. Almost without exception, the great collectors whose names are now legendary—the Bradley Martins, Tom Streeters, and Robert Taylors—worked closely with one dealer, or in the case of a mega-collector like Paul Mellon, several. Collector Mark Samuels Lasner recently put me in touch with a fellow collector who was selling his library. The library consisted of a collection the current owner had acquired from another collector en bloc around 1960. Going through the books, I discovered that in the vast majority was a letter or a postcard from one or the other bookseller offering the then owner the item. This correspondence testified to a substantial network of relationships. Sometimes one could follow them as they gradually evolved through formality to friendship. I cannot tell you what an exciting day I had going through the collection and reading the correspondence, which brought to life so many long gone names, many of whom I had known. In cases where such relationships still exist, unfortunately, e-mail will have buried their tracks, making such nostalgic pilgrimages impossible.

As the institutions became the biggest buyers of books, a relationship with a bookseller became even more important, if one was to have any hope of obtaining items before they made the journey of no return. Collectors faced stiff competition on two levels. First, institutions (mainly but not exclusively American) all of a sudden were combining seemingly unlimited budgets with inexhaustible appetites. Second, some of the great libraries were under the stewardship of a unique generation of librarians. Legendary figures, such

A Brief Survey of the Way Books Change Hands

as Philip Hofer, Dave Randall, and Harry Ransom, to name just three, not only had money to spend but also the taste and vision to assemble collections of breathtaking size and importance. Having access to dealers was key to building all the great collections.

One only has to read Gordon Ray's celebrated surveys of the book-collecting world in 1965, 1974, and 1982 to see that collectors feared they were being run off the field. In fact, for a short time, they were. But nothing stays the same forever, and the landscape has changed again. Institutions are no longer the all-conquering, acquisitive beasts they once were. Collectors have regained the upper hand; as I have said, there have been two vast changes. The shops with sagging shelves that populated the landscape have gone, and the books, which remain, offer vastly different collecting opportunities.

Fortunately, book collecting is a living process. The vast majority of the books that are sought after today, and which fetch the highest prices, were not published at the time of the Roxburghe sale, and many were still not published a century later. From the great color plate books of which Audubon's *Birds of America* is perhaps most famous, to books illustrated by the twentieth-century masters of which Matisse's *Jazz* is the star, the last two centuries have provided book collectors with a seemingly endless supply of fields from which to choose. The most obvious area of collecting has always been literary first editions, and visitors to most book fairs might be forgiven if they were to think that this was the primary area of collecting and dealing for most people. I am fortunate enough to have a daughter who wrote a best-selling book in 2002. I have observed people approach her at book signings with up to six copies carefully glassined, and at the time I prepared this there were already two signed copies online at over $100. Beyond fiction, there has been no shortage of other subjects. Vast areas of the globe were explored, scientific and medical breakthroughs have been legion, and there is the whole private press movement, which still continues.

Grolier bindings might be scarce, and beyond the budgets of all but a few, but there are modern binders, and new bindings can even be commissioned, just as Jean Grolier commissioned them. Early editions of Shakespeare's plays might be unfindable or unaffordable should they turn up, but the works of Tom Stoppard and his contemporaries not only abound, but at relatively modest prices. One of the positive aspects of book collecting is that it depends largely on taste—and taste changes. Of course, collectors can follow in the footsteps of their predecessors, but they can also create their own pathways. Unfortunately, there is no escaping that fact that the current landscape offers vastly reduced options. One of the great hopes for the future might lie in the disparity in prices, which has arisen between the prices for twentieth-century fiction and everything else; a situation not unlike that in the art market, where Rothko has outpaced Rembrandt. When an inscribed copy of *Ulysses* fetches more than twice the price of the editio princeps of Homer, and an unsigned first edition of the first Harry Potter book sells for more than most people can imagine in their wildest guess, there has to be a glimmer of hope for serious book collectors. Not only early printed books, but also pretty much everything printed before 1900 looks cheap when compared with the prices of modern first editions. Supplies have diminished, but the books have not completely disappeared, and hopefully a new generation of collectors will awaken to the marvels of books without dust jackets.

The health of their age-old primary suppliers is more of a question. Where once there was one source, the bookshop, there are now four. I will discuss each in what I feel is ascending order of importance. First, is the auction—the least sensible place for a collector to acquire books, in my opinion. Difficult as it may be to imagine, prior to the 1970s, it was virtually unheard of for a collector to buy at auction. These were the times when auctions were strictly for the trade, and the prices were largely wholesale. However, set against the fact that prices were much lower, was the fact that in many cases the books were by and large not fully described. So, it made more sense to buy from a dealer who had collated and catalogued the book, and to whom you could even return it, if you decided you did not like it. Of course, people and institutions did buy at auction, but almost without exception through a dealer acting on their behalf. One of the effects of the Ring was to exclude the private buyer in addition to enabling the trade to purchase books advantageously. Following my acclaimed debut in Utrecht, I was dispatched to a sale in Glasgow, with strict instructions to decline any invitation to participate in a Ring. I was duly approached and politely explained that I could not join in. I subsequently spent two days being outbid on every single lot I was supposed to buy. In a reprise of Utrecht, at one point I noticed that no one was bidding on a set of the *Index* to the *London Times*, so I quickly raised my hand, and the set was knocked down to me. It was my sole purchase in the sale. When I triumphantly reported this to New York, I was rudely brought down to earth with the information that the set was utterly worthless, as it consisted of the monthly volumes, which were superseded by an annual volume once a year. No wonder I was the only bidder.

Ironically, unlike in the "good old days," in many cases auction prices are now higher, in some cases vastly so, than retail. This is simply because an auction is about competition, and there are very few people more competitive than book collectors. If this sounds like sour grapes, you do not have to take my word for it. Check the auction prices—again and again, you will find prices that bear no relationship to the marketplace. For years, many dealers have been steadily consigning books to auction, fully confident that they will realize higher prices that way. This is a sad state of affairs, akin to the suicidal act of selling to institutions, but since reserves enable one to protect the price, this would seem to make this behavior inevitable. Obviously, since auctions exist, I am not advocating that collectors ignore them. However, I feel that even here, the advice of a dealer is invaluable, and people who go it alone do so at their peril.

The second place to find books is at a book fair. Gordon Ray and his fellow collectors were much put out by the advent of the book fair, and they would be stunned by the proliferation that has taken place. The rise in the number of book fairs would appear to have risen in direct proportion to the decline in the quality of the available material. Here the problem is simply that there are now so many fairs, that the limited supply of good books means that much of what is on display at any given fair is neither fresh nor important. It might be hard to imagine that book fairs were once glamorous events. The annual June fair in London was the top one. It coincided with the London Season and, in addition to various auctions, a visitor to London could also visit Henley, Royal Ascot, and Wimbledon. America boasted two important fairs per year, New York and the West Coast fair, which alternates between San Francisco and Los Angeles. Most of the leading international booksellers participated, and one was guaranteed to see a fabulous array of books. Many people (among them Gordon Ray) claimed that so many of the books had changed hands before the fair opened that the fairs were "unfair." I have always disputed this charge, and can only respond that of course some books change hands before a fair opens, but to view this as a mass migration is to believe that the bulk of the exhibitors do not know how to price their books properly. Just as dealers saved books in order to make a catalogue, they held books back for fairs, and this created a tremendous level of anticipation and excitement. Alas, both these elements have vanished from the book fair scene along with all pretense at elegance, and accompanied by a precipitous decline in the quality of participants and books.

Nevertheless, book fairs provide the missing link to the human contact with the bookseller and other collectors, and for that alone they are hugely important. They also offer collectors the chance actually to handle books. At the end of the day, a book is a physical object, and for most collectors the feel of a book is of crucial importance. At fairs, collectors can easily meet large numbers of dealers under one roof, and by seeing the books on display, get an idea of the quality and type of book each dealer handles. Obviously, one can buy books at fairs. However, the situation is much like that at an auction and certain questions arise. Are the decisions made in a calm and rational way, or is the book being bought before someone else can get to it? Have you examined the book carefully enough? Often the lighting is not great, and the physical atmosphere in the booth is not conducive to serious decision-making. Nevertheless, the fact remains the book fairs are now a key part of the book-collecting scene, and they represent a great place to meet people, learn, and, yes, even to buy something.

Third, there is the Internet. While this is a godsend for the used book market, it is, in my opinion, an imperfect tool for collectors. Serious bibliophily has always had the condition of the book at its core and if there is one thing you cannot verify on the Internet, this is it. People who do not possess the bibliographical skill or knowledge to adequately describe what they are selling are the ones who offer the vast majority of books for sale on the Internet. There are thousands of sellers, but only a handful of these are bona fide bookdealers. This is the blind leading the blind. I cannot tell you how many times I have cross-examined a seller about the condition of a book only to receive the item and find it bears no resemblance to what supposedly was being offered. Of course, books can for the most part be returned, but the bottom line is that for all the vast quantity of books listed, the kinds of books serious collectors pursue are not available on the Net in significant quantities. That is not to say that the Net does not have its uses. For specialized collectors, such as people who collect the work of a particular author in all its variants, the Internet is a huge blessing, especially for minor items that most booksellers do not have time to quote. On a different note, the sad fact is that the Net has proven to be the final nail in the coffin for many shops. When booksellers flocked online, they found that the good books disappeared even faster than from shelves or from catalogues. Countless shops have closed as their owners saw they could achieve similar or better results with smaller overheads. When it started, there were indeed marvelous books to be found on the Internet. Now it is quickly becoming a vast sea of unsellable or undesirable books, as the good books have been siphoned off, and there is no real source of resupply.

This brings me to eBay. Several years ago, a good client told me I was becoming obsolete. Collectors would trade back and forth via the Internet, and dealers would become a thing of the past. Naturally, I thought this person was not serious, but he assured me he was. Well I am not obsolete yet, but the Internet has changed the dynamic of the book-collecting world forever. On the one hand are search engines like ABE and Amazon; on the other hand is eBay. I do not feel seriously threatened by these things, but it would be equally foolish to pretend they did not exist. People can buy and sell on eBay, making them independent of the book trade if they so choose. The same caveats apply to eBay as to the Internet in general, only more so for buyers, since returning is not usually an option.

This leaves the fourth, final, and in my opinion best option, the bookseller. I end by briefly outlining what booksellers do and stating why I think they should be patronized. One definition of a good bookseller would be "A collector who has to sell in order to keep collecting." Booksellers do for books what bankers do for money, or supermarkets for food. We hold on to books through thick and thin, and make them available when the collector or librarian is ready to buy. Unlike auctions or fairs, which are time-sensitive situations, a bookseller's stock is maintained over time; thus books can be had on approval and studied with appropriate diligence. The bookseller does much of the work that most collectors do not have time for, or, in some cases, are not equipped to do. Beyond the initial selection process, the dealer is responsible for seeing that the book is complete and bibliographically correct, not always a simple task. Lastly, and not insignificantly, the dealer should have a better idea than anyone of a book's true worth. Price is a contentious issue. Simply put, in the long run if a dealer overcharges he will not sell, and if he undercharges he will have no stock. As I mentioned earlier, auctions have resulted in the tail wagging the dog. Price is related to a complex mixture of such things as supply, demand, and condition (not, contrary to popular belief, what the dealer paid for it).

The great dealers of the past may be gone, but their worthy successors are active today. Recent dealer publications reveal booksellers issuing highly important catalogues in many different fields. The level of scholarship in the trade is still remarkably high, and if the catalogues themselves are not as thick and treasure laden as those of a generation ago, their quality remains high and the taste and imagination that goes into assembling them is also extremely impressive. Booksellers are still among the pioneers in creating new fields of collecting. Sadly, the shops have almost vanished, but book dealers have not, and if collectors are to continue to flourish, the dealers who survive will need their support. If collectors withhold it, they do so to their own detriment and to that of the world of bibliophily as a whole.

Some Thoughts on the Maturing of the Rare Book Market

Ken Lopez

I WANT TO address what I see as dramatic changes that have taken place in the rare book market in the last fifteen or so years, and even more dramatic changes in the past ten years. What kinds of changes have we seen? What has caused them? What do they mean for the here and now? And what are their implications for the future?

The changes I discuss refer to the market in general and are not limited to, or focused on, my own specialty of modern first editions. Probably most of my examples—to the extent that I illustrate my theses with examples—will come from modern firsts, since that is my specialty and where most of my experience lies. This may sometimes result in a bias, or even in getting something plain wrong—generalizing from a phenomenon in modern firsts when in fact that phenomenon is specific to modern firsts.

For the most part, I feel confident in this approach for two reasons. One is that the modern firsts are a legitimate and inextricable part of the current rare books market, especially in the United States and Britain, but also around the world. And secondly, especially in the United States, modern firsts make up a more volatile part of the rare book market than many other segments and, therefore, trends in the overall market are often more readily visible in this segment than elsewhere.

As early as the early 1990s, we began to see prices accelerating at an unprecedented rate, especially prices of "high spots," or those books most universally agreed to be valuable and collectible. Several factors contributed to this: the beginning of the longest economic boom in American history played a part: more people were beginning to have more disposable income than before. Ironically, the recession that preceded the boom contributed to this by encouraging a small but relatively wealthy segment of the population to diversify their investment holdings, with rare books being added to the list that previously included stocks, bonds, real estate, fine art, and other collectibles. In this context, books were rightly seen as having been undervalued for a long time: fine first editions of significant books were selling for anywhere from one-tenth to one–one hundredth of the prices of, say, a similarly scarce Picasso print.

In addition, in certain circles—notably including, but not limited to, Hollywood—there began to be a certain cachet, or sexiness, to book collecting that occasionally brought it to the general public consciousness in a way that had not happened before.

Finally, the building and sale of, certain notable collections— the Garden collection, in particular, being one—lent credence to the notion that there was still a challenge to assembling a fine book collection, even one built upon, as the Garden was, the "received knowledge" of previous collectors, bibliophiles, bibliographers, and scholars.

All told, the early 1990s were an auspicious time for book collectors and the game was pursued with money, verve, and a discriminating, and, at times, partly mercenary, eye.

All this contributed to good times for book collectors and booksellers, and a general increase in prices, which included a sometimes astounding increase in prices of high spots: as more people pursued the rarer books, they became even rarer and the ratio of demand to supply skyrocketed, dragging prices of the most sought-after books upward at a frenetic pace. The trend was exacerbated by the fact that

Some Thoughts on the Maturing of the Rare Book Market

as more money came into the market, new collectors were more likely than in previous times to start at the top—buying the best and most expensive works—rather than beginning with modest collections and inexpensive books and gradually working their way up to more expensive rare books.

As a result, much of the pressure was focused on the top end of the market, and drove those prices upward disproportionately fast and disproportionately high. A corollary effect of this was to bring a larger number of collectors' copies of these high spots into the market more rapidly than ever before, also creating an upward pressure on prices. You may wonder: how does an increase in supply force prices upward?

In the past when prices were moderately stable or increasing at a slow, even pace, collectors had to wait until their books doubled in value, more or less, before they could break even. For them to realize a substantial profit when they sold their books they would have to triple in value, at least, and this could take not just years but even decades.

In the early 1990s, however, we were seeing books—high spots at least—begin to sell at ten times what they had brought only a decade earlier. Even at the dramatic wholesale to retail differential in the rare book trade—often a 100 percent markup is involved—a collector who had bought a book in 1982 for $125 could sell it for five times that much in 1992, and the dealer could still double the price he paid for it. As a result, an unusually large number of copies of these high spots began to be recycled within the collectors' market, always predicated on the fact that the price increase has been so great. Since these were collectors' copies—that is, already selected a decade or more earlier as being among the best copies available—they typically came into the market at the high end of the current price range. Collectors wanting to maximize their profits on these books that they were disbursing from their own collection—in other words, to get as high as possible a percentage of current retail—and dealers wanting to have these best possible copies in their stock combined to further fuel the upward pressure on prices of the rarest, or at least most sought-after and collected volumes.

The early 1990s saw price records broken one after another in a continuous stream, at least for the most collected books. This trend continued and increased through the mid-1990s and was fueled by what we now call the "dot-com bubble," but which at the time was more generally known as the "new economy." Thousands, maybe tens of thousands, of overnight millionaires contributed to this simply by virtue of the fact that in any demographic there will be a certain percentage of book collectors. The dot-com millionaires were no exception and they were both a wealthy and educated group. And, despite some efforts in the marketplace to the contrary, they tended to be more inclined to collect a first edition of *Moby Dick* than a first edition of Lotus 1-2-3.

As we know, the dot-com bubble burst, but the technological revolution continued to alter the rare book market, most notably by harnessing the power of computers to match databases of books wanted with databases of books available. As this process gained momentum, the networking capabilities of the Internet began to influence not only the availability of books—or viewed from the other side, the availability of customers—but, more importantly, the availability of information.

For generations, the rare book market had operated by means of a rigidly defined hierarchy, or food chain. There were book scouts, who scoured the land for valuable books of all sorts (here I mean "valuable" in terms of books that would have some value to someone, in other words, saleable but not necessarily expensive books). There were a large number of general bookstores in most big cities that would buy books in great volume and had sufficiently educated and experienced staff to recognize when a book was particularly rare and valuable (here I do mean, in general, expensive). Moreover, the personnel at these establishments knew whether they had likely retail customers for such books or whether the best way to sell such items was to funnel them to a specialist bookseller, someone whose stock consisted exclusively or primarily of the rarest books and who thus was more likely to have an actual customer for such books.

Some Thoughts on the Maturing of the Rare Book Market

This basic way books moved through the market continued into the early and mid-1990s. It was predicated on two things—market position for the bookstore and specialist, that is, being in a position to move those books, whether to another dealer or a retail customer, and, more importantly for all three—especially the scout—a body of information about what was valuable, what people wanted and would pay for, and what was not commonly available. This body of information came slowly, over time, through much experience and trial-and-error (usually including a lot of errors), and eventually the market resembled an efficient vehicle for moving rare books out of attics and tag sales and into the hands of collectors and institutions.

The advent of the Internet changed all that profoundly, although it has taken years for the change to permeate the marketplace fully. I remember, in 1997, we issued our third catalogue of Native American literature—books written by American Indian writers. It was actually our fourth such catalogue, although one was never issued. We did our first in 1992 and it was received very well, especially by institutions. No one I know had ever done a catalogue of that field before and we got a very favorable response. In terms of the percentage of books sold, we did 50–75 percent better than our general literature catalogues, and those were already doing quite well by the general trade standards. Our second Native American catalogue, published in 1994, did even better, and with our third catalogue, we sent out a half-dozen advance copies to the heaviest buyers from the first two. We sold so many books from those advance copies that we cancelled the print run: the catalogue had mostly sold out and the remaining books, even if every one of them sold, would not have covered the printing and mailing costs.

Then, in August 1997, we sent out our fourth, the third to be generally issued, and on the first day it hit I got a call from a librarian, effusively thanking me for my very informative catalogue and telling me that he had found two-thirds of the books on the Internet for one-third the price. I do not know if he thought he was being clever and catching me out, as though this were a game and he had scored a point, or if he was sincere but oblivious. I do know he did not buy any books from that catalogue—despite the fact that he was deeply interested in and committed to Native American literature. This was the clearest wake-up call I could have gotten. The rules were changing, the playing field was changing, and the market was changing. What was changing fastest of all, however, was the availability of information. All those books he had found on the Internet had been available the day before, but he did not have the information to recognize them. Now that he had the information, which I had freely given out in a kind of transaction that had worked for both sides in the earlier market, he did not need my books.

Native American literature is a field primarily of scarce, not rare, books. Scarce because small publishers printed them in small editions to capture what they knew to be a limited market. Many were books an average collector might not have stumbled across in a year's worth of browsing used bookstores, or might have missed even if they were there. When encountered, they could often be purchased for a few dollars and we could price it at $45 (roughly double what a new, widely available book might cost). Given the cost of printing and mailing catalogues, not to mention compensation for the time and effort it took to find and catalogue the books, $45 was little better than a break-even point. We made a few dollars on a book at that price, but not much more. Our customers benefited by our having done the work for them of finding and recognizing the worth of these books, and they would get a book that might be ten to one-hundred times scarcer than a new book (or more) for roughly twice the price of a new book. We felt we were doing a good thing, for ourselves, for our customers, and for posterity, by ensuring these books were preserved.

This market was in its own way efficient—in other words, it worked. The books got from wherever they were located—a small, used bookstore in Kansas or Idaho, for example—to where they belonged—that is, where they would complement an existing collection or be seen in context, often someplace like Yale's Beinecke Library or the Newberry libraries. Still, in terms of efficiency, it left a lot to be desired. Often it took a year and a half to amass enough books for a catalogues and a couple of months to prepare the catalogue, and only then would the books begin to sell and the customers be able to add to their collections. There were plenty of other inefficiencies, too. We might print two thousand copies of a catalogue and mail them; but in the end, 80 percent of the buying was done by 20 percent of the customers—a typical scenario in any kind of business. However, if you do not know which 20 percent that might be, you must print and send catalogues to as many potential buyers as possible.

We did the calculations a number of times and concluded that every book we sold in such a catalogue cost us about $30 to sell, not including the cost of the book. On the $500 and $1000 books, that is not so bad, but spending $30 to sell a $45 book can hardly be characterized as efficient. (One could, of course, calculate this differently, with those costs amortized over the total dollar value of sales as opposed to figured on a per book basis; this would make a more reasonable number, but in a field like Native American literature— where the books tended to be scarce but not rare, it is not a huge difference: there tend to be a lot more books under $50 in those catalogues than over $500.) What made this approach work, however, or at least be viable, was that there was a scarcity of information as much as, or more than, an absolute scarcity of books. While many of these books were, and are, in fact truly scarce, customers for them are just as scarce, or more so. In absolute terms, the supply usually outstripped the demand for all but the scarcest of them. However, the supply was not available to fill the demand except through the intermediary of the book catalogue (and more generally, the entire "food chain" of the rare book market referred to earlier).

The advent of the Internet changed this dynamic, and booksellers were among the first large group of retailers to embrace the World Wide Web en masse. As far back as 1997, there were six thousand used booksellers on the Internet—this at a time when a census of booksellers counted slightly over seven thousand used book dealers in the country. (Today, the number on-line is somewhere north of ten thousand, but a significant portion of these would be excluded in a census because they are part-time hobbyists or individual collectors selling off small portions of their collections.) A recent *New York Times* article pointed out that 65 percent of the used booksellers on the Advanced Book Exchange—the largest database of used books and used booksellers on the Internet—have *only* an Internet presence: no bookstore, no catalogues, no book fairs. The total, however, does include a significant number of full-time booksellers, who either have closed their brick-and-mortar stores or, more commonly, who began their bookselling careers at a point where having only an Internet presence was, and is, sufficient to support a legitimate full-time business. Whatever the actual numbers, the percentage of knowledgeable full-time booksellers who have their books listed on the web is extraordinarily high—probably as high as or higher than any other comparable field.

The Internet suddenly made all books available in effect to everyone, directly, and pretty much instantly laid waste to the traditional hierarchy, or food chain, that had existed within the book trade in years past—scout, general bookseller, specialist. The disparities that remained were in the area of information: the bookseller listing a Maurice Kenny title, for example, might not recognize him as being a Native American writer. Similarly, a librarian building a collection might not know that George Plymell was a Beat writer and the first publisher of *Zap Comix*.

In the first years of the Internet's prolific growth, it was not uncommon to find specialist dealers trying to figure out how to hold onto their specialized knowledge—which they had generally worked long and hard to acquire—rather than giving it away for free, once and for all, by posting their listings on the web. Their concerns and fears were justified. In the early years of the Internet, some computer-savvy people copied and posted dealers' listings as their own, running an algorithm on the prices to mark them up, so that if a book sold they could buy it from the dealer who actually had it, sell it to their customer and make the markup as free and clear profit. This happened numerous times and one large database actually made this a feature of their offering: they gave customers software that allowed them to re-list books that other dealers had posted on the database, mark the prices up en bloc, and make it appear that you were the bookseller with the books. These so-called "super-sites" provided an inducement to get dealers, or at least aspiring "dealers," to list with them. From a marketing perspective, the technique was quite clever: if any individual could overnight become the owner, or at least lister, of millions of books, then the potential number of subscribers to the site was not limited by the actual number of booksellers who actually had books to sell, but could include anybody and everybody.

There were, however, problems with the super-site approach. For dealers who had written catalogue descriptions based on exhaustive knowledge and research and who had put the books in their historical and literary context, there was the question of copyright violation. Such writings belonged to the dealers who wrote them, and appropriating them without permission and attribution is forbidden under copyright law. The Antiquarian Booksellers Association of America (ABAA) took a strong stand against this on behalf of its members, many of whom were the very dealers who had written the most thoroughgoing catalogue entries. Practical problems also existed: if a dealer appropriated the listing for a jacketed first issue of, say, *The Sun Also Rises*, what was he supposed to do if a customer asked a technical question that required specific knowledge? "What's the issue point on the dust jacket?" is a question that many novice booksellers would be hard pressed to answer. Worse were cases in which customers asked simple questions to which the "dealer" had no response: "What's an issue point?" or "What does 'first issue' mean?" Such instances happened far too often when information was available to people who did not have the expertise to interpret it to their customers who were similarly uninformed.

For all its limitations, the Internet has made essential information readily available to collectors, librarians, and booksellers—and information, in any market, is the key to efficiency. Almost by definition, a market in which every participant has 100 percent of the available and relevant information will tend toward being the most efficient. Such information-rich environments reward creativity, ingenuity, and innovation: if everyone knows exactly what it costs to put a new roof on a house in terms of time, materials, and incidentals, then the person who figures out how to make a higher quality roofing tile for the same price as existing ones, or an equivalent tile that costs less than current ones, will have the market advantage. Innovators are rewarded for effort and knowledge; customers receive the benefit of a better product (and the knowledge invested in that product) and the best deal possible; and the remaining players in the market (the competitors) are encouraged to be similarly creative or risk falling behind.

What does all this mean for booksellers and collectors? The answer is yet unclear, but some guesses can be made based on general knowledge about markets and what we know about the book market in particular. For one thing, as I have told collectors—and even other dealers—numerous times in the past couple of years, we are probably going to look back on these few years before and after the turn of the twenty-first century as a Golden Age for book buyers. More books have become more readily available to more people at one time than has ever been the case before or will likely ever be the case again. There simply are not another ten thousand dealers out there to list their stock on-line beyond those who have done it already. (Although here I should introduce qualifiers: Europe, South America, and the Far East have been several years behind the United States in this process and are just beginning to approach the kind of market saturation that has been the case here for several years. For those people whose collecting interests run to books more likely to be found in those countries than in the United States, your Golden Age is just beginning.)

During this Golden Age, tremendous competitive pressure has been driving prices downward for all but the most scarce or highly sought-after books. When twenty copies of a legitimately scarce book are available on-line, the dealer with the twenty-first copy must keep the price down to compete with those already available. There are unlikely simultaneously to be twenty-two customers for those twenty-one copies, and each dealer wants to sell his own copy to the next customer who turns up. However, over time, I think we will see more than twenty-two customers for that book at the same time as those first twenty-one copies sell out, with far fewer replacements. Thus the number of available copies of legitimately scarce books (and if there are only twenty copies available of a book among the stock of 10,000 book dealers that represent the vast majority of books on the market in a country of 300 million people, we can feel safe in calling them "legitimately scarce") will tend to dwindle over time by attrition; in the meantime, strong competitive pressures will keep prices down.

In some sense, customers these days are in the position of book searchers back in the days of *AB Bookmans Weekly* (book searching being another niche in the book trade effectively obliterated by the Internet). Then, a searcher advertised for books a customer wanted, got quotes for several, sometimes dozens, of copies, and then picked the ones to buy. The buyer had all the options, knew all that was available, and could choose among them. Now individual customers can do that. The difference today is that dealers can also see at what prices books are being offered and they can, and do, condition their listings accordingly. By far the largest amount of bandwidth used by the major book database search engines involves booksellers pricing their books, not customers buying them. But buyers have the advantage of seeing all the books available, and since no corresponding database of collectors on the Internet exists, buyers are at a great advantage.

The buyers' advantage, however, is only true for those books that are not in high enough demand, at a single moment, to outstrip the available supply. For books in high demand, or which are truly rare, or both, the same situation works toward an opposite end: dealers who have copies of one of these high spots can see what is available and price their book competitively, but such copies will tend to cluster at the top end of the price range and, if a dealer has a particularly special or nice copy, it may be in his interest to price it higher than any other copy, signifying that it is indeed a superior copy.

In this way, the same market forces that exert a downward pressure on prices for "medium-rare" books exert an upward pressure on prices of rare books and high spots. In a market that is, for the reason previously discussed, tending to emphasize high spots more than in the past, this upward acceleration of prices can be truly astounding.

In 1999, I wrote an article called "Trends in Modern Book Collecting" that discussed some of the phenomena and processes I have outlined here.* One thing I said, however, bears noting because it was so wrong: The price of a fine first edition of *The Catcher in the Rye* had recently gone from about $1250—where it had been for quite some time—to about $3000, fairly suddenly. Then virtually overnight (somewhere between 6 months and a year) it shot up to $6000. I said at the time that we could be fairly certain it would take longer to double from $6000 to $12,000 than it had taken to get from $3000 to $6000. I could not have been more incorrect: in April 2001, a copy sold at auction for about $33,000 and a month later another copy sold in the market for $35,000. These days, even shabby copies of the book command over $12,000. My mistake, I believe, was in only seeing one side of how these pressures are working on the market; in fact, my guess is that as this Golden Age of book buying passes, and even medium-rare books become scarcer by attrition, a similar upward pressure on prices will be felt on an ever-larger pool of books.

As promised, all the examples I have presented thus far have been from the realm of modern firsts, but I believe similar examples could be drawn from a wide range of collecting areas in the rare book world, although perhaps sometimes not quite as starkly obvious as the ones I have outlined. In 1992, I bought a collection of Western Americana manuscripts with several other dealers, and we put out a joint catalogue. Americana is a field I know very little about, and I had to do a great deal of research to do my share of the cataloguing. It was more than just learning about the material: I had to understand how the Americana market—which seemed to work

---

*"Trends in Modern Book Collecting," *Firsts* (1999); also available online at http://www.lopezbooks.com/articles/trends01.html.

very differently from the market for modern firsts—functioned. A friend of mine who dealt in Americana, used to tell me that he would get a copy of a book, catalogue it for $50, get ten orders for it, and then when he got another copy of it—maybe a year or two later—he would catalogue it for $50 again. When I asked him why, he said, "Because it's a $50 book." In the field of modern firsts, where one assumes a certain volatility in the prices—in part because they are so new and the passage of a few more years makes a significant difference in terms of availability—we would take ten orders for a $50 book as a sign that our estimation of supply and demand was skewed and surmise that the price of the next copy, especially if it were going to take a year or two to turn up, should be much higher.

Many areas of the book trade work more like Americana than like modern firsts: prices change more slowly because the books have a longer track record. Nonetheless, in the past decade or so, books in a wide variety of fields have broken all previous price records. The Frank T. Siebert collection of American Indian and American frontier books and manuscripts set a number of astonishing records: many of the items sold for several times what any previous copy had ever brought. Our 1992 Western Americana catalogue, which was scoffed at for its high prices at the time (three of the four dealers involved in purchasing the collection were primarily modern literature dealers, and we tended to apply our own rationales to pricing the material) now looks almost like a bargain catalogue, and prices in the Western Americana field—especially for truly rare material—have escalated to unprecedented new levels, not just incrementally but often, like the Siebert collection, multiples of previous highest prices.

Similar price escalations have occurred with manuscript archives. In 1992, shortly after she won the Nobel Prize for Literature, Nadine Gordimer's archive sold for $300,000. A few years later, the Allen Ginsberg archive sold for almost a million dollars; then, the manuscript of one novel — "Jack Kerouac's *On the Road* — sold for $2.6 million, helping to put a value on the rest of his archive, which went to the New York Public Library for an estimated $8 to

$10 million. Susan Sontag's archive sold for $1.1 million and Norman Mailer's went on the market at an asking price of $2.5 million and reportedly sold at that price. In this field as well, the top end is reaching unprecedented levels at an ever-increasing rate. (I could here also illustrate the corollary that I discussed earlier with modern firsts: that "medium-rare" material has had downward pressure on the prices, and is in many cases much harder to sell today than it was in the past; but with manuscript archives, even though that is approximately true, forces affecting prices are somewhat different than those I have identified for medium-rare books.)

Audubon folios and quartos have broken price records repeatedly through the 1990s, often by a large margin, as have the Edward Curtis North American Indian portfolios. And getting back to literature: a copy of *Moby Dick* that sold to a dealer for $48,000 at the California Book Fair in 2002 (breaking the previous price record for that book by about $12,000) then sold to a collector for $76,000. Another copy of the same title sold a few months later for $85,000. In 2001, at the New York Book Fair, a children's book dealer put out a copy of *The Hobbit*, which he had held onto for many years, at the world-record price of $50,000. It sold to a dealer instantly, who sold it a few minutes later to another dealer for $80,000, who then put it on the market at something like $125,000 or $150,000. Now, even so-so copies of *The Hobbit*, when they turn up, are priced in the $30,000 to $50,000 price range.

The changes in the market in recent years are not random, nor are they successful attempts by a small group of booksellers to manipulate the market: few people in the field have enough clout to do that and those with such power do not need to. On the contrary, these changes have come about as a result of specific forces at work in the current marketplace that are different—sometimes in degree, sometimes in kind—from those that long governed the rare book market. Understanding those forces and the changes they have produced should help all of us—collectors, librarians, and booksellers alike—view this new market from a more informed perspective, and navigate it with a surer hand.

Some Thoughts on the Maturing of the Rare Book Market

Far more information is available today than ever before about what books are available, what they are priced, and the like. In addition, more books are available to buyers than ever before and there are more potential customers readily available to dealers than has ever been the case. Such factors combine to keep a lid on prices of scarce, but not rare, material and, at the same time, help force prices of the truly rare and/or most sought-after books to new highs. What it boils down to is this: we live in a Golden Age for book buyers, so buy now and buy as much as you can; prices will only rise in the future, for both rare and medium-rare material, which, at the moment, is still artificially low. If that sounds like what booksellers have forever been saying to collectors and librarians, I suppose that should come as no surprise: as a bookseller, I have to believe that it is a good thing. I hope, in elucidating how and why I believe these various factors have combined to make that true, I will have persuaded you to believe it as well.

My Adventures in Academe

Anthony Garnett

THE NAME of Garnett has been a significant one in the literary field for over a hundred years—with Richard, Edward, Constance, David, and a few others as representative. I wish I could say that I was related to them but, although our two families come from only a few miles apart in the north of England, there appears to be no connection, at least not for the past four hundred years. If I was a closer relative, I would almost certainly be writing my own books instead of peddling other people's.

My own connection with, and love of, books began at school in the late 1940s when I worked with the librarian to reorganize and recatalogue the collection to which, by setting aside a small part of his inadequate budget, he had always been careful to add occasional examples of fine printing. Hence I gained an early familiarity with the work of Eric Gill and Robert Gibbings, for example, which gave me an abiding love for the wood-engraver's art, as did my introduction to Dickens through the Nonesuch Press edition which, in those happy, far-off days, was on the open shelves, and a set of which I have longed to own ever since.

The next stage was obviously to start collecting for myself — a slow process that began on a very small scale on a virtually nonexistent income. While doing my National Service in the army, the then newly founded Folio Society offered attractive editions of significant (though sometimes infuriatingly abridged) works. The Oxford bookshops also were for me a constant lure and source of delight and impoverishment — particularly the Turl Cash Bookshop, which belonged to Blackwell's and to which they used to send all their overstock or unwanted books. These were delivered in large canvas bags and were then priced by the two charming ladies who ran the shop and who clearly judged the books by their outsides. Sixpence or a shilling were fairly standard prices — though a first edition of Dickens would probably be half-a-crown. And, during the last week of term, virtually the entire stock was available at half the marked price.

After university I spent thirteen years working for a large industrial corporation, first in England and then in Canada, which provided a steady, though not overgenerous, income of which a large part was spent on books. Montreal in the late 1950s had an excellent charity shop, run by the Junior League, where three-for-a-dollar was the going rate, and their stock usually contained a goodly supply of literary first editions. At the same time, I began to get catalogues from English dealers and would indulge myself by buying private press books — even the occasional Ashendene when times were good.

The realization that advancement in the corporate world was closely linked to office politics led me to resign from what was actually a very promising career, without having any notion of what I would do instead. To give me some thinking time, I climbed into my car and drove to Guatemala. (It was the end of February, when the Canadian climate is especially depressing and what passes for spring up there is still months away.)

Apart from being introduced to my future wife in a Chinese restaurant Mexico City, I crashed the car on the return journey (the two events were *not* connected), which resulted in a much longer trip than intended, but the upshot of two months of newfound independence was the decision that running one's own affairs was the thing to do and that maybe turning a hobby into a business was the answer — and that, for somewhat complex reasons, in which a distinctly misguided idea about the local climate played a part, St. Louis was the place to do it.

St. Louis was, as it still is, a culturally very active city, with a large and fairly wealthy community, a {to me) surprising number of colleges, most of which appeared to have minimal libraries, and no good bookshops — in fact, an open field. So, in the summer of 1967, I moved south.

Now, although I had some business experience, I had had absolutely no involvement in the book trade except as an enthusiastic customer whose delight was in browsing in old-established English bookshops with huge general stocks and wonderfully low prices. Without any training in, or knowledge of, the selling end of the book business, or even an understanding of what was going on in the book world in general, it was probably inevitable that I would make some basic mistakes.

My first disappointment was the discovery that the absence of decent bookshops in the area appeared to be due to an absence (at least to the naked eye) of private book collectors. St. Louis was a city of large houses, many of them dating from the great days at the turn of the last century — when there was a real book collector in the person of William Bixby. Many of the houses had libraries, but these all appeared to have been stocked by the architects or interior decorators with those pseudolimited editions, bound in cheap half-leather, often referred to as books-by-the-yard, which by now were disintegrating, although they were usually still unopened.

So I turned to school libraries. It was clear to me that the libraries in all the colleges (most of which had not yet taken on the misleading title of "universities") desperately needed to build their collections. At that time even Washington University was frantically searching for books and their bibliographers were usually to be found scouring the shelves of such bookshops as then existed in the city, of which Pat Dunaway's newly established business was the best. They, at least, had a highly active collection development policy, both for the general collection and for the Rare Book Department where Bill Matheson was the inspired head (before he was lured away by the Library of Congress). For a while St. Louis University was also building its collection, but was about to enter a period of acute financial concern. Even so, it took me a while to realize that attempting to sell to the other, smaller, colleges was a total waste of time: they simply had neither the resources nor, in most cases, the inclination to build what would pass as basic core collections. The fact that one local college (which now calls itself a university) finally broke down and bought a book from me (it was a copy of *Alice in Wonderland*) was the first wake-up call.

This was a time when some more farsighted universities were acquiring books in huge quantities. The University of Illinois was known to buy a good bookshop's entire stock and almost every item in many sales at Sotheby's in London went to the University of Texas. The dollar was strong, prices in Britain were low, and everyone thought that the supply was bottomless — the falsity of which assumption only gradually began to sink in — and I was able to buy books in England, literally by the ton. Postage on books was inexpensive, and shipping them in quantity by sea freight was extraordinarily cheap. The volume of my acquisitions was boosted substantially by the fact that I had an entrée into a number of the big country houses in the north of England at a time when landowners were heavily taxed and often anxious to sell their books to raise some cash. At one such house the family had been collecting for some three hundred fifty years. In several rooms the shelves were ranked three-deep with books. The removal of about three tons of books made not the slightest visual difference to their holdings.

The most difficult decision to make was foregoing the idea of being a collector and using my own books as my starting stock. I was able to build a larger stock quickly, but was restricted to the less expensive kind of material by lack of funds. Trying to borrow money from St. Louis banks to buy books was frustratingly difficult. If it had been a matter of opening a grocery store, they would have understood the value of inventory, but books merely raised eyebrows. Typically they would be impressed by the value of my stock, admit that they would love to lend me money but, please, what did I have as collateral? It was some years before I did finally manage to find one bank that went some way to help, but even this one understood what I was up to so clearly that my file there apparently recorded my collateral as "a collection of old boots."

Limited funds had one other unfortunate corollary which was that acquiring a really good collection, as I did in Belleville in about 1975, involved some complicated financial arrangements and forced me to do the worst possible thing — to sell the best items first to pay for the rest. In this case it meant bidding a quick farewell to the shelves of first editions of John Milton, Fanny Burney, Jane Austen, Jonathan Swift, Daniel Defoe, and even such treasures as Mary Shelley's *Frankenstein*, a complete set of Giambattista Piranesi's *Vedute di Roma*, and a large collection of first edition opera scores ranging from Jean-Baptiste Lully to Richard Strauss.

At that time, I was still selling books to libraries by typing up lists and sending them out in the mail. My catalogues were not well presented (I was, and probably still am, too much of a cheapskate to have them printed), and they met with only a scattered response as bibliographers were overwhelmed by such offerings. I started traveling and visiting libraries in person to find out in detail just where their individual priorities lay. The first discovery was that every library is differently organized and that, in each case, it is essential to establish just who is responsible for making purchase decisions. It might be someone in the Acquisitions Department, or a subject bibliographer, or it might even be the Library Director since, in those precomputer days, the top job was most frequently still held by someone who was actually connected with books rather than machines.

Today most university libraries have far fewer subject bibliographers than formerly — those people with a sound knowledge of their subject areas and of their library's holdings — and a high percentage of book buying is limited by the escalating prices of new books that are supplied by vendors on the basis of the subject "profile" given them by the library, an impersonal system, the efficiency of which depends on the clarity of the definition combined with the accuracy of the vendor's analytical classification of the books.

But back in the 1970s, those libraries with good budgets were heavily involved in retrospective buying to build their core collections. My second discovery then was that the most frustrating thing for a librarian was to work through a catalogue, establish which titles were needed, and then find that most of them had already been sold. Wasted work, wasted time — and almost equally aggravating to the bookseller involved. On a visit to the University of North Carolina at Chapel Hill, where the English Department did its own book selection and even had a full-time secretary at work on processing orders, I showed them the draft of a catalogue I was planning to send out. They asked if they could borrow it and on my return to St. Louis I found an order for over 30 percent of the entire list. They were hungry, they knew that everything on the list was available, and it was therefore worth their while to check the whole thing thoroughly. No wasted work, no wasted time.

Needless to say, the list never was sent out, and I have never sent out a list in a general mailing since, but have always given the lists to libraries on an exclusive basis. For a long time this involved updating and retyping the lists each time they came back to me. It was certainly time-consuming but the system worked extremely well, at least so long as library budgets held up and before the cost of new books and journal subscriptions had begun to skyrocket, and large chunks of money were being syphoned off for technical improvements.

The advent of computers has changed many things. When they first appeared in libraries, the general impression seemed to be that investment in machines and software was a one-time deal. It seemed not to occur to people that they would continue to run away with ever-increasing sums year after year. This has drained much funding away from the purchase of books but, in a different direction, it has made my method of working with libraries on an individual basis much easier. Now from my database I can produce a subject list that is tailored to a library's specific current interests, check that list on the Net against their existing holdings, and already hold. It certainly beats typing, and works just as well — when there is money in the budget. In addition, individual lists of this sort, printed from the database, enables one to offer low-priced items that would be impossible to include in general-mailing catalogues, which are expensive to produce and mail.

One of the more interesting things about working with university libraries is doing appraisals for them — or, more often, for donors whose collections are headed in that direction. Sometimes these are straightforward enough, involving books that, even if unique (inscribed by the author to his mother, for example, or perhaps enclosing a letter discussing the writing of the book), are easy to ascribe a current fair market value to. On the other hand, they can involve an area of expertise that is outside a dealer's experience and necessitate a good deal of homework before one is able to come up with a competent assessment. Here are three examplary cases in which I had to engage in considerable self-education:

1. A large collection of Martin Luther pamphlets from the first half of the sixteenth century.
2. A huge archive of largely ephemeral material relating to the early, and extremely confusing, history of Colombia, much of which was not even held by the National Library in Bogotá.
3. The extensive and detailed papers of a lawyer involved in, among other things, the Watergate hearings in which he was responsible for asking the crucial question that revealed the existence of the White House tapes.

Apart from the excitement involved in learning enough to be able to make an intelligent assessment of value for tax purposes on behalf of the donors, this part of one's work highlights the enormous importance to libraries of the gifts they have received over the years, and are still receiving, from private collectors whose passion for specific, sometimes quite narrow and sometimes very broad, subject areas have done so much to enhance the learning resources of so many universities. The Chapin Library at Williams College and Eli Lilly's huge collection at Indiana University are just two great collections that immediately spring to mind because they retain their original identity but, obviously, the vast collections at Harvard, Yale, UCLA, University of California at Berkeley or the New York Public Library are made up in substantial part of a multiplicity of magnificent individual gifts.

This brings up what is sometimes a thorny problem that faces a library in its dealings with a prospective donor — the request that a donation be kept together as a discrete collection. Clearly, in the case of a Chapin or a Lilly this request can be readily acceded to, but take, for example, the lifetime accumulation of a distinguished professor retiring from the faculty. It may contain some nice rare materials relating to the good doctor's field of study that the library is keen to add, but it probably also contains a lot of lesser material duplicated in their existing holdings. To keep this material and add it to their collection is expensive, would take up space, which most libraries are desperately short of, and is probably not needed. As a result, most donations of the more general kind are accepted with the proviso that the library is free to dispose of (or return to the donor) such duplicates or material deemed unsuited to their needs. As for retaining a collection as a physical unit, this produces additional expense and inconvenience that can only be justified in the case of a really outstanding collection or one where completeness may be a significant feature of its importance, for example, the working library of a major author whose reading habits form an integral factor in the study of his or her work. In such a case, dispersing even minor material into the general collections would make no sense.

Some donors who perhaps have an exaggerated view of their own importance or of that of their collection can make a major nuisance of themselves and, if given an inch, will want to take a mile. I know of one library that has been caught in such a situation and refers to a particular family as "the donors from hell."

On the other hand, in a well-developed library, duplicate

material received in gifts may include some highly desirable and valuable items. The Folger Library possesses more copies of Shakespeare folios than most people thought existed and firmly hangs on to all of them, but most libraries prefer to use duplicates to trade with dealers for material they do not already have. A goodly part of my own stock has been acquired in this way, mainly from private schools since they tend to have more dedicated alumni with book-collecting habits than the big state schools whose alumni seem more inclined to donate funds for sports facilities than intellectual resources. A significant exception to this is Penn State University where the rare book library is named after an enthusiastic supporter: the football coach.

Duplicate material is not the only source of my stock but it does supply the bulk. This has the unfortunate side effect of building a substantial residue of basic material of the sort that is still needed by the smaller libraries that cannot afford it but not by those that can. This perhaps highlights the fact that I am by nature a book collector who cannot resist nice general books even if by now I instinctively know I should pass them up and be far more selective, concentrating only on the rarer material — Special Collections material rather than fodder for the general stacks.

This raises the question of why I do not have an open shop? It would provide both an outlet for general material and a venue where individuals could offer items they wish to sell.

The flip side of this is that shop premises are expensive (which is why an increasing number of dealers today specialize in narrow fields and work, as I do, from a private address) and need either one's constant presence or the employment of assistants. I have always been a one-man band and have resisted the idea of an open store for those reasons. Besides, I need to be free to travel, not only to distance myself from St. Louis during the hottest months of the year, but mainly to do that part of my selling that I enjoy most: the trade in modern fine printing and private press books. While there is theoretically no reason why press books cannot be sold from lists, it is virtually impossible to do justice to the more imaginative offerings from the better current book artists by mere description. Customers really have to see such books, particularly when the works cost several thousand dollars each. Ironically, in these days of restricted budgets, it is these books that seem to be the easiest to sell and are certainly the most fun to deal in.

I am often asked what effect the Internet has had on the book trade. A leading London bookseller who deals in high-end art books told me that he had been quite seriously affected by other offerings of similar material at appreciably lower prices. While I am sure this is so. I think there is another, opposite, side to this. Certainly websites on which hundreds (indeed, thousands) of dealers can offer their wares allow comparison shopping and provides an outlet to huge numbers of sellers offering small numbers of cheap books from their kitchen. Checking offerings on the Net usually reveals a wide range of prices for any given fairly common title. But most of those the low-end back-kitchen outfits are, from their lack of descriptive ability, amateurs who do not offer serious competition. Rather, my impression is that many professional dealers can see what prices others are asking for titles they own, and tend to adjust their own upwards.

As for me, I do not offer books on the Net because I am not set up to sell single items, but I do find the Net useful in one important regard, which is that when I get a book about which I have no idea of its rarity or value, a quick check on the Net can give me a ballpark figure.

University libraries certainly use the Net to search for out-of-print items they need in a hurry, while before they typically worked through dealers. Now they seem only to give dealers lists of wanted titles that are impossible to find.

There have been a number of cases in recent years where a newly established institution has announced its intention of eschewing the idea of printed material altogether and of relying totally on electronic resources. This, to the best of my knowledge, has proved to be impossible, but it does indicate the current trend in thinking at institutions for whom budget restraints are a constant concern, and this has been heavily reinforced, as you may have read in a May 2005 issue of the *New York Times*, by the fact that the University of Texas and a couple of other very large institutions have, in fact, decided to close their undergraduate libraries and to replace them altogether by computer facilities. This is perhaps not so dire as it might first appear since for most undergraduate courses students have to buy their own texts, but it will mean that the most enquiring students will not have access to that library browsing which can give real meat to their papers.

In the book market, in general, the trend has been similar to that in the art and antique fields. Prices for first-class material seem to go ever upwards while the more pedestrian material lags way behind. I believe that anyone who wishes to build a good reading library in this country can do so these days without a huge outlay of capital. The same does not seem to be true of the English book market where my experience is that in second-hand bookstores any book costs about the same number of pounds as it would dollars in the United States, which is a complete reversal from my early days in the business.

If there are any modern-day Astors or Houghtons or Chapins or Lillys out there, I am sure they have found this to be true. Curiously enough, until the recent slide in the value of the dollar against European currencies, the one area in which England, in particular, remained surprisingly inexpensive vis-à-vis the United States was that of private press books, but the change from about $1.40 to the pound to the $1.90 or so since 2004 has to a large extent leveled the playing field.

However, there is still a great deal of very fine work being done particularly, I would say, in books illustrated with wood engravings, and it is still an area in which many of my university customers remain very active, especially those in which the library works closely with the art department and offers courses on the art of the book.

In connection with this, some schools also run annual competitions among their students to encourage them to build and exhibit their own book collections, with sometimes very imaginative results.

So there is hope yet that there will be a new generation of bibliophiles, and surely there are some great new collectors waiting in the wings.

From personal experience, I would say that it is very difficult to be both a book dealer and a book collector. The best one can do is to try to satisfy one's collecting instincts by buying books, and then paying for lunch by letting them go again.

To return to those literary Garnetts, the novelist David said that the only piece of advice that he was given by his father, Edward, who ran the Poetry Bookshop as well as being a writer, was "Never be a bookseller." My nearly forty years of helping libraries build their collections has given me enormous pleasure, as well as a great many friends both in libraries and in the trade, for which I am hugely grateful. Still, I often wish I could have afforded to take Edward Garnett's advice and just indulge the instincts of a collector.

COLLECTING

Will the Book Collector of Today be the Donor of Tomorrow?

Robert H. Jackson

S PECIAL COLLECTIONS are a recent development in our history. They are among the legacies of the capitalists of the last century, along with most of our orchestras, art museums, and even the buildings that define some of our cities. Over the years, these collections have flourished and multiplied with the growth of college and university budgets. Today, the special collection is a mature phenomenon, one that is in danger of becoming ossified or static. Whereas once, the future of the special collection was in the hands of the private collector, today it is in the hand of the institutional treasurer. The questions before us now are: Will that hand be a closed fist? Will we need to pry it open? Or can it be made to give of its own free will? One answer to these questions depends on the psychology of the collector.

Collecting has been around since the beginning of time, or at least of human time. Is it instinctive or acquired? Rational or

Note: This essay originally appeared in Collectors and Special Collections, published by the Library of Congress in 2002. It was part of symposium entitled, "Private Collectors and Special Collections Libraries" which was organized by the Rare Book and Special Collections Division of The Library of Congress in 2001.

obsessive? No one knows. The word "mania" is often applied to collectors, and not always with affection. Collectors are motivated by an obscure craving, harkening back to childhood. Walter Benjamin speaks of the "profound enchantment" of the collector, who seeks to lock "individual items within a magic circle."

This magic circle is not open to everybody. There are rituals of entry that rival those of *The Magic Flute*, especially in rare books. The novice needs mentors and guides if he or she is to navigate the flaming landscape. But that landscape is changing. Reliable guides are harder to find. The Internet supplies information, but not wisdom.

Well into the century past, book collecting was like politics: a gentleman's game. It was a bastion of the wealthy male. This was true not for any sinister reasons, but because men of leisure were the only ones with the time and means to pursue it. Entry called for a leather armchair, a tweed jacket, and a mahogany-paneled library. That has changed. A visit to The Grolier Club in the twenty-first century will tell you that interest in rare books has undergone a swirling demographic sea change. This interest now captivates young and old, men and women. The magic circle becomes wider.

When I began collecting in the mid-1970s, I found book collecting to be primarily a solitary activity, requiring an aggressive, proactive approach to knowledge. Written guides were few, and no *Book Collecting for Dummies* existed. You were on your own. I was fortunate enough to have the advice of a few knowledgeable dealers who guided me toward an introspective understanding of market dynamics.

Book collecting was a quiet field then, periodically punctuated by well-hyped auctions or promoted by writers such as A. Edward Newton or, earlier, the books of Holbrook Jackson. The domain of the book collector was a backwater of the high-powered art and antiques market. In the 1980s and 1990s, however, books picked up the pace. Today, the book market is probably ahead of art and antiques, at least as measured by its use of computers and the Internet.

Back in the 1970s, book auctions were a distant rumor—they existed primarily for the trade. Today, auctions are the Grammys, the Oscars, and the Golden Globes of the game. The big houses market like Hollywood super-agents. They find properties with crossover appeal and polish them to a high gleam. We have all had the experience of losing our heads and purse at auctions. Today, auction enthusiasms threaten to become a way of life. Irrational exuberance is not confined to the stock market.

All eyes are on the "trophy book." You do not have to be elitist to see something vulgar and grasping in all the outlandish bidding for these books that arrive on a pile of press releases. The effect is like that of inflated star salaries of the movie business. A few big names soak up all the resources, and many other items starve.

Actually, starving is far too strong a word. A decade of prosperity has opened the field to thousands of people who might never have passed the browsing stage. The real problem is paucity of product, a condition not likely to reverse. As a result, new fields and new subjects for collecting are opening up every day. Specialization has become broader and deeper. There are new theaters of value. Dealers seek a finer grain. Collectors see that it might be possible to achieve the nirvana of a small, yet complete collection.

No one is born with special interests. Ideally, we cast about the same way we look for a spouse or life partner. We survey the generality and let ourselves be drawn by the mysterious forces of affinity. When it comes time to cast about, many of us begin in the antiquarian bookstore. Christopher Morley wrote of *The Haunted Bookshop* (1919) and my fellow collectors and I were the ones who haunted it. We took the measure of the field and learned about books by touch, by feel, by comparative intuition. For us, bookshops were temples of initiation. But the day of such bookstores has passed, because real estate and the cost of doing business have made them impractical. Nevertheless, books captivate through personal encounter, and to meet a book for the first time at an auction has all the warmth of an arranged marriage.

Personal relations are at the heart of the book field. Mentors and advisers teach us the folk wisdom of the trade. The best relationships cannot be formed overnight. Valuable chains of acquaintance may begin at the bookshop level. There is something symbolically democratic about store-front access that we shall be sorry to lose.

In many ways, today's beginning book collector is expected to begin with fully formed tastes. Although there are many opportunities to start small at modest cost and to make modest mistakes, it is still difficult to grow rich in experience. Today, it helps to know somebody. But everybody knows that if you are a nobody, you cannot meet anybody. So it is not easy to get started.

You might meet somebody at a book fair. The book fair is the last remaining place on earth where all the players in the rare book game come into one another's physical presence. Many of us remain jaded and cynical about book fairs. But they still hold the possibility of surprise. They are our equivalent of the Quattrocento masked ball. People trade identities. Dealers become buyers, buyers become sellers, and the unexpected crouches behind the tapestry.

Today, with the Internet and the availability of material from a broad spectrum of dealers, the number of collectors has boomed. Correspondingly, the amount of important earlier material coming to market has rapidly diminished. These two facts, in turn, will affect the quality of the next generation of collectors. A large supply of material brings increased knowledge, a more highly developed connoisseurship, and refined appreciation. A shrinkage diminishes the collective knowledge pool, and the connoisseurship of individual collectors.

We all know the spectacular effects of the Internet on all aspects of trading. Rare books and manuscripts are bought and sold at lightning speed. Whole libraries evaporate in seconds to buyers made knowing by instant access to comparative pricing and sellers who can tell at a glance what their competitors are asking and adjust their prices accordingly. Ten years ago, no one could have predicted what book collecting has become today.

So what does the future hold for collectors? For that matter, what does the future hold for the book?

The answer to this question contains the future of book collecting. For whatever happens to the book will have a decisive affect on

Will the Book Collector of Today be the Donor of Tomorrow?

the way we collect, what we collect, and how we pass items on for future generations.

At the turn of the twentieth to the twenty-first century, we are living in the heyday of the printed book. Today, there are more books being read by more people in more different walks of life then at any time in human history. More books have been printed in the past five years alone than were printed in all the years of the seventeenth and eighteenth centuries combined. Shops that specialize in new books groan with titles. Second-hand bookshops do a lively trade. Libraries are jammed with patrons and overwhelmed with titles. Antiquarian booksellers try to satisfy the burgeoning pool of collectors with ever-odder materials. Far from killing the book, the invention of the computer has been responsible for killing more trees than any event in human history, spawning mountains of handbooks, how-to books, users' guides, repair manuals, and volumes of cybernetic philosophy. And the well-named Amazon.com has turned the United States Postal Service and UPS into great rolling rivers of print products. This was already the great age of the book even before Oprah got into the act and turned television into a publicity platform for them.

If we look around us, the triumph of the printed word would seem to be complete. There was a time when you had to travel to Harvard Square to find a good newsstand. Today, the Amish in Holmes County, Ohio, live only a short carriage ride from a newsstand at Borders that is just as good as any in America.

Yet when anyone speaks of the future of the book, a certain nervousness creeps into the voice. This is particularly so when we are talking about the book as an object in space with six sides, two covers, and a spine. There is something in the air. Everyone can sense it. Vast changes are in store for the book and everything that is associated with it. Something is waiting to be born. Only a few simple details remain to be ironed out. For instance: what it will look like, how it will be read, and how it will be sold.

Jason Epstein, with whom Dan De Simone and I recently spent some time, has written extensively about these issues and remarkably "has been repeatedly successful in anticipating the future," as Larry Kirshbaum has noted. Epstein believes we are approaching the era of the instant printed book on demand.

We seem to be at that proverbial moment when the past has yet to die, and the future has yet to be born. Among our own symptoms we might include the e-book, the Rocket E-Book, downloadable text, and other efforts to wipe out the sensual pleasure of reading, owning, and collecting books. But what comes next?

I happen to own a page of Dickens's manuscript of *The Pickwick Papers*—a notable icon. The page is of little interest to scholars, except as evidence that Dickens—like Shakespeare and Mozart—never, as Ben Jonson said, blotted out a line. Nevertheless, this single page may be the most emotionally precious item I own. By contrast, I recently saw pages of Joyce's manuscript of *Ulysses*, a draft of the Circe episode. Unlike Dickens's smooth production, Joyce's pages are almost black with additions, emendations, and other rewriting. As a reader, not a collector, I found the insight I gained from seeing those pages to be, in its own way, priceless.

The end of the twentieth century may have seen the end of that kind of artifact. Tomorrow's collector may not own or donate original manuscripts, because the original manuscript has more or less ceased to exist. Today's younger authors almost universally type their books into a word processor and send them to their publishers in the form of an electronic file. Early drafts are deleted to make room on hard drives. Or a writer may simply work on a single draft, changing and correcting and leaving no trace of the creative struggle.

It appears that in the future, literature will cease to produce the unique paper artifact. The manuscript page, with its erasures, additions, and tear stains will vanish. The vanguard of this trend is already with us in the form of e-mail, which has increased letter writing, if you call it real letter writing, but eliminated the physical letter.

All that is solid will not melt into pixels, however. There is some resistance. Children's books are at the forefront of this effort. Among the children's literature set, there seems to be no lessening of

Will the Book Collector of Today be the Donor of Tomorrow?

interest in books with pages and pictures. Their enthusiasm actually gives hope to the future. For do we not begin to love the form of a book in early age? And are not the books we cherish as grown-ups simply elaborations of that same form? In this way, perhaps, all books are essentially children's books. Do we not take a child's pleasure in their shape and feel and tactile qualities? Is this not the same pleasure we take in fine private press editions? Sometimes we even like the story the edition contains. What stamps our character as children has remarkable staying power. For this reason alone, I believe in the persistence of the book.

Those who predict the disappearance of the book are in a strange position today. They are like the climatologist who is asked about global warming in the midst of the blizzard of the century. The book may disappear and the ice caps may melt. But at the moment, we are still digging out.

The difference between short-term phenomena and long-term change makes it hard to predict the future of the book. But what about the future of book collectors? Who will they be? What will they collect? Will they donate to special collections?

It is a fact that today's class of collectors is a heterogeneous one. They may be men or women of any age, race, or level of affluence. How knowledgeable are they? William S. Reese recently suggested that the most knowledgeable collectors are those over the age of sixty-five, but I would differ with him. Among the collectors I meet and those I am currently mentoring, the younger—and I mean those from thirty to sixty—are well educated on the topic of the book and everything else, or so they think. The affluent young are more likely to be from the professional or computer-smart dot-com classes, and therefore to have extensive educational backgrounds. They differ from earlier collectors, the top-hatted capitalist, the self-made man, for whom books signaled the possession of knowledge. For this earlier type of collector, the possession of a library may have served both in his own eyes and as notice to the world to confirm that he had "arrived" in the world of culture. Today's younger collectors do not have to prove themselves this way. At the same time, the

Manuscript page from the *Pickwick Papers* (author's collection).

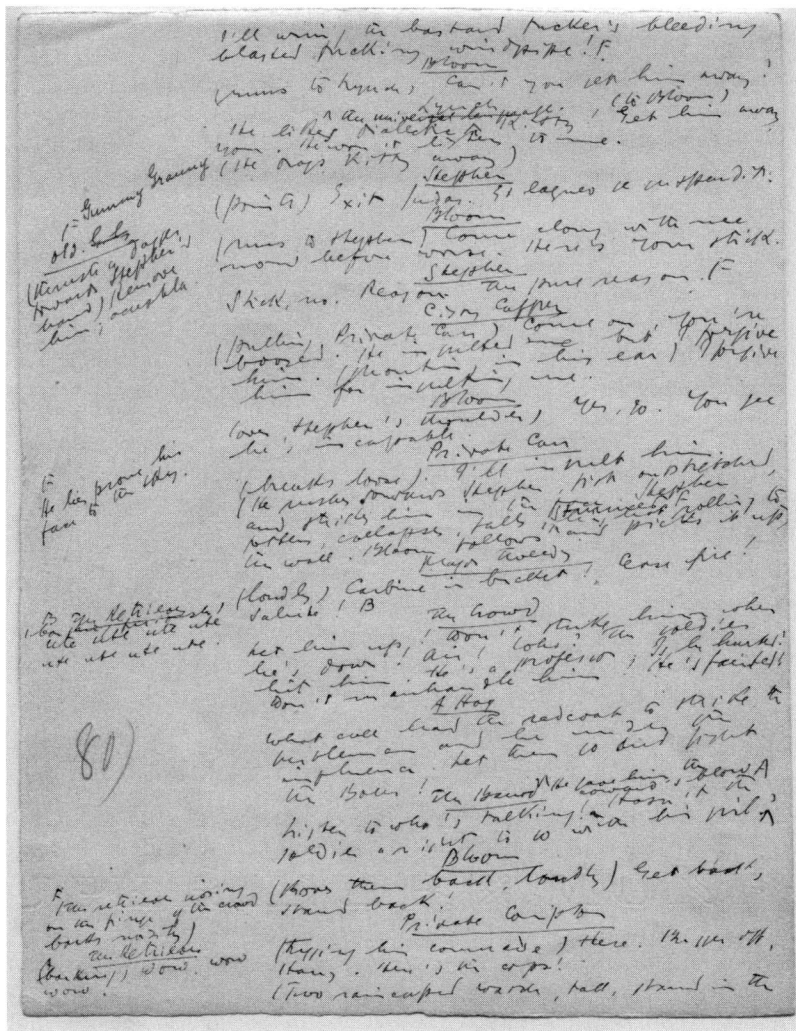

James Joyce, *Ulysses*. Autograph manuscript.
[Rosenbach Manuscript.] "Circe" episode, *p*. 80. *n.d.* [Fall 1920].

affluent members of today's society less frequently constitute a "leisure class." They do not have time to "play" at collecting. If they do not study the topic themselves and learn it down to the ground, they rely on experts.

Book collecting offers a rare opportunity to those who are only modestly wealthy or of means that have limits. Unlike the art market, which is driven by the truly wealthy, the book market is a place where a moderate fortune can still compete.

So we are all out there collecting. Men and women. Young and old. Creating for ourselves shadow lives of books and print, passion and possession, pursuit and capture. Our collections themselves are not static things. They are born, they flourish, and, ultimately, they travel out of our possession as we either die, or sell them, or give them away. It is this ultimate dispersion that concerns us here. Will the book collector of today be the donor of tomorrow? In many ways, it is to be hoped not. As collectors die and their collections are sold or auctioned, their books go back into circulation. They return to nourish a new generation of collectors and collections.

But book collecting's gain is a loss to those scholars and that posterity which justifiably wish to see artifacts gathered and preserved in a unitary fashion, in a place where they are both easily accessible and easy to keep track of. A private collection that is arduously compiled and exhaustively complete is a collection at rest. Its final home should be an institution, where it can be preserved and consulted by future generations.

That is the special collection. The remarkable expansion of special collections over the past century at universities and public institutions has radically altered the pursuit of scholarship and knowledge. The unique and rare manuscripts and material that were once the private hoard of the church or the wealthy collector are today relatively accessible to academic investigators and the curious layperson. As special collections mature and metamorphose in research institutions and electronic repositories, the need for preserving the past in its original form becomes more critical than ever.

Clearly, it is the right thing to give books to special collections.

But motives for doing the right thing are often mixed. Some donors give out of the goodness of their hearts. Others, for the tax advantage. The latter is not to be despised. At the moment, the tax motive is very much in favor of special collections.

A great deal of material is about to become available. Private collectors who started collecting in the 1960s and 1970s or earlier were able to obtain important items at a very low cost, compared to today's values. They will obtain a very good tax advantage based on the present fair market value of their holdings. Not so today's beginning collectors, who are entering a market where prices and value are very much in line. They, too, will have to wait their time.

For collectors who began their collecting much earlier, it is to their advantage to donate to special collections. Why sell to a dealer? A dealer will only give you about half the retail value of your collection (unless on consignment or private treaty). There is a significant advantage in going to auction, but mainly for trophy books and highly promoted items. Even with capital gains rates plus state income tax rates at a fairly reasonable level, donating or selling and donating—rather than selling the bulk of a collection—is an attractive option.

Those who are beginning to collect today, however, are buying high. The tax advantage will be far less. What will happen to all these collections?

It is always fashionable to be cynical, and the fashionably cynical view is that without artificial tax support, donation will die, which may be true. On the other hand, it is undeniable that the great age of American philanthropy took place in the early part of the past century, when great fortunes went virtually untaxed. And it might be added, that the authors of this philanthropy were that generation known to us as the "robber barons." Popular history tells us that they were as cynical and cut-throat a crew of bloodthirsty pirates as ever sailed the bounding main. Yet the cultural infrastructure of the museums, universities, libraries, and orchestras that we enjoy today is largely a creation of their generosity. It may be that, being greater sinners, they had more to atone for. But it is difficult to believe that today's gentler and better-educated generation of affluence will be any less likely to give.

But now, let us turn the tables. Too often, discussions of philanthropy turn on an analysis of the donor and his or her responsibilities. As a collector and a donor to special collections, I would like to address the other partner in this ménage: the special collection. I would like give my perspective on the future of special collections.

The past half century has seen the development of hundreds of special collections in libraries and research institutions. Today, most of these are flourishing. But more recently formed collections are having identity problems. Most of the "good stuff," by which I mean that at the high end or in "canonized" areas of collecting, has been taken. The major materials that have the ability to define a collection are coming off the market. Even if those materials were on the market, the newer collections could not afford them. There is no special collection library equivalent of the Getty Museum, a new institution with an unlimited acquisition budget and carte blanche to buy. With shrinking budgets and a lack of outstanding material available, libraries or other institutions with special collections are in a quandary.

Other factors at work include the changing face of librarianship. Many know better than I that there are currently fewer venues for training librarians. Where training is available, the current emphasis is on technology transfer and information education rather than on the traditional library school core subjects. Positions in special collections librarianship are being filled by younger people who may have greater comfort and familiarity with computers than with books. Nor are the ranks of librarians, like those of nurses and other formerly female-dominated professions, being replenished at the same rate as in the past. Women have more options and can make better money elsewhere. As time goes on, preservation will become more important. But special collections were founded mainly as the heart of research institutions. For researchers, preservation of materials continues to be of secondary importance.

Now and in the future, special collections librarians will need to develop and expand their relationship with the donor. It is not enough to presume an alumnus will give to a university library simply because of some nostalgic college or teenage memories. Some universities are developing parent and community programs aimed at cultivating donors. One librarian in Florida learned Spanish for the specific purpose of reaching out to a large Hispanic community.

Although I have never performed or read of a scientific survey on the subject, I suspect very few collectors are aware of the needs and goals of special collections. The world is full of people who would be quite happy to donate their collections, taxes or no taxes. But they have to be reminded that special collections are out there and that special collections people would love to make their acquaintance. You don't get anything if you don't ask for it.

If established collections do not move first, these collectors may establish new special collections. But are these really necessary? Perhaps for expanding active subjects like science, medicine, and business, they are. But for the rest, there is not enough money out there, and most new collections will simply lead to diffusion and mediocrity. We need to build on what has already been started.

Our current special collections were created in a different climate, when universities and institutions had huge acquisition budgets and played the six-hundred-pound gorilla at auctions and with dealers. Today, that gorilla is a very quiet little marmoset. Too quiet.

When acquisition budgets shrank, most special collections slowed in developing and growing their collections. Now it is a real challenge, even for curators of historically strong special collections to effectively persuade the library's senior administration that these collections are central to the teaching and research goals of the parent institution. With only a few notable exceptions, many began to see themselves as caretakers rather than wise stewards.

As I have said, special collections may be able to rely on the tax-motivated giver today. But down the line, giving will be a matter of pure altruism. In the future, special collections libraries will need to act like other successful nonprofit organizations. They will need to assess their wants, survey the pool of potential donors, and target those individuals whose collections complement their own. They will need to hone in on those collectors. Show them that somebody cares. That somebody loves and wants their collections and is prepared to care for them in perpetuity. If not, the collector of today will not be the donor of tomorrow.

A Book Collector Builds A Life

Arthur L. Schwarz

WHAT AM I doing here?
I must confess to more than a little astonishment at being in company with notable authors and publishers, eminent scholars and librarians, and distinguished dealers, as well as presidents of the ABAA. And me—just a book collector. Not to put too fine a point on it, but I am not a professional. However, I have managed to build a life around collecting books and making a place for myself among professionals who know so much more than I do but who, nevertheless, are willing to help amateurs wanting to learn and expand their horizons, to work with and to teach them, and to welcome them as colleagues in the world of books.

Several threads have created the fabric of my book life. I read books, but I must admit to a terrible impatience with most contemporary fiction and I am out of the loop at many social gatherings. I hunger for the substance of English history; give me a good new biography of Henry VIII any day. I love reading history but, in truth, if it happened after 1688 I really do not care. Unless it is royal. Or London. Or just plain interesting. I collect books as objects, yes, but content is important. I treasure my collection, finding it hard to part even with out-of-scope books, although sometimes I find it necessary to sell books to provide the funds to acquire others that I would prefer to have in my library.

Like all boys, I was a collector; I collected stamps, coins, bugs and, of course, books. My first collection was the work of Edward Stratemeyer, better known by his pseudonym, Franklin W. Dixon, the author of the *Hardy Boys*; I got rid of all the dust jackets because they ruined the uniform look of the shelved books. (I learned recently that this passion for uniform shelves is an English trait, so maybe I come by my Anglophilia naturally. You know, Samuel Pepys put little wooden blocks under his smaller volumes to raise them in order that the tops of his books would create a straight line, but I have yet to go that far.) In addition to the *Hardy Boys*, there were other nice books that I systematically destroyed: I submitted my father's boyhood copies of Heinrich Hoffman's *Der Struwwelpeter* to attacks of crayons, and I simply wore out my copies of *Treasure Island*, *Mutiny on the Bounty*, and other books with wonderful N. C. Wyeth illustrations.

My father was a book collector, with very eclectic interests: he bought English, French, German, and Latin literature (he read all four languages), history, mathematics, illustrated books, anything that appealed. Dad once complained that my interest in English history from the eleventh to the twentieth century was too narrow. At one time he owned a second folio Shakespeare, which I loved to look through; for me, the best part was seeing the stains from the candle drippings that remained after some long-ago reader enjoyed his book of an evening.

My father loved book collecting, I admired my father, and the combination led me to wet my feet; I found that I enjoyed it, so we shared the interest and enjoyed it together, until the end of his very long life.

In my working life, I was in the investment world, and from 1977 to 1979 I was situated in London. I have no idea why my firm sent a municipal bond guy to live and work in London, but it did, and, undoubtedly, living there stimulated my book collecting interest.

In the late 1970s, Dad started giving his books to his kids—for tax purposes—and he gave me one of my current treasures, Francesco Bartolozzi's engravings of Hans Holbein's drawings of the court of Henry VIII. During the two-and-a-half years I lived in London, I bought the 1754 edition of John Stow's *Survey of London* from Stanley Crowe for a few hundred dollars. There are wonderful plates in that edition, along with its fascinating text. Some collectors may remember Stanley; he was not easy to buy books from—somehow he did not seem to want to part with his stock. It bothers me that my Stow is missing one plate, though it appears never to have been bound into this copy, and was not removed by a print dealer. I am reminded of the late Leonard Hansen, book enthusiast and Grolier Club member, who bought damaged books with great abandon for relatively few dollars. "After all," Leonard said, "the Metropolitan Museum is perfectly happy to buy statues with arms, or legs—or who knows what else—missing!"

I was pleasantly surprised, and still am, at how reasonably priced unusual, old books can be. For a few hundred dollars—or a few thousand—you can buy, and own, fascinating bits of history. Now I know that a few hundred dollars—or certainly a few thousand dollars—is real money, but compare the prices of books with some of the purchases people put on their walls! Maybe this is because book spines do not dress up a wall as well as paintings and prints do, and "art" is a better weapon in the competition which Thorstein Veblen termed "conspicuous consumption." Whatever the reasons, these wonderful pieces of history seem relatively undervalued, with no offense intended to my friends who collect modern prints.

While living there, I started to collect books about London: these included publisher Rudolph Ackermann's *Microcosm of London* and his *Westminster Abbey*, which led me to see what else might be out there, like Ackermann's *Oxford*, *Cambridge*, and the *Public Schools*. And, although I did not have the courage to bid on it at the Prescott sale at Christie's in 1981, I was able to buy, more than a year after the sale, Christopher Wren's own copy of Sir William Dugdale's *History of St. Paul's Cathedral* (1558). I had not bid because, in all candor, I was scared to death, as a relatively new and very naïve collector, of making some horrendously expensive mistake. But I have never regretted buying it; this is history that I can hold in my hands.

So here I was, an investment manager who had bought a few books (and been given others). Although I am now an avid student of history, in college I was not a student at all. I had no interest in history or literature; I spent too much time on other activities. I got my "gentleman's C's" at the beginning of the time when a "C" was no longer really gentlemanly. Now my whole life is "book learning," in several senses of the phrase.

In 1992, I was standing in the Harvard Club coat-check line with William Manchester's biography of Winston Churchill under my arm, when a fellow standee suggested that if I enjoyed that, I should try Jasper Ridley's biography of Henry VIII; I was not 100 percent sure of the connection between Churchill and Henry VIII, but I followed his advice. Loved the book. I then read John Guy's *Tudor England* and the J. J. Scarisbrick biography of Henry. I was hooked.

Two years later my wife, Susie, and I went off to Cambridge, England, each to take a two-week summer course. She took Dickens; I took Tudor history. I had recently purchased a copy of the *Bishops' Book* (1537) and I brought it along, together with some other bits of English Reformation material—they are all octavo, easily carried. I was not taking the course for credit but I decided to write a paper about the *Bishops' Book*, just for the hell of it. I had not penned an "*ibid.*" or "*op. cit.*" since receiving my bachelor's degree, many years earlier, but here, when it was not required, I enjoyed it.

The mid-1990s found me buying a few books here and there, and filling most of my nonworking, waking hours with reading about Tudor England, much to Susie's distress. Among our non–Grolier Club friends, almost no one cares about the history or the books of sixteenth-century England, but I have to admit that that is one of their attractions for me. Somehow, I rather enjoy doing something that others think is a little offbeat.

A few years earlier, my Dad had a book on which he wanted an opinion. I went with him to Christie's, then on Park Avenue and

59th Street, where we met Chris Coover, now head of their manuscripts department in New York. He took us around the corner to see The Grolier Club (of which I had never heard) and I thought it was quite splendid but well above my level. I did keep up with Chris and in 1996 he suggested that I should join. He asked me to give him the names of the collector members whom he could ask for supporting letters, as one or two letters from nondealers was preferred. But I knew only dealers, such as the wonderful Nicholas Poole-Wilson and others at Quaritch. My reason for joining the club was just that: to meet other collectors, and librarians.

The required letters were garnered from a couple of generous souls willing to perjure themselves and I joined The Grolier Club in mid-1997. I found the club to be just what I had hoped, replete with fellowship and proffered friendship. Members said, "Tell me about yourself; what do you collect?" not, "Oh, you're a new member, may I tell you about myself?" These are the kind of people who have "biblio," "byron," and "firstfolio" as their e-mail addresses. There is one couple, both of whom are members, where the husband gave his wife, for Christmas a couple of years ago, shelf space. He actually emptied a bookcase and gave her so-and-so-many linear feet. Now that is devotion. And the wife of one collector told me that she *knows* that her husband is not having an affair, "He would not spend good book money that way."

Less than a year after I joined The Grolier Club, I retired from full-time work, although I continued the part-time role of marketing my firm's services in London, which took Susie and me there at least four times a year; "tough duty," as they say, but this came to an end in October 2001.

In retirement, I had four projected areas to keep myself occupied: to take classes at Columbia and NYU, to work on my book collection, to read more English history, and to build a model railroad. I have more than managed the first three; the model railroad still awaits another day or, more likely, another life.

One of the first highlights in my Grolier Club activities came when I, along with other new members, was invited to exhibit a few books in the "New Members' Collect," an annual show in which recently admitted members display a few items from their collections. This gave me a bit of a view of the work—and the rewards—that are part of the physical mounting of exhibitions. My Club involvement grew when I was asked to join the Publications and Members' Exhibitions committees, then chaired by Carol Rothkopf and Mary Schlosser, respectively. By demonstrating a little interest, you can get very involved.

What better way was there to fill my time in an interesting and productive manner than to do some volunteer work at The Grolier Club? I spoke with Eric Holzenberg, the director/librarian, and he suggested I work in the library with curator Michael North, who started me cataloguing the Club's collection of eighteenth-century Sotheby's catalogues on the Research Libraries Information Network (RLIN). This was pretty interesting—for a while—looking at the catalogues themselves, and seeing books listed by format (folios, octavos, and so on, rather than strictly by author) and RLIN was okay, if bizarre. I have to confess, though, that I tired of this project after some months of doing it for a day or so a week. There is just so much RLIN cataloguing that you can stand. It is awfully repetitive, so I asked Michael and Eric for another project—and this next one kept me happily occupied for a couple of years.

This time they wanted me to work on the Sydney Cockerell/Harold Peirce correspondence, which continued from 1897 to 1931, a collection of which The Grolier Club had purchased in 1998. Few people knew of Peirce, but it seemed that everyone knew of the redoubtable Sydney Cockerell. Everyone, that is, except me. I not only did not know who he was, I could not even remember his name, and I had to write it on a slip of paper as a memory jog. Well, I now know who he was. I spent over a year going through more than five hundred file folders of the letters between these gentlemen, creating what was to be a finding aid but which ended up being an article in The Grolier Club *Gazette* and then a book of the edited and annotated letters which detailed many aspects of the book world in the first third of the twentieth century. As interesting as the letters, themselves, were, I never could have completed this project without the help of one of the great scholar-collectors, Mark Samuels Lasner. He added many insights about the myriad people whose names come up in the correspondence, always with generosity of spirit and never with a suggestion of the surprise he must have felt at how little I knew about matters that are almost second nature to him. This is an example of the kind of relationship that The Grolier Club and Fellowship of American Bibliophilic Societies (FABS) foster.

While I was working on the Cockerell project, my younger son, Alan, said he had been concerned that I would be at loose ends after I retired. Apparently relieved, he said after I got so involved in this and other club projects, "The Grolier Club is your fraternity house!"

To augment my book collecting and interest in English history, I started to audit classes at Columbia: "The Reformation," "*Beowulf*," "*Canterbury Tales*," "Depiction of London in Renaissance Literature," and the like. Among the great aspects of auditing college courses at my age are the opportunities to get to know the professors without being accused of grade grubbing, and I have brought a couple of my instructors to The Grolier Club as my guests. I have also brought my books to classes, and that has worked out very well. Just doing that may have encouraged some undergraduates to become collectors. I was excited to learn that one of my professors at Columbia, Alan Stewart, would be co-curating, with Heather Wolfe, an exhibition at the Folger Shakespeare Library in fall 2004 on the "Culture of Letter-Writing in Renaissance England." I offered to lend him one of my treasures, four letters from George I, written in 1724 to members of the French nobility; two of them have never been opened and still bear their red ribbons and wax seals, just as they were affixed nearly three hundred years ago. It sounded good to Alan and Heather, and it sounded good to me that a bit of my modest collection would be exhibited on loan at the Folger.

Along with this, I started to do some teaching. Before I lived in London, I had taught investment banking as an adjunct, at the Columbia and Harvard Business Schools, and I had loved it. Maybe,

Book Talk

I thought, I could teach English history, tying in my book collection. Lorella Brocklesby, whom I had met when I took a couple of her English history courses at NYU, asked me out of the blue if I would like to conduct a full-day NYU workshop on Henry VIII. I realized that although I knew a lot more about English history than most Americans, I was really not equipped to teach a course in it. "Why not let's do it together?" I asked her. I could talk about Catherine of Aragon and the divorce, the split with Rome, and the five other wives, as well as the early years of the English Reformation. Lorella could cover her areas of expertise: art and architecture of the period, fashion, and theater, and we could share the political-historical bits. But what would make this class different would be the books: I would—and did—bring into the workshop a couple dozen books from or relating to the period—to share the thrill at holding history in your hands. The books ranged from Holbein's drawings of the court of Henry VIII (not the original drawings, Her Majesty the Queen owns *them*, but, rather, the almost equally spectacular Bartolozzi engravings which my father had given me twenty-five years earlier) to Ackermann's *Oxford* and *Cambridge*, and from Henry's *Assertion of the Seven Sacraments against Martin Luther* to John Foxe's *Book of Martyrs* to Gilbert Abbott À Beckett's *Comic History of England*. Lorella and I turned out to be a good combination; we still call Henry "Herny," in remembrance of a typo in one of our e-mails.

I went on to teach three classes at my local adult school, at which Lorella has taught for many years. She gave four sessions on the age of the Tudors, and I complemented this with some of my books in a kind of "hold history in your hands" show-and-tell. The following semester we did the Stuarts, and the next spring the four Georges. My classes give a dozen or so people the opportunity to see and touch some unusual items; they also had a chance to chat about "rare books."

Funny things happen. I was preparing a handout for the Georgian class in which one of the books to be included was an immensely heavy copy of Hogarth's engravings. The volume was to be open to one of his most famous works, "Gin Lane," and when I looked at the text on my brand new computer screen, I was surprised to see a light underlining below that just-inserted title. Placing my cursor there produced a tiny icon, with a broad, lower case letter "i"—you know, like an "information" sign. Clicking on the icon, I was offered a map of, and driving directions to, "Gin Lane." Wonder of wonders! I tried for the map, and was offered, as the closest fit that "MSN Maps and Directions" could find, "Gina Street" in London, Kentucky. Computers do not know everything. What else could I offer at NYU? I suggested "A Day at The Grolier Club," and in spring 2004 it ran on a Saturday, from 11 to 4, with an hour break for lunch. We started with Eric Holzenberg giving a 45-minute tour, then I talked for an hour or so about books I had brought. Following lunch, a half hour was spent viewing Garrett Herman's splendid Darwin show, we had another hour of show-and-tell and hands-on book examination, and ended with a half hour at the exhibition of Bill Drenttel's and Jessica Helfand's spectacular collection of volvelles.

For fall 2004, NYU asked me to give a course on rare books. Me? What can I do? I am very aware of what I know and what I do not know (remember what I said about teaching English history?). I do not feel comfortable at the prospect of pretending expertise on descriptive bibliography, binding, illustration processes, identification, and other details of the rare book world, but I have gotten to know a lot of experts, who shine where I barely glimmer, so I ran a sixteen-hour NYU course, *Introduction to Rare Books*—with no fewer than ten Grolier Club members as guests. Think about how *you* might maximize your knowledge and contacts. I guarantee you will get pleasure from it.

One school thing reminds me of another: Rare Book School (RBS), in Charlottesville, Virginia. RBS is one of the great experiences a book collector can have. Susie and I have been there twice. First we took Terry Belanger's "Descriptive Bibliography"; I loved it, treated it like solving a puzzle, and Susie, well, she weathered it. A couple of years ago we went back and, again with Terry, took "Book Illustration Processes," which, I am glad to report, Susie enjoyed more than "Des Bib." RBS is grand, not only for the course content, but for the opportunity to meet and work closely with other likeminded people. Lunches and dinners are full of as much book talk as one can stomach, so to speak.

When Susie and I married, she had little interest in and no knowledge of "rare books," but, over time and through the process of osmosis, she and I came to share an enthusiasm for much of my collection. While she really does not care about my major passion, Tudor England and the English Reformation, she loves and, indeed, urged me to buy, several of our choicest items: a complete run of Ackermann's *Repository of Arts*, the English magazine published from 1809 to 1828, and our Duke of Windsor material, including the former Edward VIII's own presentation copy of the warrant granting him his ducal title.

Another way to meet fellow biblio types is on trips, such as the FABS excursion to New York. Susie and I went on the Grolier's *Iter Britannicum* in 2001, where she lost count at fifteen libraries in six days. We did not just look around these libraries; each of them took out its greatest treasures for us to enjoy. For example, at the Royal Library at Windsor, we saw a small notebook in which a ten-year-old child had written charmingly about sitting and waiting, restless and hungry as only a child can be, through "Daddy's" and "Mum's" coronation. It was, of course, Princess, now Queen, Elizabeth, writing about the coronation ceremony of her parents, George VI and Queen Elizabeth, the late queen mother. "Granny" (the formidable Queen Mary) assured her that there would be ample tea and cakes at the ceremony's conclusion. And while "Granny" claimed not to remember her own coronation in 1911 (of which "Uncle David's" copy of the *Form and Order* is in my collection), ten-year-old Elizabeth asserted that she would *never* forget hers.

More recently, we traveled to Washington, Amherst, and Northampton, and again to England, although this time it was only for a day each in London and Cambridge. Taking advantage of these travel opportunities gave us hours of contact with people interested in the same things as we are, as well as enabling us and our fellow travelers to reminisce about common experiences when we met again in home territory.

One of the wonderful things you can do at The Grolier Club is work on setting up exhibitions, nine per year. I mean physically setting them up—handling all kinds of wonderful material and seeing more than just the exhibited openings, without having to buy the books. A wonderful camaraderie develops.

Even better than setting up others' shows is the opportunity to curate an exhibition drawn from your own collection. In 2000, I was lucky enough to mount one at The Grolier Club, on the second floor. Like every other exhibition curator, I brought in too much material, and had to leave some items out, but so it goes. But I did get to see about eighty of my books open at one time. I felt like an old man with several children and numerous grandchildren. These people would come to visit me occasionally, and we would have a nice, quiet chat, or a cup of tea. But for this birthday celebration, or whatever, here they were all together, talking animatedly among themselves, and relating to one another. That is what these eighty books were doing.

If you choose to write an exhibition catalogue, as I did, it is worth the ton of work, more than you can possibly imagine, that goes into it. You learn a great deal about your own subject and your collection.

As this is being written, I am working on another show. In, I think, April 2001, I was at a Grolier Club lunch, seated next to Werner Gundersheimer, then director of the Folger. "What would you think of working together on an exhibition in 2009, commemorating the five hundredth anniversary of the accession of Henry VIII to the throne?" I asked, somewhat hesitantly. "Good idea," he said, but he pointed out that he would be retired by then. I brought it up again, to Folger's Richard Kuhta and Bill Stoneman of the Houghton Library, who liked the idea. Then John Bidwell of the Morgan Library signed on, so here I am, leading this commemoration of my friend, "Herny," at the Grolier, in very distinguished company. I think we can pull it off.

Most of the projects I have discussed: working in the Grolier Library or mounting and setting up an exhibition, take a fair amount of time. But even if you have time constraints, and we all do, there is always something worthwhile in which you can become involved. For example, The Grolier Club has about ten committees, ranging from Members' and Public Exhibitions to Library to Admissions, and from Finance to Publications to Special Functions to the House Committee. Joining one, or more, of such committees is a great way to become involved in your club, and who knows where it will lead?

I am sure by now you get the idea. One can build a wonderful life around books, as I have. As in a spider web, the threads just come together.

The Future of Book Collecting

Paul T. Ruxin

WHAT IS collecting? The root word of "amateur" is the Latin *amo, amare*, "to love," and as an amateur collector, I am passionate about, but not an expert on, collecting. In fact, I had not even thought much about it until I was asked to contribute to this discussion. Trying to prepare, I went to Amazon.com and searched for all the books about "collecting." Amazon provided the information that, at that exact time in space, there were 5,730 different titles on the subject. Although a cursory review of the results suggested at least some of these books were about credit and collection policies rather than book collecting, the number still astounded me.

What kind of collecting am I talking about? Take the copy of the magazine *Collector's Mart* I recently found in an antique shop. The publication is geared to collectors of such things as Dean Middleton Original Dolls, Harbor Lights, and cocktail swizzle sticks. The edition I found featured an artist named Gaylord Ho in what appeared like the old-style ads for brands of scotch whiskey wherein famous people revealed what they did and did not like. In the ad, Ho answers a series of seemingly banal questions—for example, What is his favorite food?—and then reveals his philosophy of the art he creates (Ho makes ceramic angels and glitter domes): "I believe art should help make the world a better place." Of course, this is a profoundly generous statement that is hard to argue with. But, at least in my view, book collectors have a different take on the meaning of what they collect than the people who read *Collector's Mart*. Samuel Johnson once reviewed a book that he found to be "both good and original." "Unfortunately," he went on to point out, "that which is good is not original, and that which is original, is not good." The pack rat instinct will always be with us, and there will always be people who buy and collect books, whether they are recognized classics on erudite topics, Nancy Drew books, or something less ephemeral. There will also be book collecting like ours in the age of the Internet, no question about it. The most popular program on public television is *Antiques Road Show*, proving that for virtually everything available there is an audience and a demand.

Serious book collectors are engaged in a different kind of activity than the audience *Collector's Mart* addresses. Ours is a more rarefied kind of collecting, and I am going to intersperse some history among my few thoughts on this. Let us begin by remembering George Santayana's famous observation that "Those who do not learn from history are doomed to repeat it." It is worthwhile to ask who the serious collectors of the future will be as well as who were the collectors of the past. One of the first and most notable European book collectors was Jean Grolier. Grolier was a great scholar and a great man and although he began the book-collecting tradition in many respects, others who may not have had his intellectual capacity have continued it. Through this line of descent we came to Thomas Dibden, for example, who, in a sense, popularized the collection of books. Some people do, in fact, collect the works of Dibden himself. However, beginning in the nineteenth century, men of means who were not necessarily interested in or able to understand the content of books began nonetheless to purchase them in large quantities.

Book collecting became a status symbol under the example of people like Henry E. Huntington, J. P. Morgan, and members of the Folger family. It is useful to remember, of course, that J. P. Morgan

The Future of Book Collecting

himself had the redoubtable Belle da Costa Greene as his librarian and adviser. Other great collectors of the age also had their own advisers and favorite dealers. But book collecting in the golden age of the last part of the nineteenth and first part of the twentieth centuries, unlike during Grolier's time, was perhaps not always driven by serious interest in the books' contents. For a time, book collecting seems to have become the thing to do if one could afford it. Over time, however, the ability of collectors to find suitable material diminished, and the nature of the collectors changed for the better, in my opinion, because some of the great collectors who followed that golden age were more serious about their books than had been their predecessors. People like Haskell Norman (who assembled an extraordinary collection of medical books) or, as famously, H. Bradley Martin and Estelle Doheny, were seriously interested in books and what they contained. More recently, there have been exemplary collectors who have built extraordinary collections and became profoundly knowledgeable about them. The outstanding example, of course, was Mary Hyde, Viscountess Eccles, who began with her first husband, Donald Hyde, to assemble the great Johnson-Boswell collection, which is now at Harvard. Another example is Gwin J. Kolb, whose astonishing *Rasselas* collection is now at the University of Chicago.

Many serious collectors exist today, and it is important to think about and compare some of the current collectors with the Huntingtons and the Morgans of the past. I can think of three or four people who are assembling or who have assembled great collections of great books. With the advice of Stephen Massey, Stuart Rose of Dayton, Ohio, is building a fine "high points" collection. Another great collection—built over the last sixty years and just put back in the market through his sale at Christie's—is that of Abel Berland of Chicago; and of course the collections of people like Jon Lindseth, Fred Kittle, and others, who have built extraordinary focused collections about which they have become prominent scholars.

An interesting question is why the enormous new wealth created by the Internet and e-commerce has not led to a wave of new collectors. I can only think of two who have participated in a serious way. Bill Gates, for example, bought the Da Vinci notebooks for an astonishing amount of money, and has bought a fair number of other books. However, like his nineteenth-century antecedents, it is not clear whether Gates spends any time reading or studying these books. John Warnock, creator, founder, and former CEO of Adobe Systems, is also building an extraordinary collection and is indeed a lover of those books and their contents.

What will the collectors of the next century collect? It is hard to collect the things that have been collected because most of those collections were, or will be, passed on to institutions. The Hyde's Johnson-Boswell collection, as noted, is at Harvard, removing a great deal of Johnson-Boswell materials from the market. Kittle's Conan Doyle collection has gone to the Newberry Library. You can certainly find first editions of Johnson's dictionary and Sherlock Holmes books, but many of the crucial works you would need to create a truly great collection around these literary giants are unlikely ever again to be on the market. The same is true of Jon Lindseth's Lewis Carroll collection at Cornell, and Kolb's *Rasselas* collection at the University of Chicago. I have been looking for Johnson's "Prologue to Comus" for twenty-five years and I have never seen one offered. But there will always be serious collections to be created. Jim Hagy in Chicago, for example, is now building an extraordinary collection of books about magic.

Our notion of what is worth collecting and what is important to collect changes in response to availability and taste. Suppose someone today wished to create a great collection of detective fiction. Perhaps not knowing much about where to begin, that person might choose as a likely place to start, say, Edgar Allen Poe. Then that collector might decide to move on to Sir Arthur Conan Doyle—certainly no one would argue about the appropriateness of collecting Doyle. The collector might then say, "I probably ought to have Agatha Christie, and, I don't know, maybe Dashiell Hammett—who would not want to have that in a collection—then Mickey Spillane, Sara Paretsky, Dick Francis...." And why not, if that is what this person

The Future of Book Collecting

wished to collect? Is Dick Francis less important to collect than Edgar Allan Poe? Some collectors might argue that relative scarcity, for example—Francis is not scarce, and Poe is—renders one more desirable to collect than another. Scarcity, however, is not the only mark of an important book for a collection. To have a complete collection and to understand the genre, you need them both. I doubt most serious collectors believe simply that the fact a book is scarce and expensive makes it worth having or makes it important to collect; conversely, the fact that a book is available does not necessarily diminish its importance or make it not worth collecting.

Plenty of things exist for collection in the future, even if they are not the same things we collected in the past. How will collectors of the future go about it? Probably in much the same way as we always have, with some differences. When I started to collect Boswell and Johnson, it was simple to use the Courtney and Smith bibliography and I naïvely thought at the time that I might just be able to find everything on their list.[1] Now the Fleeman bibliography, which consists of two of the thickest volumes I have ever seen, demonstrates this to be an impossible task. Fleeman should be used as the basis for judging the success or failure of a Johnson collection only if one is prepared to accept failure as the result.[2]

Book fairs still exist—perhaps in even larger numbers than they did previously. However, they seem to be less interesting than they were formerly. Many of the leading dealers now appear at only the largest fairs: London, New York, Los Angeles, or San Francisco. Many dealers no longer have shops that are open to the public. For example, I was disappointed at a recent show in Chicago that had only three or four dealers, and even they had little to offer, really more used books than rare books. Catalogues remain a prime source for collectors, as do occasional auctions, like the Abel Berland sale.

Perhaps most important, building a serious collection in the

---

1. William Prideaux Courtney and David Nichol Smith, *A Bibliography of Samuel Johnson* (Oxford: Oxford University Press, 1915).

2. J. D. Fleeman, *A Bibliography of the Works of Samuel Johnson*, 2 vols. (Oxford: Clarendon Press, 2000).

twenty-first century will require an established relationship with a specialized dealer or group of dealers. Berland admits, for instance, that without the help of John Fleming he would never have been able to create his great collection. I could not have progressed with my own collection without the help of a number of dealers, including Ruth Igelhart, Stephen Weissman from Ximenes, and others. Identifying the serious and knowledgeable dealers in the areas in which you intend to be a serious collector remains essential, and becoming a favorite client of such dealers will no doubt aid you in your search. Indeed, great dealers of the past have always had their top clients. One of the problems this raises, however, is favoritism. There are at least three of us who are serious about our collections of Boswell and Johnson: Gerry Goldberg, Loren Rothschild, and I. Unsurprisingly, seldom do three copies of the same important or scarce book come up simultaneously—and, if the book goes to Stephen Weissman or Simon Finch or Christopher Edwards, all of whom know the three of us, these men are put in a terrible spot. Whom do they call? What do they do with the book?

Dealers are of crucial importance, even in the age of the Internet and despite the wealth of Internet sites available to booksellers and buyers. While such sites are easy to use and accessible for purchasing certain items—usually inexpensive and common—serious collectors' books of real value and scarcity will rarely be traded on the Internet. Buyers will continue to patronize knowledgeable dealers who will always call their favorite clients first when something juicy arrives, and it is dealers and serious collectors who will continue to buy and sell the great books. Internet sites can be useful for building the beginnings of a serious collection or filling in basic spots, but the treasures will always come from dealers. Some readers may have had the pleasure of dealing with Simon Finch, Stephen Weissman, or Christopher Edwards. Connected to all kinds of British sources, including old families, and country homes, they know when people with libraries die, and heirs without fail call them, but not you, the collector, to sell these estates. Through dealers like these, a book that has been on the shelf for hundreds of years might enter your possession without ever going to market at all. Indeed, I have acquired some extraordinary association copies in this manner.

I conclude with a few questions and the answers they elicit: Why do we love and collect books? Why is it such an important exercise to us? Why do we care whether book collecting as we know it continues in the twenty-first century? To answer the first question, one need look no further than The Rowfant Club, which takes as its creed the "critical study of books in their various capacities to please the mind of man." Books and book collecting at this level are a mental endeavor; but collecting is not only about the mind. Books resemble architecture, which is truly unique among the fine arts because it alone deals with both form and function—it serves a practical purpose as well as having an aesthetic importance. The book, like a building, is a combination of form and function; interacting with one is a unique human experience. Books appeal to humans at every level: from the physical sensations of holding an old book in your hands, feeling the rag paper, and admiring a beautiful binding or printing to the intellectual experiences reading fine writings elicit. Books define us as human beings—through them, we absorb ideas and memories from the printed words of people who have gone before us. And so, the study of books, the love of books, will continue to be important to those of us who value those basic elements of what make us human.

There is a final reason in the age of the Internet why book collecting will endure. People often assume that reading is a solitary pursuit and that book collecting by extension must also be a lonely endeavor; the pleasure of it comes from sitting alone in your library, surrounded by books and removed from human contact. Of course, the falsity of such a notion is obvious to FABS members both separately and collectively. In the age of the Internet, when electronic communication has increasingly replaced face-to-face interaction, the fellowship of the book is an extraordinarily rewarding part of life. The collective nature of book collecting leads us to each other and it is our human connections that ensure the future of our passion for books in the twenty-first century.

SPECIAL COLLECTIONS

What Can A Librarian Do?

Roger E. Stoddard*

I: My Vienna

EVERY OTHER year between 1994 and 2002 I would spend a few days in Vienna as part of a tour of Germanophone book dealers I inherited from James Walsh, the original manager of the German collections in Houghton Library. On my final visit, I arrived in the city at nine Saturday morning, May 25, 2002, and taxied to the hotel. My room was not yet ready, so I headed instead for the breakfast room. Along the way, I ran into my old friend the concierge. I raised my arms and shouted: "Welcome to Vienna!" which garnered some snickers from behind the counter. Then I challenged him: "Anton Bruckner is forgotten in Vienna!" That sent him to his concert calendar. I admitted that I was leaving the city on Wednesday morning, and he agreed that nothing by Bruckner would be performed during my visit. "Have you ever gone to a concert in the Musikverein?" he asked. I responded that I knew it only vicariously from the New Year's Day concerts telecast in the United States with Walter Cronkite as the announcer. "Then you must go tomorrow morning to one of our Vienna Festival concerts. It will be conducted

---

* I dedicate this essay to my friend James Needham, consummate book collector.

by Previn.""Thank you very much, I am grateful," I replied as I went for breakfast.

I had been on the road for twelve days, I had five to go, so I had allotted a bit of extra time in the city. From Amsterdam and Vestrenen, Stuttgart, Köln and Bad Honnef, Hamburg, Eutin, and Altona, and Berlin I had visited fifteen bookshops and knocked off a few hundred books from our desiderata lists of two hundred German authors. Among them were long-sought and formerly mysterious rarities by the likes of Theodor Fontane, Thomas Mann, Johann Heinrich Pestalozzi, Oskar Kokoschka, Joachim Ringelnatz, Heinrich Heine, and Georg Christoph Lichtenberg. For instance, the twelve-volume collected works (1890-1891) of Fontane in publisher's gilt-stamped cloth—*with the portrait*: how many times had I failed to find all twelve volumes without the portrait or the portrait without all the volumes! Reminds me of the Turgenev set, *with the portrait*, that I had bought many years before and of choosing the right set (1846) of Karl Postl (a.k.a. Charles Sealsfield), the one revised by the author. This time there was Mann's *Herr und Hund* (1918), copy C on Zanders (Bütten Papier), inscribed to the author's close friend and supporter, both early and late, Ernst Bertram; all three volumes of Pestalozzi's didactic *Lienhard und Gertrud* (1790); the first book, *Hiob, ein Drama* (1917), authored and illustrated by Kokoschka; the second, third, and fifth books by Ringelnatz, all of them illustrated stories for children; Heine's French book from Paris, *De l'Allemagne* (1835), the missing volumes from his *Gedichte* (1854-1857), and a run of *Agrippina* (Köln, 1824) with seven youthful poems; and a complete run of the *Göttingisches Magazin der Wissenschaften* (1780-1785) edited by Lichtenberg ("the German Voltaire") and brilliant translator Georg Forster.

And, there had been surprises: two books of Dutch verse (1617, 1624) by the Anglo (Rowlands) Dutch (Verstegen) author of, among other things, *Restitution of decayed intelligence* (London, 1605); one of two known copies of the two-volume *Gedichte* by Friedrich Hölderlin's *Catcher in the Rye*, 'Crisalin' (a.k.a. Isaac Sinclair); the fourth-known copy of a teaching edition, with sets of questions, of

Lucan's play *Timon* (Worms, 1530); Erasmus's *Catalogi duo operum* (Antwerp, 1537); two volumes from the library of Georg Friedrich Hegel; and, a truly wonderful author's copy, with tabs and MS. indices, of P. Johannes Findling's *Lutheri antilutherana* (1528), the Donaueschingen copy.

After a bite to eat, I strolled over to the Dorotheum quarter, with its antique shops and art galleries, named for the old Viennese auction house. I was hunting for a dentist and his son who had been operating a business in antique medical instruments. Two years before I had teased them into selling me a stack of turn-of-the-century catalogues of central European manufacturers of scientific instruments; none of the firms were represented at Harvard, and my library holds and collects the *usuels* for the Harvard Collection of Historic Scientific Instruments. The dentist had disappeared, but not my old pal Peter Hardy. On a former visit, he had sold to me for

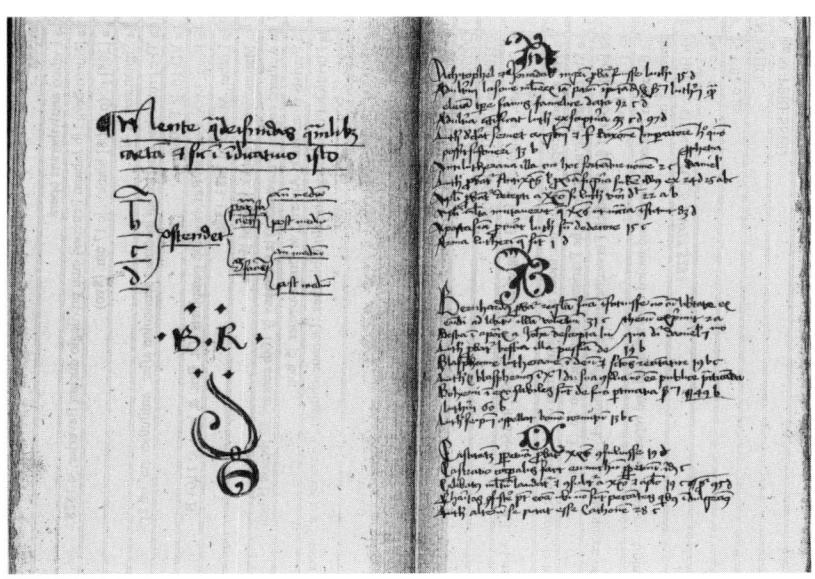

First opening of the MS. Index in the author's copy of *Lutheri antilutherana opera* by Johannes Findling (Nuremberg, 1528). Reproduced by permission of the Houghton Library of the Harvard College Library.

my personal demonstration collection what he calls a "Wachs-Stock." Not quite wax taper, but fashioned out of tapers, it is a little book molded out of colored wax tapers with a Madonna inside the cover. The perfect memento of a pilgrimage, mine as well as the original purchaser's.

After I had had seen enough paintings and religious articles, I strolled across the Opera Ring at the Staatsoper to find my streetcar for some nontourist Vienna and the apartment house of Wolfgang Mantler. You want to keep in close touch with him if you care for alchemy and science. Four years earlier, I had bought out of his vitrine an unrecorded Venetian thesis printed by Antonio Zatta in 1759, a huge broadside three feet square, illustrated with an engraving of the solar system, Halley's Comet and all. Before that, I purchased a German translation of a book by George Starkey, the magus who had roamed New England before returning to London and perishing in the Plague. This time, Mantler had two pocket-sized German ornament books, bound together, 1687 and 1695. Then off I went for some window-shopping and supper in preparation for *Tannhäuser* at the Staatsoper that evening and for "Sunday morning service."

By eleven o'clock Sunday morning I had found my way to a seat in the center of the balcony of the Musikverein, so I could see the depth of the hall in perspective and its inner crust of gold close up. Sir André Previn led the Vienna Philharmonic in *Four Interludes from "Peter Grimes"* by Benjamin Britten and the Harp Concerto by Alberto Ginistera before crowning the performance with a piece I did not know, Sergei Rachmaninov's Second Symphony. From the ominous opening bars of the Largo the music does not loosen its grip on you, but I held my own through all the quick turns until the Adagio when I broke up—and the woodwind duets, like birds courting in flight, could not comfort me. Sir André took three bows, but the musicians started to leave the stage, so he came out into the hall for his final acknowledgment. Then, amidst all those hard-hearted Viennese, I left with tears still in my eyes to walk down to the Johannes Brahms memorial. You will recall that Brahms appears to sleep, with his head resting on the back of the bench, but the Muse has fallen headlong, smashing her lyre on the tarmac. Then I went on to the Kunsthistorisches Museum for an afternoon with Parmigianino and friends. I was hoping that the beautiful waitress with the gimpy leg would still be serving in the café. She was, but she never waits on me.

On Monday morning I presented myself at ten the bookshop of Georg Fritsch, our principal source for books by Austrian authors. Immediately he produced on request from my desiderata *Weinachtspiel* (1924) by Max Mell, an author whose friend I have become, as I had found not only his first but also his third work in complement to the second one already here. This Christmas play was printed in only fifty copies. Far more important was his second offer, Karl Kraus's *Die Chinesische Maurer* (1914), one of two hundred copies with Expressionist lithographs by Kokoschka. After eluding us all these years, this find brought us ever closer to completing the work of the artist. (Later that week I would buy the final Kokoschka desideratum out of a bookshop window on a Zürich hillside.) Then I thanked him for Paul Celan.

Two years before, you see, I had begged Georg and his bright assistant, Bernhard Steiner, to find for me a Viennese anthology with translations by Celan, *Die Lyra des Orpheus*, published by one Zsolnay in 1952. Speaking through my hat, I had said it sounded like a book of household verse sold door-to-door and that it probably looked like "that"—pointing to a fat volume in the midst of their poetry anthology section. "That" turned out to be a reprint of the very book, so Georg promised to sell me his own copy of the first edition. They must have recalled that incident; for when I was making appointments for May back in February, they informed me that they were purchasing a set of Celan books inscribed to a friend. I returned their fax, typing all in capitals: "PAUL CELAN IS THE MOST IMPORTANT GERMAN AUTHOR FOR US THESE DAYS, AND WE ARE TRYING TO GET ALL THE BOOKS, INCLUDING THOSE FROM BUCURESTI. PLEASE SEND US YOUR PRICED LIST . . . ."

I rushed them more than a bit, got the list and the price, begged some funds from my German book-selector colleague, Michael Olson, and got the books. Most are inscribed to Klaus Demus, Celan's Viennese friend who helped get *Der Sand aus den Urnen* published in 1948. Thanks to diligence over the years, capped by that purchase, we now have all eighty or so books that you need, except for the Modern Book Club *Gedichte* of 1966,[1] the Brunidor edition of *Fadensonnen/Schlafbroken* (1967) with etchings by Celan's wife, Cécile Celan-Lestrange, and two ephemera; the Fogg Art Museum has purchased from the same cache a collection of twenty etchings by Lestrange, for which we are grateful.

The next day found me at Inlibris, the shop of Hugo Wetscherek, located now in an expansive apartment on Rathausstrasse near the palatial town hall. I have been visiting the brilliant Jüngling Hugo since he started selling books out of a cellar room. This time I intended to examine two collections of Viennese drawings for a library benefactor and to check out a copy of Leo Tolstoy's late novel, *Resurrection*. Now if you are looking for the heartbreak of bibliography, then try Tolstoy.

By the end of his career, Tolstoy had acquired an English publisher, one V. G. Chertkov of Maldon, Essex, who customarily published a complete, authorized text in Russian. There are lots of philosophical tracts by Tolstoy published in Maldon, as well as an edition of *Resurrection*. There were central European editions of indeterminate authority, but the Russian editions had to pass the censor. Hugo's edition was published by Bonch-Bruevicha in Moscow in 1900, an edition missing from the bibliography; Tolstoy inscribed the copy at Yasnaya Polyana to Tatianie Al., a person who remains unidentified. Naturally, we bought it. On the way out of Boston, I had purchased one of those early cyclostyle editions of *The Kreutzer Sonata*. What is my point? Sooner or later, people will pay attention, do the bibliography and the philology—even the censorship. The books will be waiting in strings and sets for that.

1. Thanks to the generous agency of the Berlin publisher, Thomas Günther, I was able to purchase a copy for the library on July 14, 2004.

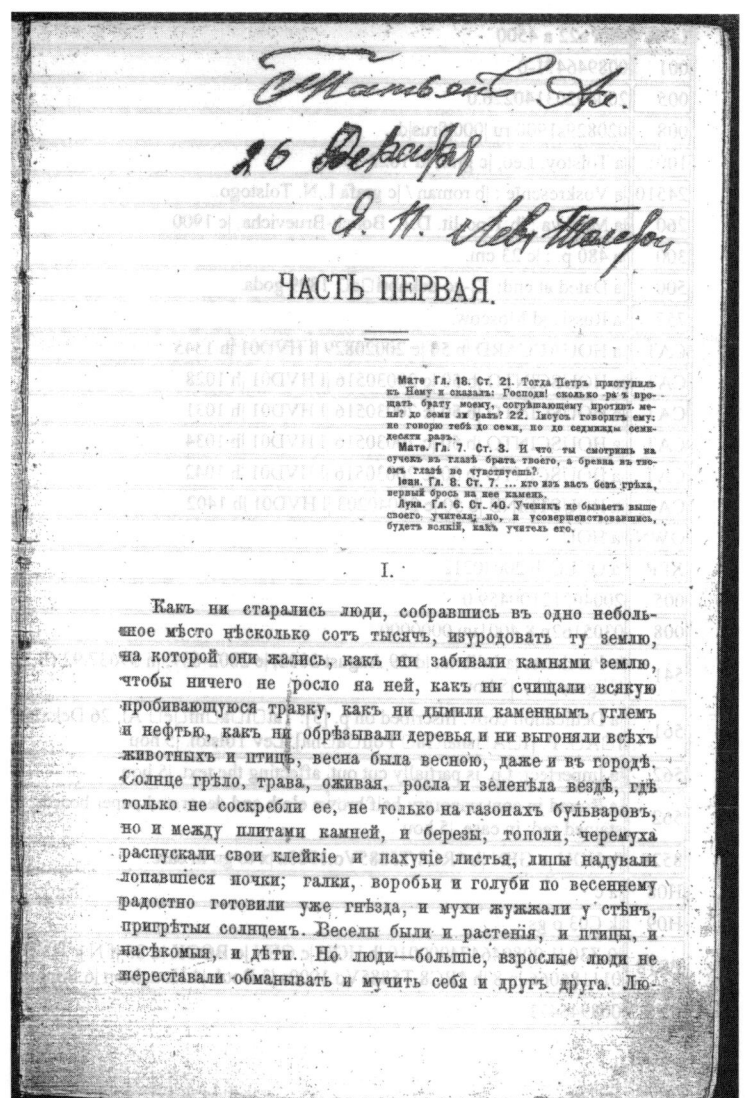

Inscription by Tolstoi in a copy of his *Resurrection* (Moskva, 1900). Reproduced by permission of the Houghton Library of the Harvard Collage Library.

Book Talk

II: Solzhnenitsyn and Me

On Commencement Day, June 8, 1978, Aleksandr Solzhenitsyn came to us like some giant of a metropolitan to deliver the principal address. "'Veritas' may be your motto," he told us, "but you have fallen far, far, far away from it." He spoke in Russian, his wife delivering the English (voice over). Afterward, I rushed to the News Office to get the English version so I could send it to Bayard Kilgour, founder and supporter of Harvard's Russian Literature collections, but I never heard from him about it. Great Son of the Crimson that he was, he probably threw it in the wastebasket. But Solzhenitsyn's strong voice cannot be denied in Russian culture.

I had been laid on to entertain Mr. Solzhenitsyn beforehand with a look at the Trotsky Archive and some classics from the Kilgour Collection. I met him at the front door with his motley accompaniment of bodyguards, and I led him down to the Graphic Arts study room where I had arranged a two-tiered exhibition. On top were all the great classics of nineteenth-century Russian literature from Pushkin to Chekhov, but I will never reveal what he said about them. Beneath these classics, I spread out the copies of his own work that I had been collecting, books not only from Russia, but also from Italy, Germany, England, Netherlands, France, and the United States. I was surprised to hear him say (in translation) that he had never seen most of them. Virtually all were unauthorized editions in Russian of work by an author whose country avoided international copyright agreements, but it took me a while to discover a parallel between Solzhenitsyn, author of *A Day in the Life of Ivan Denisevich* and the Gulag Archipelago series and Henry Fielding, author of the novel *Tom Jones* and the play *Tom Thumb*. Let me explain.

Donald Hyde had formed an excellent Fielding collection, which we worked hard to earn as the gift of his widow Mary. I determined to extend it, and with the particular help of book dealer, Stephen Weissman, and aided by the stocks and catalogues of European book dealers, the collection has been enriched both by English rariora and by Continental editions both in English and in translation. Fielding, like Solzhenitsyn, could not have seen all those Continental agents of his work as they made their way to coffeehouses, stages, drawing rooms, and libraries. I did not forget those unauthorized editions of Solzhenitsyn.

Downstairs in the manuscript stack I showed Solzhenitsyn the Trotsky Archive and the Diary. He liked our manuscript boxes, so we sent him a dozen of them after his visit. I shall never forget shaking his big, bony hand as I unlocked the tunnel door into the Widener Library. (It took months to extract from him the reading copy of his address, "Veritas" inscribed in the midst of all those typed cyrillics.)

In 1994, the International Bibliophiles visited St. Petersburg, and I got the chance to organize and deliver at Akademiia NAUK a talk about the five hundred years of Russian books at Harvard: "Red Star and the Crimson: Harvard's Love Affair with Russian Books." Solzhenitsyn and his visit were not omitted. One afternoon we found ourselves outside an old hippodrome with an artist's book fair in progress. A book on a far table turned out to be a new edition of *Rakovyi korpus* (*Cancer Ward*), just printed by "Glagol" in St. Petersburg. I begged our Russian guide to get me a copy, and the next day I returned to the bus to find the driver reading "my" book. Censored passages restored and corrected by the author, it was one of ten copies in a special binding. I gave it to the library in honor of Kate Gray Kilgour, Bayard's widow, but we could never locate "Glagol" to find out what else they were publishing.

And the unauthorized editions? The principal publisher was Alec Flegon in London. When "A Day in the Life of Ivan Denisevich" was published in *Novyi Mir* in 1962, Flegon offset the magazine pages and brought out a pamphlet edition. When the Russians published their pamphlet edition, Flegon offset it; and when the Gulag series came out in Paris with the YMCA Press, Flegon offset those volumes also. Whenever I would mention his name to members of the Russian Research Center, they would hold their noses as if detecting a bad smell, for they knew him as author/publisher of Soviet erotica—"Sex Life of the Commissars," and the like. I tried

Front cover of one of Alec Flegon's unauthorized printings of Aleksandr Solzhenitsyn's *A Day in the Life of Ivan Denisevich* (London, 1963). Reproduced by permission of the Houghton Library of the Harvard College Library.

and failed to find him on one of my book-buying visits to London. Eventually, I turned to that very savvy bookwoman at Quaritch, a specialist in modern first editions in every language but English, Wendy Delamore Cruise.

Wendy located Flegon, struck a deal for his file copies and archive, and my College Library colleagues found the funds. When I first checked Flegon in the Harvard catalogue I found only a dozen entries; now there are 151, and thirty-five boxes of papers, including dossiers on his court cases. Flegon would claim that he established and maintained Solzhenitsyn's reputation by keeping the books in print—as the Russians did not. Some fortunate scholar will determine what he published and where he sold it. Flegon has died, all his literary effects are here, he was delighted that they were coming to Harvard, but I am not so sure that Solzhenitsyn would approve.

III: A Yank at Cerisy-la-Salle

In the middle of vacation, summer before last, I was strolling the grand arc of the Ogunquit Beach in Maine with my wife, Helen, on a Saturday morning in August. By early afternoon, we had returned home to Lincoln and I was correcting some files and printouts. By midafternoon, my car was parked in Cambridge and I was on the subway for Logan airport. We departed at 6:10, arriving before 7:00 the next morning at De Gaulle, where I bought a phone card and a bus ticket for Opéra and then found my way to St.-Lazare railroad station. I phoned ahead to reserve a taxi, bought my return ticket, got a bite to eat, and was on my way west by noon, changing trains at Caen and arriving at St Lô just after 3:00 p.m. Mine was the only taxi in sight, and we drove speedily through several old towns with Romanesque churches and finally onto the rolling pasture of an old chateau with remnants of its moat and long lengths of stables out behind.

Cerisy-la-Salle came into the hands of the French state about a century ago, and, with part of the stables and most of the chateâu converted to bedchambers, it has been the classic locus for the *colloque*—close in definition to our symposium—first for the generation of Gide, then for Sartre, and now for Derrida. The French tend to extemporize, holding in hand *le texte*, stuffed with place markers. Everything is taped and God bless those who transcribe and those who edit.

Yank that I am, I delivered the diskette and printouts of my lecture in English, of the French version I had commissioned from a Harvard graduate student, and of various bibliographica. But what was a Harvard librarian doing in Cerisy?

The colloque was called "Edmond Jabès, Hors Genres"—beyond the categories. A provocative title, I thought, for conversations about a Francophone from outside France, an author whose poetry attracted attention in the Mediterranean world in the 1930s, 1940s, and 1950s and whose poetic dialogues in the seven volumes of *Le Livre des questions* established his reputation worldwide from the 1960's on. My friend Robert Graff had told me to pay attention to Jabès, and I became his bibliographer. The Caen publisher, Lettres Modernes Minard, brought out the first edition of my bibliography in 1997 and the second in 2001. There are sixty-nine books in many editions printed all over God's earth and some *hors monde*, if you ask me. I published an account of the fugitive works in the *Australian Journal of French Studies* in 2000.

I am sure that the French participants were puzzled to see me embrace my faithful correspondents Daniel Lançon, a French scholar who spent a decade in Cairo tracing the roots of the elegant French literary culture that flourished there in order to publish his hefty volume, *Jabès l'Égyptien* (1998), and Steven Jaron, author of *Edmond Jabès: The Hazard of Exile* (2003) and husband of a Jabès granddaughter. Or to see me speaking familiarly with another helpful friend, Viviane Crasson, one of Jabès's daughters. After I settled in, we had a buffet supper on the back lawn and then watched a movie of Jabès speaking about Cairo before his forced exile (he never went back after the Suez crisis of 1956).

What Can A Librarian Do?

On Monday morning we gathered in the old library, walls embellished with the published volumes of previous colloques. I sat at the speaker's table on a dais beside the moderator, E.-K. Kaplan, a professor from Brandeis. The audience did not come from places with names like Brandeis or Wellesley or Columbia, but from universities named V or VIII or III. They received copies of the French translation and my bibliographies and then I fired away.

I had concluded from the advance notices that they believed Jabès was a nomad crossing borderlines in the desert and composing commentary on Kabbala, fashionable sightlines of the moment, but obvious malarkey: an indulgence of the critic but an insult to the poet. So, I humanized him, and I internationalized him: "'How do I read Edmond Jabès / Wie ich Edmond Jabès lese / Comment je lis Edmond Jabès?: hear the bibliographer's answer.' With an appendix, 'Edmond Jabès: supplement to the bibliographies of printed books (2001) and fugitive work (2000).'" I carried on:

> Here is a librarian, a librarian of historical collections, therefore a book historian, this one a bibliographer as well.... While you are studying texts in all genres and making comparisons ... I am doing that with printed things in all genres.... So, what can I do to help you up there in the reading room, what can I do for our beloved Edmond Jabès, how can I conflict your mind about texts—those electrical charges trailing through matter and materialized by print? ...
>
> Desiderius Erasmus was the first international author.... Like so many scholars of his time and of ours, he wandered. When he wandered he made friends with the printers, and he kept printing all over Europe.... W. G. Sebald is the most recent International, a German national who took his training in German and Austrian Literature at Germanophone institutions.... The Sebald case for internationality came to trial when the Harvill Press in London purchased the English-language rights.... The English versions, including the American issues by New Directions, circulated in a new and much larger language group....

There are 100 million German speakers in 40 countries, 341 million English speakers in 104 countries, and 77 million French speakers in 53 countries.... The life of Erasmus in the Holy Roman Empire, even the literary life of Sebald in the Anglo-German sphere, seem so simple when we compare them with the life of our Cairene hero, Egyptian and Jewish by birth and family, Italian by inherited citizenship, Francophone by education and culture....

The world of Jabès expanded in 1963 with the publication of *Le Livre des questions*, but no one could say that it was the work of an unknown Paris poet, or that it did not crown a considerable oeuvre, well received and well respected.

But 1963 did change the world for Jabès, for the serious French critics of the day, and for literary culture, initiating a Fête de Jabès both inside and outside the borders of his new home in France.... Three of his own books were printed first in French in Italy, and commissions of texts, requests for texts, and invitations to read his work and to participate in colloquia came from many different countries. Some of his texts were published first in translation or only in translation. In his work he was always addressing an international audience.

I made two demonstrations before laying out an action plan for future Jabès studies. First Jabès as his own editor: he established his own selected works, *Je bâtis ma demeure* (Gallimard, 1959), and for a German publisher he made a sampler, *Vom Buch zum Buch* (Hanser, 1989) which was translated into English (Wesleyan, 1991), but never published in French. He invented a locus for collecting his fugitive work, *Le Livre des marges* (Fata Morgana, 1975 and 1984), and he spiced it up with quotations from other writers. His devoted reader, Antoni Tàpies, contributed "marginal" illustrations and color etchings. Unique with him, I believe, was his method of choosing lines here and there from a large work and offering them as a new "composite assembly" as his contribution to a *Livre d'artiste*, "where text and art share the power of the book and its meaning," I reminded

What Can A Librarian Do?

Front wrapper, etched and embossed in silver and black ink by Antoni Tàpies, of *Dans la Double Dépendance du Dit* (Montpellier, 1984) by Edmond Jabès. Reproduced by permission of Roger Stoddard.

the audience. "That is a dangerous territory for a poet," I said, "as text can be reduced to caption or undermined by art." Now that I think of it, for the author a *Livre d'artiste* is not a solo with accompaniment, but a duet in which either party can make a bad entrance, get off key, forget the score, and so on.

My other demonstration concerned the final fifty, very spacey pages of the current collected edition, *Le Seuil Le Sable* (Gallimard, 1990), an obvious anomaly. I showed that the page layout, derived from a "Book Happening" created and performed by poet Emmanuel Hocquard and his then partner, Raquel [Levy], who in a single day would compose, print, and sew up a nine-copy edition of a text. They called the result "Chutes," "a fixed forme, strictly constrained: five pages of text (verse or prose) with a maximum of five or six lines on a page. Unlike the sonnet, for example, the formal unity is not established by the poem but by the volume," as Hocquard explained. Jabès loved it: "Words from the abyss, spaceless in immense and senseless space, here, dear Raquel and dear Emmanuel Hocquard, you have created for them a universe to their measure, and their own universe to your measure," he wrote.

The audience did not exactly love me. They did not like the idea of artists mingling with the texts. (Actually, Jabès loved artists and they reciprocated; he wrote prefaces for their exhibition catalogues.) They tried to find out where I was coming from, what did I do? I responded that I published bibliographies of difficult subjects, for instance Julien Offray de La Mettrie, author of *L'Homme machine*, and Etienne Pivert de Sénancour, author of *Obermann*, and Jacques-Charles Brunet, author of the *Manuel du Libraire et de l'Amateur de Livres*. I detected no sign of recognition. As an American librarian collecting five centuries of French books for Harvard, building strings and sets in hierarchies, probing deep and ranging wide, I had been living in a different world from theirs, and we shut down.

I got up at three o'clock on Monday morning, my cab took me to a deserted country railway station, and I stood beneath a streetlight hoping that the milk train still stopped there. It did, and I made my way back to Caen, to Paris, to De Gaulle, and, finally, to Boston.

What Can A Librarian Do?

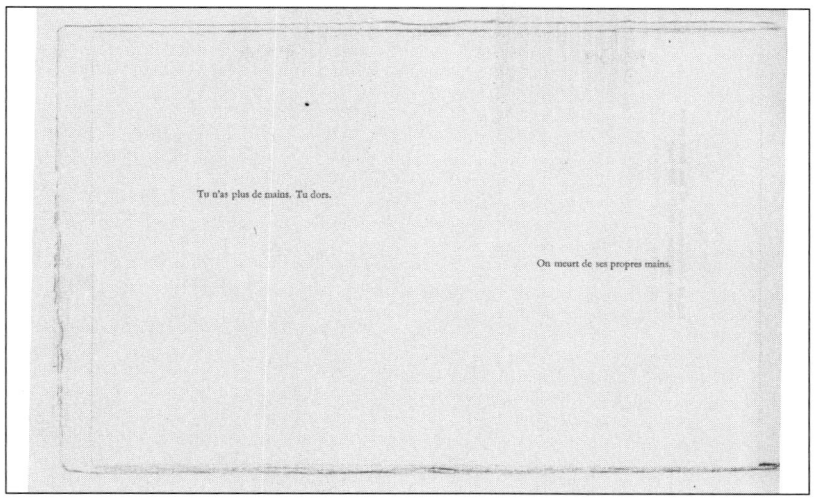

A typical spacey opening of the 'Chutes' edition of *Des Deux Mains* (Paris, 1975) by Edmond Jabès. Reproduced by permission of Roger Stoddard.

Next day I was back in Maine. Later I learned that the colloque decided that Jabès did not know much Hebrew, so the Kabbala theory was out. Perhaps I will learn the replacement when they have printed our lectures. I wonder if they will include my bibliographical supplement? Maybe it was too much for them. *Hors genres?*

So, what can a librarian do? Frustrate scholarship for a generation or more? Are there opposing parties, a scholar who knows it all and a librarian who proves otherwise? Materially the librarian builds the anti-thesis, over and over and over, challenging first with matériel, then with indexes. The historical record of mankind may be preserved in libraries on account of their focused attention span over the decades and centuries, but it will always be incomplete: most of it was never represented materially, much of the matériel is either lost forever or temporarily misplaced, and history exceeds in volume and speed the capacity of libraries to accommodate it. Would you give it up? What would you do?

An Embarrassment of Riches: Collecting Trends in Institutional Special Collections

Samuel Streit

THERE IS a fairly common, though by no means unanimous, perception that everything worth collecting has been collected, that all the good stuff in well-established areas of collecting interest has long ago vanished, and private collectors often grouse that it has vanished into the omnivorous jaws of institutional libraries. It is also sometimes perceived that there are no new areas in which to collect, that every scrap of printed or manuscript documentation on every conceivable subject, no matter how cutting edge or idiosyncratic, enjoys the attention of legions of collectors, both private and institutional, all fighting tooth and claw to snap it up.

I do not really agree with either of these lines of thought—witness ever-growing number of booksellers, steady continuation of auctions, book fairs, and such Internet services as Bibliofind, and succeeding generations of book collectors and collecting organizations. I daresay if there were nothing left to collect, there would be no collectors and no collecting groups. In fact, as my title indicates, I think there is an embarrassment of riches available. The trick, especially for institutional collectors, is to discriminate among the possibilities in ways that enhance the institution's research capabilities and to make the best use of insufficient acquisitions funds without overwhelming the institution's capacity to catalogue, preserve, and house the collections it acquires.

In times past, institutions as well as private collectors usually built their holdings based largely upon "canonized" rare books and manuscripts. This perception may at least partly be one of hindsight, since what we today consider rare may not have been accepted as such by earlier generations. Still, especially in the last thirty years or so, efforts to collect in traditional areas have been balanced by a more expansive, nontraditional, ever-emerging concept of what makes up worthwhile areas for collecting. In this essay, I shall address both traditional and untraditional areas of collecting using my own library, the John Hay at Brown University, as an example. However, I will concentrate upon the latter since the theme of this volume is changing trends in book collecting.

Brown is old as American universities go, and it has been fortunate that its library has never been the victim of fire, flood, or warfare. Hay has always possessed books that received special care—which is to say they were locked up—and, as early as the 1880s, entire collections received such special treatment, some in their own rooms, a practice that continued into the early decades of the twentieth century. Special Collections in the more modern sense, though, did not come about until the 1940s, and a coherent, gathering together of the collections only began in 1964. This leaves aside the John Carter Brown Library, of course, which came to the campus in 1904 and was established as a separate entity because the donor wished his collection to maintain a unique identity within the larger library context.

The result of this essentially unplanned accumulation of rare books and manuscripts as a component of a larger library or library system, both individually and as discrete collections, has long been typical of American universities and contributed to both the strengths and weaknesses of such collections. Essentially, this broad scope makes Special Collections at Brown and elsewhere into a microcosm of the library system of which it is part, from A to Z in the Library of Congress classification. At Brown, there are both a general rare books collection and a general manuscript collection, which assimilates individual items that are not part of a discrete bloc. If one includes manuscript collections, several hundred distinct collections exist within this system. We have continued to develop some collections over the years, especially those that arrived with endowments. Some, thanks to curatorial nurturing, have been supported using the library's undesignated funds. Others were sufficiently complete within their intellectual boundaries upon arrival that the library has not felt compelled to add to them. But some, many of them quite old, have not been supported; the result has been that they are not very important today. This is not to say such collections are unused or have no function within an academic environment where curricular and research interests are broad, sometimes abstruse, even quixotic, and certainly never static. Such collections, however, place a burden upon the library, both in terms of making decisions about which collections and subject areas to sustain or allow to suffer from benign neglect and which new areas it should explore. Given its wide-ranging holdings, one might conclude that Special Collections at Brown (and, by extension, special collections in similar institutions) has no focus and that this breadth but not depth renders its overall collection weak. To the contrary, I believe a broad scope and mission can allow Special Collections to pursue new opportunities that may add significantly to the library's overall strength. The challenge is to make wise decisions, balancing traditional collecting with newer initiatives, which may be very untraditional both as to subject and scope, and to make those decisions based not only upon the appetite to acquire, but also the ability to digest what is acquired by making it accessible and preserving it for future generations.

As I stated, we at Brown have several areas of collecting emphasis, of which about one-half are of long-standing importance and tend to be traditional in nature: American literature, American history, the history of science and mathematics, and the book arts. Others are of more recent vintage, being no more than thirty years old, and some quite a bit younger than that; these are a mixture of traditional and untraditional areas and include early twentieth-century English literature, military history (especially iconography), publishing history, and that great catchall, popular culture. These in themselves are quite broad by definition, and we believe it is important to keep them broad — elastic, if you will. On the one hand, this gives us boundaries; on the other hand, however, we are not too restricted, and indeed add collections outside these categories as long as they are strong in their own right and support our faculty's teaching and research agendas.

For the purposes of this essay, I looked back over the past ten years to see what major collections we have taken in and how well they fit into the broad collecting areas I previously outlined. The collections themselves number about forty and include books, manuscripts, ephemera, and art. To list all forty would be tedious and time-consuming, so I will outline here only two areas: American literature and its close ally, American publishing history. In part, I selected this area because it is one of the most traditional of all subjects collected by special collections libraries and departments. However, this area is also infinitely expandable into untraditional realms, the idea being to show how special collections libraries, as typified by my own, continues in tried and true directions while also venturing into less familiar territory.

Literature is undoubtedly the most common and the most sacrosanct, and sometimes the stodgiest of areas collected by rare book and special collections libraries. In Brown's case, the Harris Collection of American Poetry and Plays is probably our oldest identifiable special collection, having arrived in 1884 as an endowed gift. The prior owners of the collection had a radical, for the time, collecting scope: they had set out to collect every volume of published poetry and plays by a citizen of the U.S. or Canada. When a catalogue of the collection was published in 1886, it was vilified in print by William Cullen Bryant and praised by Walt Whitman, who wrote a review called "5000 Poems" in its praise. Bryant hated its inclusiveness, Whitman loved it; I rest my case. Thanks to the accompanying endowment, Brown has been able to maintain the collection's scope, so that the Harris Collection today is the largest of its kind, numbering somewhere in excess of 250,000 volumes. The point is that the Harris Collection was in its day considered untraditional because it set out to be comprehensive rather than canonical in its field; today, however, it is considered to be, by and large, a traditional literary collection, albeit what sometimes passes for poetry and is thus included in its scope is rather strange.

In American prose literature, our holdings are much more erratic, with a large number of individual titles held in the general rare book collection and a handful of strong, primarily nineteenth-century author collections. Nonetheless, since we have such strong holdings in poetry and plays, we have set out selectively to build our prose holdings as well.

During the past ten years, we have added approximately seven collections to our American literary holdings, including some collections that might qualify as popular culture, if one takes a more canonical approach to what constitutes literature. Two of the collections are acceptably canonical by just about any modern standard: the Martha Dickinson Bianchi Collection and the personal library of James Laughlin, founder of New Directions press, both of which came to us as bequests.

An author in her own right, Martha Dickinson Bianchi was Emily Dickinson's niece and inherited The Evergreens, the Dickinson family home next door to Emily's own house in Amherst, Massachusetts. Through Bianchi's heir Mary Landis Hampson and the good offices of two Brown faculty members who are Dickinson scholars, The Evergreens' library and substantial Dickinson family archive was bequeathed to Brown. Although Harvard purchased everything pertaining directly to Emily years ago, the Bianchi Collection provides scholars both a context for Emily and her family as well as a wider understanding of printed holdings by Emily that the Harris Collection holds.

The Laughlin Collection builds upon both our poetry and our prose holdings. The relationship between New Directions, which in essence means publisher James Laughlin, and Ezra Pound, William

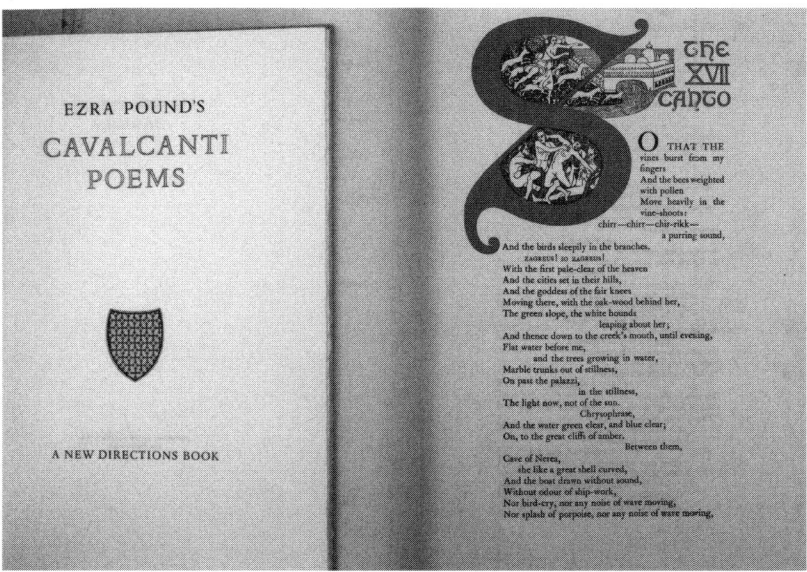

Among the significant Pound editions in the Laughlin Collection are one of 70 copies of the Rodker Edition of *A Draft of the Cantos* 17-27 with initials by Gladys Hynes and copy 2 of 115 of the *Cavalcanti Poems* published by Laughlin's New Directions Press.

Carlos Williams, and Thomas Merton, among others, was long and profoundly important. Laughlin bequeathed the New Directions archive to Harvard, his alma mater, but he left most of his library to Brown, where he had taught for a year in the mid-1980s. As you would expect, the Harris Collection has long collected all three of the poets I mentioned, but Laughlin's collection is often inscribed, sometimes annotated, and generally in superb condition. There is the occasional item, too—often a variant—that we had missed. In addition to the poets just mentioned, Laughlin graciously allowed us to prowl through the remainder of his library where we identified additional poetry and, perhaps even more important, some excellent prose as well. This includes a significant collection of Gertrude Stein's work, both poetry and prose, and works by another thirty or forty authors. For the most part, these are incomplete collections of the authors in question, but they provide a solid base for us to build upon systematically, something we will likely do with at least some of the authors. Additionally, we picked up a number of British authors, which complements another of our developing collecting areas and several continental authors as well, to name just a few: Henry Miller, Paul Eluard, Wyndham Lewis, D. H. Lawrence, Jean Cocteau, Ronald Firbank, Edward Dahlberg, and E. M. Forster.

So much for the canon. Among the American prose writers whom Brown has long collected, and one of the most significant in terms of interest and use, is H. P. Lovecraft, Rhode Island's best-known and probably most influential author. Dismissed in his lifetime and excluded from the critical canon even today, Lovecraft is a very important figure in the area of fantasy literature, even more so than Edgar Allen Poe in Stephen King's view. We own the bulk of his manuscripts and his enormous correspondence, as well as printed work from first appearances to the present day. Because of the strength of Brown's Lovecraft holdings, we have concentrated upon the books and manuscripts of other fantasy authors, many of whom corresponded with Lovecraft. Joining such collections as that of Clark Ashton Smith, we have in the last decade purchased the papers of Joseph Payne Brennan, Manley Wade Wellman, and a sizable group of correspondence from August Derleth to Donald Wandrei. Unless you are a fantasy collector, chances are good these names are unfamiliar, save for Lovecraft. But that is the point. Many libraries and those in the critical establishment ignore or even disdain this untraditional, genre literature. Nonetheless, serious scholars use the collection heavily and we will continue to collect in the area.

Humor is a second form of genre writing we have collected lately. Research libraries rarely collect humor; indeed, Brown had never collected it either, except in its incarnation as American poetry and plays. However, a few years ago we received a collection of nineteenth- and twentieth-century, primarily American, humor numbering approximately thirty thousand volumes. Textual (as well as sexual) humor, along with visual humor—for example, cartoon books—are well represented and both famous names and nonentities are given equal importance. Had the Miller Collection not been

Book Talk

Selections from the Miller Collection, illustrating nineteenth-century dialect and ethnic jokes and themes of social satire, cartoon and topical humor.

An Embarrassment of Riches

Examples from the Ciaraldi Collection that demonstrate the close relationship between comics and popular film.

so vast we would not have taken it, and I expect we will not attempt to add to it by purchase unless an entire complementary collection comes our way. However, it is important because of its size. Alas, also because of its size, the collection is not yet fully catalogued, and until we can make it more widely accessible it likely will not receive the use it deserves. Even so, scholars are using it: a class in Irish history, for example, has used the late-nineteenth-century Irish and Irish-American books to examine how stereotypes of the Irish made their way into popular imagination. As a reflection of trends in popular culture, the Miller Collection will no doubt provide future insights into society that other forms of the written record may not reveal.

Another recent genre collection of note is the Ciaraldi Collection of comic books, graphic novels, and other forms of comic art, which numbers some sixty thousand items and is growing, thanks to the donor. The Ciaraldi Collection contains runs of "superhero" comics by both obscure publishers and such mainstream houses as DC. The illustrated novels, of which there are over three hundred, range from Ann Rice's *The Vampire Lestat* to Art Spiegelman's *Maus*, the rodent allegory based upon Nazi Germany. There are also compilations of newspaper comic strips, such as "Prince Valiant" and "Terry and the Pirates." There is the French metal burlant (adult science fiction) and Japanese manga and anime comics, which derive from Japanese animated film. And this is only the tip of the iceberg. Even with the gift only partially processed, this collection has seen extremely heavy use. Not surprisingly, many undergraduates utilize the collection, although not necessarily in a frivolous way (and we never discourage reading for pleasure). Two of our students have been looking at comic book depictions of the Viet Cong from the 1960s and 1970s and comparing their findings to depictions of the Japanese during World War II.

As with the Miller Collection, of which the Ciaraldi Collection in many ways is a logical extension, our interest was partly based upon its large size and partly on the fact that we continue to receive infusions of new titles several times a year. The collection is large enough to be nearly comprehensive within its genre, and it is a major source for documenting an aspect of popular culture that few other institutions are duplicating: only one, to be exact.

A more recent collecting area that complements our American literature holdings is publishing history. By their very nature, special collections libraries contain much raw material for the study of publishing history; building upon that, Brown decided fifteen years ago to go about it in a more organized fashion than they had previously. Initially and for obvious reasons, we concentrated upon small and fine press publishers, especially those that produced American poetry, and we now have a dozen or more such publishing archives. In the past decade, this has included purchasing the archives of Unicorn Press, Palaemon Press, and Burning Deck Press. We also have purchased the archive of *Conjunctions*, a leading literary journal that publishes work by many Brown faculty and alumni, although it has no formal ties to the university. By gift, we received the Third and Elm Press archive and the library and personal papers of Rollo Silver, a Brown alumnus best known for his standard histories of American printing, bookselling, and publishing. His voluminous and wonderfully organized research notes provide an enormous amount of data for American publishing of the last century in particular.

Most recently, we received the archive of St Martin's Press, founded in the early 1950s and today one of the major U.S. trade houses. The two recently retired chief executives of the company are Brown alumni; through their efforts, the archive came to us with an agreement that every three years another shipment will arrive. This is obviously a quantum leap from small press publishing, colleagues at other institutions that possess such archives in their collections (e.g., the New York Public Library, Princeton, Columbia, and the Lilly Library) advised us that such archives provide insight not only into the publishing industry but also into the entire biography of individual books, from receipt of the manuscripts through the editorial, design, printing, advertising, and distribution processes. And, for many authors whose personal papers may never be saved, these archives preserve perhaps the only record of their lives. As publishing undergoes massive changes due to the computer, even one such large archive provides a remarkable window into twentieth-century life and culture. We have hopes for an endowment that will see to the continued processing and preservation of the archive.

In sum, what does all this discussion of Brown's collections say about trends in institutional collecting? Most important, it suggests that while things change much also remains the same. Most special collections try to maintain their significant historical strengths while expanding their boundaries to incorporate the evolution of the collections subject matter, or to add complementary collections. Simultaneously, we are branching out into entirely new areas, documenting contemporary life and culture in manifestations that only a couple of decades ago would have been considered outré, at best. This is also true of the media upon which or within which specific subjects are presented. I began by observing that there is an embarrassment of riches remaining to be collected. I hope I have convinced you that this is in fact the case.

I Didn't Know You Had That! — Resuscitating Special Collections

Geoffrey D. Smith

"I DIDN'T KNOW you had that," is among the more common yet disconcerting remarks heard in rare book and special collections libraries. Such a remark is especially discouraging when the reference is to a notable book, manuscript, or collection that may have been highlighted in special catalogues, covered by local, even regional and national media, discussed in innumerable talks to tour groups, friends groups, university classes, or a point of illustration in an address to a scholarly association. Though the material in question may have been used over the years by scores of international scholars, we must simply reassure ourselves that, even with all the outlets of modern communications, we cannot reach everyone, sometimes even our local users. As will be discussed in some more detail below, ever more sophisticated technology is improving access to well-documented materials, especially renowned books and manuscripts. On the other hand, there are those less renowned collections that, correspondingly, have received less extensive, if any, formal organization and little to no public promotion. These less renowned collections are the focus of this paper. The remark, "I didn't know you had that," applied to these latter collections, is not a case of bemusement, but a case of regret, for, in fact, these undocumented or under-documented collections might be of profound influence on current research, but remain difficult to access even in a preliminary record, let alone a detailed inventory or catalogue record.

Without doubt renowned book and manuscript collections merit that designation if only by age, reputation, and rarity. In the theory and methodology of collecting, be it the private or institutional collector, renowned collections tend to be composed of "high spot" items, a term from the collectible market that designates the assembly of books typically associated with canonical authors (Shakespeare, Cervantes, Joyce), great ideas (Galileo, Newton, Einstein), historical figures (Machiavelli, Luther, Lincoln), and so on, which, in their own right, tend to be derived from established, bibliographical lists such as *Printing and the Mind of Man* or a Grolier 100, to cite but two. In the private sector, such a style of collecting is realistically restricted to individuals of means, many of whose collections do, indeed, end up in institutional holdings. Other areas of collecting for the less wealthy, whose collections also find their way to institutions, tend to focus, by fiscal necessity, on more modest materials of profound personal interest (academic, artistic, political, religious, and so on) and developed through judicious selection of closely related materials. Each type of collection can be of important research interest, but the more canonical collections have traditionally received greater institutional commitment, and hence, public attention since the early days of catalogue books through the catalogue era and into the digital era. Yet, as research evolves, both in theory and methodology, many of the less recognized and under-organized collections, those collections currently in libraries and those to come, will emerge as significant scholarly resources.

The discovery of new research resources is the métier of the academic scholar and literature on the subject, such as Richard Altick's *Scholar Adventurers* (New York, 1951) has been fascinating and enlightening reading for generations. Serious researchers scour bibliographies, catalogues, footnotes, correspondence, and, even with the least documentary note, traveling to and physically working through boxes of poorly organized papers in search of primary materials. And, still, there remain those collections that, indeed, have languished in rare book stacks without any serious note, perhaps other than an internal acquisition or accession record, and those internal records may be inaccessible to the general public.

Languishing collections are common to all repositories, from major research libraries with millions of volumes to small college libraries, and, remain, likewise, a common concern. Repetitively, I return to "renowned" collections, those established and publicly recognized institutional resources that continue to receive principal, administrative support, especially as we enter the digital age when there is an impetus to promote more widely known collections: again, the glamour of emphasizing the "high spot" collections. Today, the impetus to provide not only remote bibliographic access to a library's holdings, but also supply facsimile digital images of the contents themselves is certainly a boon for scholarship, but, still, often an enhancement of known materials at the cost of further neglect of other collections. For instance, the elaborate and colorful images of medieval manuscripts may make a greater institutional impression on the general public than the penciled diary of a World War I enlisted man; but, in reality, is one document more valuable for research than the other? Perhaps the dull, shabby, though individualistic, document, in fact, offers more original insight into actual events than yet another page from a *Book of Hours*, say, beautifully, yet conventionally designed for an aristocratic household.

I do not by any means wish to value the research importance of one document over another, and medievalists might well castigate me for any deprecation of the scholarly significance of early manuscripts. The publicity surrounding the British government's fundraising efforts to keep the Macclesfield Psalter in the United Kingdom rather than let it be sold to the Getty, speaks strongly to the insights offered from the hand-painted satiric and ribald images adorning the manuscript. Rather, this is all to suggest that there remain innumerable untouched or little utilized resources available for original research, documents that will remain plentiful for the future because human resources, despite great technological advances, cannot keep pace with the mountains of original materials that descend daily upon special collections across the nation.

Technology is making great headway with regard to access to library materials not only through online catalogues but, more effectively, through full text access to library holdings. A recent, significant technological breakthrough in intellectual access is Google's collaboration with five research libraries (Harvard, Michigan, New York Public, Oxford, and Standard) to digitize portions of their collections (each library has a separate agreement with Google regarding the number of volumes). Even if full text access were available for all the holdings of these distinguished libraries, even if the holdings of the remaining tens of thousands of libraries were available through full text—a far-reaching proposition, to say the least—broad assumptions regarding access remain, the principal one for this paper being that only identified and previously processed materials will be available. Furthermore, with regard to the very materiality of the text, it is a truism among bibliographers and specialist researchers that each copy of a book or document is unique and there is more to access than the title and author. That is to say, the prospect of including the abundant bibliographic data for each of the millions of volumes and manuscripts, both the obvious and as well as the nuanced data, is a remote possibility, yet this copy-specific information is required for much serious research. But, lest I stray too far, the focus of this article is not about digital ventures; rather, to emphasize, again, those materials that are currently difficult to access and will remain so, perhaps, even in an advanced digital environment.

As noted above and for the sake of emphasis, books from the hand-press era are almost exclusively unique documents due to the many changes made by printers during the printing process. David McKitterick, Librarian of Trinity College, Cambridge, has demonstrated clearly in his book, *Print, Manuscript and the Search for Order, 1450-1830*, that not only were early printed books constantly

I Didn't Know You Had That!

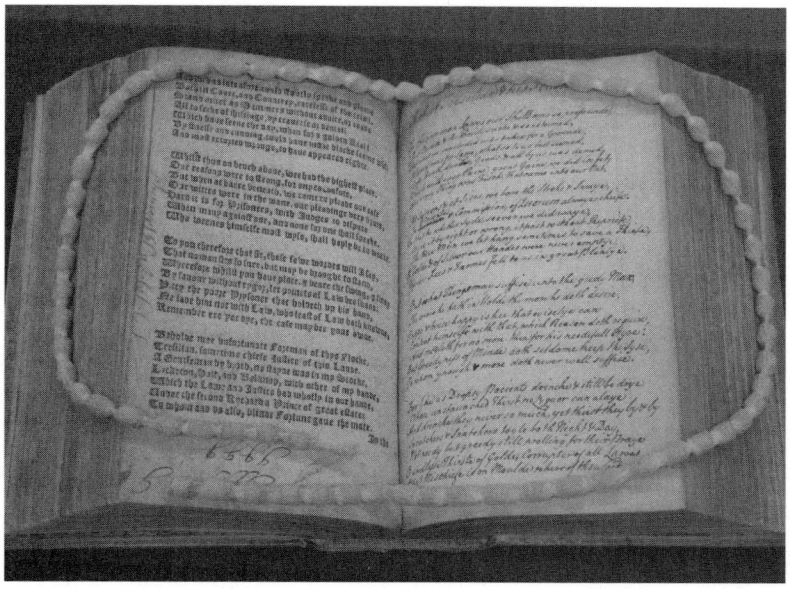

Major portions of this copy of the 1575 edition of John Higgins's *The Mirour for Magistrates* is in manuscript as well as print. Additionally, printed pages are heavily annotated throughout. (Image courtesy of the Rare Books and Manuscripts Library of The Ohio State University Libraries.)

corrected for typographical errors, but that many leaves, for various reasons, were left blank and completed with manuscript insertions. Through extensive examples, McKitterick demonstrates further that printed texts were hardly stable even into the early nineteenth century and makes stronger the assertion that a thorough digital record of primary sources would, ultimately, require the replication of not each individual title of a work but of each individual copy. McKitterick notes that "Hinman's work on the Shakespeare First Folio, and that of R. M. Flores on the earliest editions of *Don Quixote*, taught the world one aspect of what had been known to all printers from the fifteenth to the early nineteenth centuries: that printing-house practice resulted in unpredictable and incalculable variation between copies of books bound up from sheets each of whose differences in themselves could be monitored and demonstrated".[1] McKitterick speaks to important books that, presumably, would have received great scrutiny from the printers and we can only extrapolate on the number of corruptions in less ambitious printing projects.

Beyond the variations that occur due to the printing process, there is also the intervention of the owners and readers of books. In a purely physical fashion, original book sheets were frequently manipulated: "There is ample evidence of the ways in which manuscripts of all kinds were altered or rearranged so as to suit personal taste, later generations, or different circumstances.... Many owners treated printed books in similar manner, reordering them or assembling volumes from different places according to their own needs or interests."[2] Intellectually, readers annotate books and each individual book with reader's comments and thoughts make it a unique document. Comments by renowned individuals are especially important and, with early printed books in particular, the likelihood of the author being some personage of significance increases. If the person is not of political or economic significance, they are very likely part of the religious, scholastic, or artistic social fabric of the era. Still, regardless of social position, any reader response speaks for some audience of a historical time and place.

The literature on the unique qualities of early printed books and marks in books is extensive and I will not extend that literature here. Rather, the focus here is on minimally processed or unprocessed collections. In brief, there are innumerable books, manuscripts and other documents and media throughout tens of thousands of international institutions that remain largely inaccessible, sometimes totally so, because there exists no public catalogue record, or only minimally or partially accessible, because the public catalogue record is too broad (a collection level record that gives little data about individual items in the collection), outdated, or

---

1. David McKitterick, *Print, Manuscript and the Search for Order, 1450-1830* (Cambridge, 2003), 9.

2. Ibid, 66.

even inaccurate. Of course, this condition is not deliberate, but, generally, due to the lack of financial support, a condition common among all too many educational and cultural institutions. There is little doubt that, given the time and resources, the vast majority of institutional libraries, archives, and museums would make their collections known in as much detail as possible. Barring that broad support, however, institutions must designate processing priorities and certain collections are deferred for various reasons.

Research libraries, generally, and university research libraries, in particular, must consider the scholarly value of their collections. If the subject matter of an unprocessed collection is not deemed an area of current or cutting-edge research, especially among local faculty and evidence more broadly by recent scholarly books, articles, and dissertations, then processing will likely be deferred and, once deferred, often forgotten, as new collections of ample extent continue to descend upon the institution. Similarly, previously processed collections, no matter how inadequate they may be for current research access, may continue to languish in this underprocessed condition. For instance, a once prominent collection, minimally processed in the past may no longer have an active clientele—faculty and graduate students have moved on and replacements have other areas of research interest. Work done on the collection in the past seems adequate, why go back? In terms of economic return, there is little apparent research by local faculty and graduate students that might offset the dearth of research in the area on the national level; if the collections is a donation or the acquisition of a previous curator, there may be no living or active donor or administrator to advocate for the processing; and, as always, the deluge of new collections added to the system tend to receive first priority because, unlike the earlier collections, they may have current, vocal advocates.

Regardless of why collections are not processed, the issue remains that innumerable books and documents of inestimable research value remain outside the access network for scholars. These collections may constitute the archives of the less-than-renowned

A typical collection of World War II correspondence common to many libraries throughout the nation. This is one of two boxes of an unrecorded collection of correspondence (720) letters of a World War II soldier from the date of his enlistment through basic training and assignment to the African and European fronts until his separation in 1945. (Image courtesy of the Rare Books and Manuscripts Library of The Ohio State University Libraries.)

individuals, but whose papers and correspondence may be expressive of first-hand experience of significant historical events, relations with important cultural figures, or inadvertent witness to conspiracy. As a particularly apt illustration, I point to World War II collections where the diaries and correspondence of front-line soldiers will be of unique assistance to a close analysis of major battles and telling instances regarding morale and commitment by support troops and those on the home front. Certainly, the New Historicism has established the importance of popular materials for a true understanding of history and these collections of the common man and woman are among those with least access.

There are also those collections developed by individuals with clear focus on unorthodox or typically noncanonical topics that may actually precede scholarly development or, more colloquially, be ahead of the academic curve. Oftentimes, these forward thinking, nonacademic collectors have passed on and deposited their collections before the wave of scholarly interest arrives. But, again, those might well be the collections that have languished or may still languish. Collections focused on local history, commercial topics, or popular culture, for instance, often found their way to institutional collections only to be heralded as world-class research collections when discovered by the scholarly community. Collections that may have been academically déclassé a half century ago are today lauded as invaluable research collections for the study of history and culture and include such areas as jazz, blues, and other popular music, comic books and comic art, children's literature, trade catalogues, cookbooks, local level records of major social movements (civil rights, labor, student activism), and more.

In addition to the importance of the content of these collections is the very logic of their assembly and compilation: an intellectual process that exemplifies the truism that the whole is greater than its parts. An individual has played a part in the selection of each item for the collection, indubitably through recourse to related bibliographies and catalogues in the field and, very likely, in consultation with other agents such as dealers, librarians, scholars, and other collectors. The nuances of such collections can be deeply personal, varied, and diffuse and, hence, difficult to describe adequately. The materials in the collection may include author association copies with annotations; the provenances may derive from professional or familial relations; the imprints may have narrow geographical limits; books may share a common bibliographic attributes such as typography or binding designer; or narrowly dated publication dates circumscribed about some particular historical era. The subtleties can go on and the importance can always be of importance to some scholar's specialist research. In addition, the inherent order of the collection will assert itself, if, by practice, the archivist does not distort the original arrangement in an inordinate fashion or without some reason for doing so. Yet, even by maintaining the essential intellectual order of the collection, the connection of the individual parts may not always be apparent and, by most standards, well beyond the obligation for description, if, as the thesis of this paper portends, such collections receive minimal or any organization at all. Discussion on the cultural and historical insights that may be contained within these under-processed collections must, by necessity, be speculative, but hopefully not inconsequential, for there is always the opportunity of discovering within them rationales or even solutions for long hidden scholarly mysteries.

In summary, the digital age will likely bring both great boon and possible bane. One the one hand, I believe we are on the brink of a glorious and astounding period of scholarship through greater access to knowledge for a wider group of people. On the other hand, the fact that a universe of research materials lies beyond the ken of current scholarship—either because of a lack of organization or, worse yet, lack of identification—is discouraging, to say the least. Scholars can logically anticipate what surprises lie in our abundant repositories, but they cannot ascertain their speculations until they witness those materials for themselves. However, such has always been the story of research and scholarship. Electronic access tools are improving and making research easier in many ways, but myriad unidentified, undocumented, or minimally catalogued collections of books and manuscripts will guarantee, for a long time ahead, the need for old-fashioned, hands-on examination of texts.

Contributors

John C. Carson, MD is Clinical Professor of Medicine at the University of California, San Diego; Chair, The Fellowship of American Bibliophilic Societies; a past president of The American Osler Society, and president of The Zamorano Club of Los Angeles.

Tom Congalton has been secretary, vice president, and president of the Antiquarian Booksellers' Association of America, as well as co-chair, for the past eight years, of the New York Book Fair. He owns Between the Covers Rare Books, Inc., in Merchantville, N.J. His firm specializes in literary first editions, detective fiction, African American literature, and history. He also co-owns Alottabooks.com.

John Crichton is a graduate of the University of Kansas and has been the proprietor of the Brick Row Book Shop for over twenty years. He is past president of The Book Club of California and is the current president of the Antiquarian Booksellers' Association of America (ABAA).

Daniel De Simone is curator of the Lessing J. Rosenwald Collection of the Library of Congress. He has served as an advisor to libraries and private collectors. He received a B.A. from Clark University, Worcester, MA, and an M.A. in history from the University of Dayton in Ohio. He has extensive experience in printing technology, including letterpress printing and typographical design. He spent a quarter century with J. N. Bartfield Fine Books and has developed expertise in the fields of antiquarian bibliography, illustrated books, eighteenth-century French and Italian books, and eighteenth-century Irish books. His charge at the Library of Congress is to make the Rosenwald Collection a more useful and visible part of the rare book world and to help build the programs necessary to insure its future growth and development.

JASON EPSTEIN is the first recipient of the National Book Award Medal for distinguished contributions to American letters. He was first in charge of Anchor Books, established by Doubleday to capitalize on Epstein's idea to market quality paperbacks, a cofounder of the *New York Review of Books*, and editorial director of Random House for over twenty years. Jason Epstein created *The Readers Catalogue*, which revolutionized book purchasing. He currently writes a monthly column for *The New York Times*. W. W. Norton published his *Book Business: Publishing Past, Present, and Future* in 2001.

ANTHONY GARNETT was educated at Ampleforth College and, after military service, at Oxford, taking a degree in Modern Languages. He spent thirteen years working for the Courtauld Group of companies, in England and Canada, before deciding that turning a book-collecting hobby into a book-selling business would be more fun than playing office politics. He has spent almost forty years in St. Louis, dealing primarily with university libraries — specializing in the Humanities and, in particular, Modern Fine Press Printing.

MARTIN L. GREENE, M.D. Since 1991, Dr. Greene has put together a collection of more than two thousand titles on Arctic and Antarctic exploration, Pacific voyages, exploration of Russian-America, and the Northeast and Northwest passages. An enthusiastic climber in the Pacific Northwest for decades, Greene has also climbed in Alaska and Antarctica, and most recently revisited Shackleton's crossing of South Georgia Island. Greene lives in Seattle and continues to enjoy the practice of medicine when he is not reading, searching out rare books, or in the outdoors.

ROBERT H. JACKSON, co-editor and contributor to this volume, is a senior partner with the law firm of Kohrman Jackson & Krantz PLL, in Cleveland, Ohio and is a noted tribal art and rare book collector. He speaks and publishes widely on such diverse subjects as literature, particularly the Victorians and the Beats, and the psychology of collecting. A world traveler, he is a former president of

The Rowfant Club, and is one of the founders of and current vice-chair of the Fellowship of American Bibliophilic Associations (FABS), as well as chair of several arts organizations.

PRISCILLA JUVELIS is a bookseller specializing in twentieth-century book arts and literary first editions, especially women authors. She founded Pricilla Juvelis, Inc., in 1980, after working eleven years with various publishing houses. With the late John F. Fleming, Jr., she has co-authored such works as *The Book Beautiful* and *Binding as Art*. Her firm represents clients in Europe and Asia, as well as in the United States. She is a member of The Grolier Club and Association of International Bibliophiles. She served as president of the Antiquarian Booksellers' Association of America and is a member of the International League of Antiquarian Booksellers.

PETER RUTLEDGE KOCH, an internationally acclaimed Master Printer, founded Black Stone Press in Missoula, Montana, in 1974, and moved the press to San Francisco in 1978. Koch has edited, printed, and published more than thirty books and portfolios, and his masterwork, *The Fragments of Parmenides*, the first of a projected three volumes dedicated to pre-Socratic philosophers appeared under the imprint Editions Koch in early 2004. For the past thirteen years, he has taught "The Hand Printed Book in Its Historical Context" at the University of California, Berkeley's Bancroft Library. In addition to his printing and publishing life, he has a second career as an artist with exhibitions of his prints currently traveling in museums in the American West.

PETER KRAUS was born Surrey, England, and educated at Epsom College, Columbia University, and the London School of Economics. From 1963 to the end of 1971, he worked for bookseller H. P. Kraus, a cousin. In 1972, Kraus established Ursus Books, which sells art books, decorative prints, and rare books in all fields. Kraus resides in New York with his wife Evelyn.

KEN LOPEZ was born in Argentina, grew up in the Bronx, left home at seventeen, and "lived underground" for five years during the Vietnam War. He went "above ground" after the amnesty for draft offenses and attended Goddard College in Vermont, where he first worked in a bookstore. He learned from Raymond Carter and Richard Ford was one of his students. Lopez started collecting first editions by authors who were teaching or visiting Goddard. He worked in retail (i.e., "new books") in Boston for three years and continued to develop his knowledge of contemporary writers and literature. He has also been employed by computer companies and developed an expertise in the e-world early in the rise of the Internet. Lopez has developed a special expertise in Vietnam-era writers and books, as well as Native American books. His firm has issued 150 catalogues in the past twenty years and he attends book fairs around the country.

PAUL T. RUXIN is an attorney with Jones Day in Chicago. Ruxin has an important collection of works by Samuel Johnson and James Boswell, and their circle. He is the author of *Friday Lunch*, a collection of essays on literary and bibliographical topics published by The Rowfant Club, and various other articles issued by The Caxton Club, Yale University, and others. He is a frequent speaker on literary and bibliographical topics in the United States and is a member of the editorial committee of the Yale Editions of the Papers of James Boswell and the Board of Governors of the Folger Shakespeare Library.

CAROL Z. ROTHKOPF, co-editor of this volume, has had a long career as an editor and author. She has been in the book world practically from birth as her aunt and uncle were the proprietors of House of Books, Ltd., in New York, among the earliest dealers in modern firsts. Rothkopf has served on the Board of Friends of the Rare Book and Manuscript Library of Columbia University, and was a member of the Council of The Grolier Club, where she was chair of the Committee on Publications, and long-time editor of

The Grolier Club *Gazette*. Her most recent book is *The Selected Letters of Siegfried Sassoon and Edmund Blunden*.

ARTHUR L. SCHWARZ has been a book collector for over twenty-five years and is a member of the councils of The Grolier Club, where he is chair of the committee on public exhibitions, and the Bibliographical Society of America. Schwarz's article, "Sydney Cockerell, Harold Peirce, and their World of Books," appeared in The Grolier Club *Gazette* in 2002 and his book, *Dear Mr. Cockerell, Dear Mr. Peirce: An Annotated Description of the Correspondence of Sydney C. Cockerell and Harold Peirce in the Grolier Club Archive*, is to be published in 2006. He teaches "Introduction to Rare Books" at New York University.

GARRETT SCOTT has worked as an antiquarian bookseller since 1991. Since 1998, he has been the sole proprietor of Garrett Scott, Bookseller, in Ann Arbor, Michigan.

LAWRENCE N. SIEGLER was a founder of FABS and its first president. He is a former president of The Rowfant Club of Cleveland and a member of The Caxton Club, The Book Club of California, and the Northern Ohio Bibliophilic Society.

GEOFFREY D. SMITH is professor and head of the Rare Books Library at The Ohio State University. His special areas of scholarly interest are American literary culture, bibliography, and textual studies. Cambridge University Press published his *American Fiction, 1901-1925: A Bibliography* in 1997, and Smith is currently working on a successor volume, *American Fiction, 1926-1950*. Smith has published articles on Nathaniel Hawthorne, Henry James, and William Dean Howells, in addition to numerous articles and reviews related to his work in rare books. He is currently general editor for a series of textual editions of William S. Burroughs to be published by The Ohio State University Press and is a regular contributor to the FABS Newsletter.

Book Talk

ROGER E. STODDARD was curator of rare books at the Harvard College Library from 1958 until 2004, except for four years when he worked at the Brown University Library in the Harris Collection of American Poetry and Plays. In December 2004, he retired from Harvard as senior curator in the Houghton Library and senior lecturer of English. He has mounted many exhibitions at Harvard and at The Grolier Club, some of them celebrating Houghton Library and one of them presciently identifying *Marks in Books*. He has published over 125 books and articles. Thornwillow Press published a Festschrift for him in 2000, and, in 2002, a selection of his work, *A Library-Keeper's Business*, was edited by Carol Z. Rothkopf and published by Oak Knoll.

SAMUEL STREIT is associate university librarian for Special Collections at Brown University, where his duties have included renovating the John Hay Library, developing public relations strategies, and undertaking a major expansion of the Friends of the Library.

BRUCE WHITEMAN is head librarian at the William Andrews Clark Memorial Library at the University of California, Los Angeles. He has published articles and poetry in the United States and Canada. He co-edited (with Cynthia Burlingham) the catalogue for a major rare book exhibition held in Los Angeles in 2001-2002,

Index

A

ABAA *See* Antiquarian Booksellers' Association of America
ABAA (online database), 107
AB Bookmans Weekly, 149
ABE (Advanced Book Exchange) (online database), 107, 136, 146
Ackermann, Rudolph. *Cambridge*, 185, 190; *Microcosm of London*, 185; *Oxford*, 185, 190; *Repository of Arts*, 192; *Westminster Abbey*, 185
Addams, Jane, 121
Ahearn, Allen and Pat. *Collected Books: A Guide to Values*, 90
ALIBRIS (online database), 107
Allen, Paul, 87
Alottabooks (bookdealers), 89
Altick, Richard. *Scholar Adventurers* (1951), 236
Amazon.com 4, 136, 173, 195
American Philosophical Society, 42, 51
Antarctic exploration literature, 69, 71, 78
Anthony, Susan B., 119, 120, 121
antiquarian books. *See* rare books
Antiquarian Booksellers' Association of America (ABAA)
    book fairs of, 84, 87, 96–97
    copyright issues, involvement in, 147
    fraud, monitoring by, 104
    history of, 108
    Internet discussion group, 88, 91
    leadership of, 95, 105, 183
    membership of, 85, 97, 100
    online bookselling by, 107

Antiquarian Booksellers' Association of Japan, 95
Antiques Road Show, 196
Annunciation (painting), 62
Aphthonius. *Progymnasmata* (1572), 25
archives. *See* manuscripts and archives
Armstrong, Lilian, 63, 64, 68
art
    biographies, 111–13, 122, 218, 220
    book as, 39, 43, 115, 165
    books, 164
    livres d'artistes, 111–13, 122, 218, 220
    nature of, 48
    philosophy on, 195
    See also woodcuts
Association Typographique Internationale. *Language Culture Type*, 49
auction houses, 15, 93, 97, 99–100, 101, 158, 185, 186–87, 188
auctions
    benefits of, 179
    bidding at, 128–130
    booksellers at, 94
    collectors at, 132–33, 136, 199, 223
    "country," 128
    heyday of, 128–30
    online, 92, 104
    popularity of, 170–71
    prices at, 93
    "rings" at, 128
    Rosenbach, 114–115
    sale catalogues, 19
    university participation in, 181
    See also Christie's, Sotheby's
Audubon *Birds of America*, 124, 131; folios and quartos, 152

Augustine, St., *City of God*, 57
Austen, Jane, 159

B

Baker, Nicholson, 12
Bartolozzi, Francesco, 185, 190
Beard, Mark, 112
Beckett, Gilbert Abbott À. *Comic History of England*, 190
Belanger, Terry, 191
Belfortis, Andreas, 58
Bellini, Gentile, 62
Benjamin, Walter, 170
Bentivoglio, Ginevra, 65–66, 66
Bergomensis, J. P. di, *De claris mulieribus*, 59, 62–63, 64–65, 66, 66, 67
Berland, Abel, 197, 199, 200
Bertram, Ernst, 206
Between the Covers (bookstore), 86, 89
Bianchi, Martha Dickinson, 227
Bibles, Gutenberg, 124; Malermi, 63, 64
Bibliofind (Internet service), 223
bibliographies, 90–91, 199, 220, 236, 243; bibliographical research, 101–2
bibliophiles, characteristics of, 11–12
bibliophily, 123–24, 135, 137
BIBLIOPOLY (online database), 107
Biblioteca Communale Ariostae, 61, 62
Biblioteca Nazionale (Italy), 27
Bibliotheca Anglo-Poetica, 19
Bidwell, John, 193
bindings
    Bonet, 113
    commissioning of, 131
    Glaister, 112
    by hand, 53, 71
    Herakleitos, 38
    innovative, 49
    Parmenides, 46
    Semet and Plumelle, 46

Birrell, Augustine, 26
Bixby, William, 157
Blackwell, Alice Stone, 121
Blake, William, *Songs of Innocence* (1789), 21, 23
Bonet, Paul, 111, 113
Bonnard, Pierre, *Parallèlement*, 112–13
book arts
    leaves and plates, 72-73, 76-74, 78, 79
    lettering, 50
    See also binding, book printing, individual artists and titles, livres d'artistes
book collecting and collectors
    amateur, 195
    Arabs and, 83
    celebrities and, 85–86, 87, 198
    clubs, 123, 125
    continuation of, 223
    cookbooks, 243
    detective fiction, 3in5, 198–99
    as donors, 161–63, 178–79
    dust jackets, 91, 92, 104
    exhibits and displays, 165–66, 188, 193, 194
    "forgotten" books, 29–37
    future of, 175, 196, 198, 199, 201
    "high spots," 30, 107, 236, 237
    increase in, 140, 170, 171, 172, 175, 178
    and Internet, 37, 86, 223
    Japanese and, 84
    knowledge and qualifications of, 170, 172, 175, 178
    on magic, 198
    nature of, 169–170, 195, 196, 201
    networking of, 130, 170, 171–72, 187, 191, 192
    private, 127, 155–56, 170, 171, 175, 178, 183–94, 195, 196–97

Index

private press books, 163
and scarcity, 199
versus selling, 158, 166
specialized, 5–6, 131, 132, 135, 171
tips, 35–36, 37
title selection criteria, 198–99
trend setters, 94
"trophy" books, 170–71
book design, 39, 43, 44, 46, 48–49, 50, 51, 53, 54, 71, 220
book distribution, 4, 9, 97, 100
book fairs
bookseller participation in, 84–85, 87, 90, 91, 93, 94, 96–97, 99, 101, 152, 199
collector participation in, 174, 223
first editions at, 131
Florida, 90
Long Island, 90
networking opportunities at, 134, 135, 172
New York, 92, 93, 152
proliferation of, 133–35
in Russia, 213
book market
best-sellers, 6–7
future of, 172–75, 201
localized, 13
in Middle East, 83
sellers', 97
specialized, 144, 145, 146
splits in, 106
widening of, 13, 93, 102
book prices and pricing
adaptable, 86–87
appraisals, 161
at auctions, 133, 136
competitive, 143, 148–49, 153
disparities in, 132
increasing for rare books, 93, 140–42, 149–50, 151–52, 153

information and guides, 90, 143, 164
book printing
in Antarctica, 69–79
digital, 53
"fine" printing, 39–55, 109–117
in Greece, 40
in Italy, 57–59, 64
book production, 4, 50, 53–55, 54, 220
book publishing, 5, 7, 8
history of, 225, 226, 233
book purchasing, 100–101, 102–3
booksellers and bookselling
avenues of, 96–97, 99–101, 103, 132–36
book supplying, role in, 200–201
chain stores, 5, 6, 7
versus collecting, 158, 166
duplicate materials, 162, 163
business, establishing, 111–13, 156–60
English, 100–101
income, distribution of, 105–6
increasing, 223
independent, 5–6
inventories, 5–6
loans to, 158–59
merger and acquisition of, 6–7
"messiah factor" in, 83–85, 86, 87, 88, 89, 94
online, 87–88, 89–90, 92–93, 103, 107, 135, 136, 145–47, 164, 238
personalities, 109–11
within profession, 97, 101, 103, 105
qualifications of, 135 (*see also* rarity: false claims of)
role of, 136–37
successful, qualities of, 108
wholesale distribution, 97, 100
bookshops
alternatives to, 132

253

bookshops *continued*
   in Austria, 206, 209–10
   networking opportunities at, 172
   physical *versus* online, 135, 146
   post-Internet decline in, 99, 100, 103, 125–26, 127, 137, 171, 172
   pre-Internet, 96, 125, 126, 157
   private *versus* open, 127, 163
   used, 107, 173
book trade
   chain stores, 5, 6, 7
   changes in, 125
   conglomerates, 6–7
   frauds in, 103–4
   future of, 172–75, 201
   Golden Age, 21st-century, 148, 150, 153
   hierarchy, 142–43, 146
   in 1990s, 140–42
   international, 83–84, 96, 99, 100–101, 103
   Internet impact on, 7–8, 86–87, 99, 101–8, 135–36, 142, 143–44, 145–50, 153, 160–61, 164, 165, 170, 172, 197–98
Bordon, Benedetto, 63
Boswell-Johnson collections, 197, 198, 199, 200
Brahms, Johannes, 208
Braithwayte, Richard. *Times Curtaine Drawne* (1621), 20
Braun, Stephen, 43
Breckenridge, Myra, 121
Breckinridge, Sophonisba, 121
Brennan, Joseph Payne, 229
Breslauer, Bernard, 126
Brick Row Book Shop, 29, 95–96, 97, 98, 101, 102, 105, 106
Bringhurst, Robert, 44, 46
British Library, 14
British Museum, 20, 25, 26

Britten, Benjamin, 208
Browning, Robert. *Pauline*, 14–16, 23
Brown University, 224–26, 228, 229, 233, 234
Bruckner, Anton, 205
Brunet, Jacques-Charles, *Manuel du Libraire et de l'Amateur de Livres*, 220
Bryant, William Cullen, 226
Burney, Fanny, 159
Burning Deck Press, 233

C

Canerio, Augustino, 58; *Constitutiones* (1479), 59
Carr, Dan, 41, 44, 49
Carroll, Lewis, 198; *Alice in Wonderland*, 158
Carson, Rachel, 121
Carter, John, 16; *New Paths in Book Collecting* (1934), 31n5
cartoon books. *See* comic books
catalogues, library, 238, 240–41
catalogues, online, 238
catalogues, printed
   Americana literature, 150–51
   Bibliotheca Anglo-Poetica, 19
   for collectors, 199
   copyright (*versus* online information), 147
   early days of, 236
   English Short Title Catalogue (ESTC) 13
   exhibition, 193
   Fortas sale, 22
   versus Internet, 107, 135
   for libraries, 105, 160
   Native American literature, 143–45
   as outreach/marketing tool, 125
   saving books for, 134
   as selling tool, 96, 97
   Sotheby's, 188

Index

specialized, 136–37, 235, 236, 243
trade, 243
See Auctions, sale catalogues
Catt, Carrie Chapman, 121
Caxton books, 115
Caxton Club, 53
Celan, Paul, 209; *Der Sand aus den Urnen* (1948), 210; *Gedichte* (1966), 210; *Fadensonnen / Schlafbroken* (1967), 210
Celan-Lestrange, Cècile, 210
Cervantes, Miguel de, 236; *Don Quixote*, 239
Chagall, Marc, *Jerusalem Windows*, 84
Chaloner, John Armstrong, 36n10
Chalons, René, 23
Chapin Library, 162
Chaucer, Geoffrey, *Parliament of Foules*, 21
Chen, Julie. *World Without End*, 115
Chertkov, V.G., 210
Child, Lydia Maria, 121
children's books, 93, 152, 174–75, 206, 243
Chopin, Kate. *The Awakening*, 121
Christie, Agatha, 198
Christie's (auction house), 93, 97, 99, 100, 185, 186–87
Christopher, St., 67
Churchill, Winston, 186
Cicero. *De oratore*, 57; *Epistolae*, 57
Ciraldi Collection, 231, 232–33
Clark Library, 13, 27
Clement V. (pope), *Constitutiones* (1479), 58, 58–59
Cockerell, Sydney, correspondence with H. Peirce, 188–89
Cocteau, Jean, 229
Cohn, Margie, (bookdealer) 126
Collins, An. *Divine Songs and Meditacions* (1653), 20

comic books, 229–31, 232, 243
Conrad, Joseph, 26
cookbooks, 243
Coover, Chris, 187
Cornell University, 198
Cossa, Francesco del, 62
Cowley, Charlotte. *Ladies History of England* (1780), 13
Crane, Stephen, *The Red Badge of Courage*, 31
Crasson, Viviane, 216
Crichton, John, 29
Crivelli, Taddeo, 62
Cronkite, Walter, 205
Crowe, Stanley, 185
Cruise, Wendy Delamore, 215
Curle, Richard, 26

D

Dahlberg, Edward, 229
d'Alemagna, Giorgio, 62
Daniel, Samuel. *Delia* (1592), 21
Dante. *Divine Comedy*, 63
Dati, Augustino. *Elegantiae minores* (1471), 58
Davenport, Guy, 40
Davies, John. *Microcosmos* (1603), 21
Davis, Paulina Wright, 118–19
Dawson, Michael, 96
Dawson (bookdealer), 96, 125
De Chirico, Giorgio. *Calligrammes*, 113
Defoe, Daniel, 159
Demus, Klaus, 210
Depp, Johnny, 85
De Ricci, Seymour, 15
Derleth, August, 229
De Simone, Daniel, 173
Dibdin, Thomas Frognall, 17, 19, 27, 196
Dickens, Charles, 155, 156; *The Pickwick Papers*, 174, 176

Dickinson, Emily, 227; Bianchi Collection of, 227
digital revolution
    and future of book, 172–75
    versus Gutenberg revolution, 5, 9, 10
    hand-printed books and, 55
    and special collections, 244
digital technology and digitization
    benefits of, 4
    and book production, 54
    Google book project, 104
    impact of, 7–8, 104–5
    information storage and transmission, 4
    printing, 53
    and special collections access, 238
Diogenes, 42, 43; *Diogenes Defictions*, 47
Dixon, Franklin W., 184
Dodd, Mead (bookdealer), 21
Doheny, Estelle, 197
Doyle, Arthur Conan, 91, 198
Drenttel, William, 191
Drinkwater, John, 26
Dufy, Raoul. *Tartarin De Tarascon*, 113
Dugdale, William. *History of St. Paul's Cathedral* (1558), 185–86
Dumond, Annie Nelles, 29,
Dunaway, Pat (bookdealer), 157

E

eBay, 92, 104, 135, 136
e-books, 8, 174
Eccles, Lord, 30
Eccles, Viscountess (Mary Hyde), 197
Edward Curtis, North American Indian portfolios, 152
Edwards, Christopher, 200
Edwards, Francis (bookdealer), 128
Edward VIII (King), 192

electronic age. *See* digital revolution
electronic information. *See* digital technology and digitization
Eli Lilly collection, 162
Elizabeth I (Queen), 192
Elizabeth II (Queen), 192
Eluard, Paul, 229
Emericus, Johannes, 67
Emerson, Ralph Waldo, 118; *Essays*, 119
English books
    20th century literature, 226
    biographies and histories, 186, 190
    foreign-language translations of, 27
    illustrated, 115
    London titles, 185–86
    prices on, 165
    purchasing, 100–101, 158
    specializing in, 113
    Victorian, 30–31
English history, 183, 184, 186, 187, 189–90
Epstein, Jason, 173–74
Erasmus, Desiderius, 217, 218

F

Falktoft, Henrik, collection of, 93
Faulkner, William, 31; *The Sound and the Fury*, 90, 93
Fellowship of American Bibliophilic Societies (FABS), 125, 189, 192, 201
feminist literature, 117–21
Ferrara, Matteo de, 63
Ferrara (Italy)
    art in, 68
    book printing in, 58–59
    woodcuts in, 57, 58, 58, 59–62, 60, 63–65, 66–68
Ferrari, Julia, 41, 44

Index

Fielding, Henry, 13, 212, 213; *Tom Jones*, 212; *Tom Thumb*, 212
film, animated, 232; popular, 231
Finch, Simon (bookdealer), 200
Findling, P. Johannes. *Lutheri antilutherana* (1528), 207, 207
fine books, 48, 49, 51, 53, 54, 163, 175, 233
Firbank, Ronald, 229
first editions
    children's, 132
    fine, 140
    literary, 92, 93, 102, 131, 142, 159
    modern, 93, 111, 139–40, 150, 151, 152, 156
    rare, 107
FitzGerald, Edward. *Euphranor* (1851), 14
Fitzgerald, F. Scott, 31, 92
Flegon, Alec, 213, 214, 215
Fleming, John F. (bookdealer), 109–11, 112–14, 116–17, 121–22, 200
Flores, R.M., 239
Fogg Art Museum, 210
Folger Shakespeare Library, 163, 189, 196
Folio Society, 156
Fontane, Theodor, 206
Forster, E.M., 229
Forster, Georg, 206
Foxe, John. *Book of Martyrs*, 190
Fragonard, Jean-Honoré, 114
Francis, Dick, 198, 199
Francis, St., 62
frauds in book trade, 22, 23, 103–4
French books, 113, 114
Fritsch, Georg, 209
Fuller, Henry Blake. *The Cliff Dwellers: A Novel* (1893), 32n
Fuller, Margaret, 117–20, *Women in the Nineteenth Century*, 117, 118, 119–20
Furnivall, F.J., 15

G

Gable, Nelly, 44
Gage, Mathilda Joslyn, 119
Galilei, Galileo, 236
Gates, Bill, 87; Da Vinci notebooks, 198
Gay, John, *To a Lady on Her Passion for Old China* (1725), 26
George, St., 59
George VI (King), 192
German-language books, 206, 209–10; Romanticism, 118
Getty Museum, 180
Ghirlandaio, Domenico, 67
Gibbings, Robert, 155
Gill, Eric, 155; Gill Sans Greek Light capitals, 41
Gilman, Charlotte Perkins, 121; *The Yellow Wallpaper* (1892), 121; *Women and Economics* (1898), 120
Ginistera, Alberto, 208
Ginsberg, Allen, 151
Giunta, LucAntonio, 63
Glaister, Donald, 112
Goethe, Johann Wolfgang von. *Faust*, 118
Goldberg, Gerry, 200
Goldberg, Whoopi, 85
Goldschmidt, E.P. (bookdealer), 126
Goodspeed (bookdealer), 96, 125
Goodwin, Mary, 77–78
Google, 104, 107, 238
Gordimer, Nadine, 151
Gosse, Edmund, 26
Gotthold, Peggy, 46
Graeve, Oscar. *The Keys of the City* (1916), 32n
Graff, Robert, 216
Graham, Tom (S. Lewis pseudonym), *Hike and the Aeroplane*, 86
Greek poetry, 40, 43, 44

Greek philosophy, 40
Greek printing, history of, 40
Greek texts, 42–43
Greek typeface, 44, 49
Greeley, Horace, 118
Greene, Belle da Costa, 197
Grenville, Thomas, 20
Griffin, Richard. *Bug House Poetry* (1917), 33, 36n10
Grimke, Sarah and Angelina, 120, 121
Grisham, John. *A Time to Kill*, 88–89
Grolier, Jean, 131, 196
Grolier bibliographies, 236
Grolier bindings, 131
Grolier Club, 46, 53, 121, 170, 185, 186, 187–89, 191, 193; Library, 188–89, 194
Gruyer, Gustave, 59, 64, 68
Gundersheimer, Werner, 193
Gutenberg Bible, 124; Gutenberg revolution, 3, 5, 9, 10
Guthrie, W.K.C. *The Greek Philosophers from Thales to Aristotle*, 40
Guy, John. *Tudor England*, 186

H

Hagy, Jim, 198
Hamill and Barker (bookdealers), 96
Hamilton, Alice, 121
Hammett, Dashiell, 198
Hampton, Mary Landis, 227
Han, Ulrich, 57
Hansen, Leonard, 185
Harcourt Brace Jovanovich, 109
Hardy, Peter, 207–8
Harkness, Rebecca, 110–11
Harvard College Library, 207
Harvard University, 21, 27, 104, 197, 198, 212, 213, 227, 228, 236
Hegel, Georg Friedrich, 207
Heine, Heinrich, 206

Helfand, Jessica, 191
Hemingway, Ernest, 31
Henry VIII, 183, 185, 186; *Assertion of the Seven Sacraments against Martin Luther*, 190, 193
Herakleitos, 40, 48
Herakleitos, 38, 42
Heraklitean codex, 41
Heritaage Book Shop, 85
Herman, Garrett, 191
Higgins, John. *The Mirour for Magistrates* (1558), 239
Hime, Mark (bookdealer), 91
Hind, Arthur, 64
Ho, Gaylord, 195
Hocquard, Emmanuel. *Le Seuil Le Sable* (1990), 220
Hofer, Philip, 129, 131
Hoffman, Heinrich. *Der Struwwelpeter*, 184
Holbein, Hans, 185, 190
Holland, Robert. *Historie of Our Lord and Saviour Jesus Christ* (1594), 20
Holzenberg, Eric, 188
Horne, T. H. *An Introduction to the Study of Bibliography* (1814), 20n1
Houghton, Arthur, 109
Houghton Library, 205, 207
House of Books (bookdealer), 126
Howe, Julia Ward, 121
Howell (bookdealer), 125
Hoyt, Shelley, 41
Hume, David, 27
Huntington, Henry, 196
Huntington Library, 58
Hyde, Donald, 197, 212
Hyde, Mary (Viscountess Eccles), 197
Hynes, Gladys, 228

I

Igelhart, Ruth (bookdealer), 200

Index

illustrations, 44, 46, 49
   See also woodcuts
Index of Prohibited Books, 28
Indiana University, 162
institutional book market, 97, 100, 101, 105, 106, 130, 131, 133, 181
   See also libraries: as book customers; libraries: university
International Bibliophiles (organization), 213
International League of Antiquarian Booksellers (ILAB), 104, 107, 108
Internet
   authors' websites, 8
   and book collecting, 37, 86, 223
   book trade, impact on (*see under* book trade)
   and copyright, 147
   discussion groups, 88, 91
   and libraries, 160–61, 164–65, 180
   and rare books, 12, 89–90, 93, 94, 135, 142, 149–50, 153, 170
   and technology revolution, 4

J

Jabès, Edmond, 216, 217, 218, 219, 220, 221
Jackson, Holbrook, 170
Jaron, Steven. *Edmond Jabès: The Hazard of Exile* (2003), 216
Jeffers, Robinson, 39–40
Jerome, St., *Epistolae (Epistles)*, 59, 63, 64
Jewett, Sarah Orne, 120
Johns, Jasper. *Fizzles*, 117
Johnson, Henry. *Ballads of the Farm and Home* (1902), 34, 36–37n11
Johnson, Samuel, 196
Johnson-Boswell collections, 197, 198, 199, 200
Johnston, Alastair, 29–30

Jonson, Ben, 174
Joyce, Ernest, 71, 76
Joyce, James, 236; *Epiphanies*, 110; *Ulysses*, 132, 174, 176
Judaeus, Thimon, on Meteors, 25–26

K

Kabbala, 217, 221
Kahnweiler, Henry, 113
Kaplan, E.K., 217
Keller, Michael, 104
Kelm, Daniel, 46
Kenny, Maurice, 146
Ker, John, duke of Roxburghe, 125
Kerouac, Jack. *On the Road*, 151–52
Kilgour, Bayard, 212
Kilgour, Kate Gray, 213
King, Stephen, 229
Kinnear, David Mitchell. *Every Day Verses*, 33
Kirshbaum, Larry, 174
Kirshenbaum, Sandra, 50
Kittle, Fred, 197, 198
Koch, Peter, studio, 52
Kokoschka, Oskar, 206, 209
Kolb, Gwin J., 197, 198
Kondoleon, Harry. *The Côte D'Azur Triangle*, 112
Kraus, Hans P., 124, 128–130
Kraus, Karl. *Die Chinesische Mauer* (1914), 209
Kuhta, Richard, 193

L

La Fontaine, *Fables*, 114
La Mettrie, Julien Offray de. *L'Homme machine*, 220
Lançon, Daniel. *Jabès l'Egyptien* (1998), 216
Lasner, Mark Samuels, 130, 189

Lathrop, Julie, 121
Laughlin, James, 227; Laughlin Collection, 227–29
Lawrence, D.H., 229
Layton, Irving. *Here and Now* (1945), 13
Lee, Harper, *To Kill a Mockingbird* (1960), 93, 94
Leno, Jay, 85
Levy, Raquel, 220
Lewis, Sinclair, 87
Lewis, Wyndham, 229
librarians, 94, 130–31, 136, 181–82, 217, 221, 236
libraries
    accession reccords, 237
    as book customers, 96, 97, 106, 159–60
    as book sources, 105
    at Brown University: John Carter Brown Library, 224; John Hay Library, 224–226
    catalogues, 19, 238, 240–41
    donations to, 161–63, 175, 178, 179, 181–82 (*see also* special collections: donations to)
    institutional, 127, 223, 224–226
    at Harvard, *see* Houghton Library
    at Indiana, *see* Lilly Library
    and international book trade, 96
    and Internet, 160–61, 164–65, 180, 238
    leadership of, 130
    patrons and titles at, 173
    research, 241
    special collections in (*see* special collections)
    university, 101, 116, 127, 157–58, 159–61, 164–65, 181, 205–207, 224–226, 233, 241
    virtual, 9
Library of Congress, 158

Lichtenberg, Georg Christoph, 206
Lilly Library, 162, 233
Lincoln, Abraham, 236
Lindseth, Jon, 197, 198
Lippmann, Friederich, 64, 68
Lister, R.H., 21
literacy, 4, 9, 10
literary journals, 233
literature (American), 31–32, 117–21, 150–51, 225, 226, 233, 277, 259; (native American) 143–145
Livermore, Mary, 121
livres d'artistes, 111–13, 122, 218, 220
local history, 243
Locke, John, 27
Locker-Lampson, Frederick, 21
Lorimer, George Horace. *The False Gods* (1906), 31–32
Louis, St., 62
Louis XIV (King), 23
Lovecraft, H.P., 229
Lowell, Amy, 21
Lucas, E.V., 26
Lully, Jean-Baptiste, 159
Luther, Martin, 161, 236; *Lutheri antilutherana* (Findling) (1528), 207, 207
Lyly's *Woman in the Moone* (1597), 26

M

Macclesfield Psalter, 237
Machiavelli, Niccolò, 236
Madden, Samuel. *Memoirs of the Twentieth Century* (1733), 20
Maggs (bookdealers), 96, 125, 128
Mailer, Norman, 152
Malermi Bible, 63, 64
Man, John. *The Gutenberg Revolution*, 3
Manchester, William, 186
Mann, Thomas, *Herr und Hund* (1918), 206
Mantler, Wolfgang, 208

manuscripts and archives
   accessing, 178, 235, 238
   age and rarity of, 236
   Americana, 150
   of authors, 233–34
   at Brown University, 225
   collecting, 123
   content of, 241–42
   Dickens, 174, *176*
   Joyce, 177
   Lovecraft, 229
   market for, 97
   medieval, 237
   prices for, 151–52
   and print format combined, 238–39, *239*
   Trotsky, 213
   Watergate papers, 161
Marcella (St.), 65
Mardersteig, Giovanni, 44
Marks, Jeffrey, 90
Marston, George, 71, 76
Martin, H. Bradley, 16, 130, 197
Mary (Queen), 192
Massey, Stephen, 197
Matheson, William, 158
Matisse, Henri. *Jazz*, 115, 131
Maurellio, St., 59, 61
McEvilley, Thomas, 42, 43
McKitterick, David. *Print, Manuscript and the Search for Order, 1450-1830*, 238–40
McLuhan, Marshall, 53
McMurtry, Larry. *Cadillac Jack*, 111
Mell, Max. *Weinachtspiel* (1924), 209
Mellon, Paul, 130
Merton, Thomas, 228
Midgley, James, Jr., 19, 19n15
Millard, John, 77
Miller, Henry, 32n, 229
Miller Collection, 229–30, 232

Milton, John, 159
Missale secundum (1503), 63, 66, 67
Mitford, T.B. *The Inscriptions of Kourion*, 42
Moby Dick, 142, 152
Molteni, Monica. *Comsé Tura* (1999), 62
Monahan, William, 51
Morgan, J.P., 196–97
Morgan Library, 193
Morley, Christopher. *The Haunted Bookshop* (1919), 171
Morris, William, 53
Morrison, Lois. *Ostrich & St. Valentine* (2002), 117
Mott, Lucretia, 118, 121
Munby, A.N.L., 16
Murray, James, 71

N

National Library (Bogotá, Colombia), 161
National Union Catalog (NUC), 13
Needham, James, 205n
Newberry Library, 198
New Directions press, 227–28
Newman, Arthur. *Pleasure's Vision* (1619), 20
Newton, A. Edward, 170
New York Public Library, 104, 162, 233, 236
New York University, 190, 191
Nobel Prize for Literature, 151
Norman, Haskell, 197
Norris, Frank. *McTeague, a Story of San Francisco* (1899), 31n6
North, Michael, 188

O

Olson, Michael, 210
Oudry, Jean-Baptiste, 114

Oxford English Dictionary, 8, 12
Oxford University, 104, 236

P

Paep, Johannes, 67
Palaemon Press, 233
Paput, Christian, 44
Paretsky, Sara, 198
Pargellis, Stanley, 30, 36
Parmenides, 44, 49; *Parmenides*, 51
Peirce, Harold, 188–89
Penn State University, 163
Pepys, Samuel, 184
Pestalozzi, Johann Heinrich, 206
Peters, Jean, ed. *Collectible Books, Some New Paths* (1979), 31n5
Picasso, Pablo. *Le Siege De Jerusalem*, 113
Piranesi, Giambattista. *Vedute di Roma*, 159
Pitt, Brad, 85
Plato, 42
Plymell, George, 146
Poe, Edgar Allen, 118, 198, 229; *Tamerlane*, 116
poetry
    American, 226–27, 229, 233
    and art, 220
    collections, 39–40, 227–28
    little known, 32, 34
Pollard, A. W., 21
Poole-Wilson, Nicholas (bookdealer), 187
Pope, Alexander. *God's Revenge against Punning* (1716), 26
Postl, Karl (a.k.a. Charles Sealsfield), 206
Pound, Ezra, 227; *Cavalcanti Poems*, 228; *Draft of the Cantos 17-27*, 228
Previn, André, 206, 208
printed books
    copyright, 147
    on demand, 174
    history of, 238–40
    proliferation of, 173
Printing and the Mind of Man, 236
publishing, *see* book publishing

Q

Quaritch (bookdealer), 14, 125, 128, 187, 215

R

Rachmaninov, Sergei, 208
Randall, David, 131
Ransom, Harry, 131
rare books
    collecting (*see* book collecting)
    defined, 11–12
    guides to, 31n5, 90, 170
    market and trade (*see* book trade)
    prices for, 93, 140–42, 149–50, 151–52, 153
    recycling of, 141–42
    shifting status of, 12–14, 25–27, 102, 224
    teaching, 191–92
    trade, history of, 95–97, 99–101
    See also under Internet, libraries
rarity
    determining, 12–14, 14n, 15–17, 19, 30, 36, 37
    false claims of, 14, 14n, 20–21, 23, 103–4
    importance and, 30, 36
    localized, 13
    and neglected fields, 29–37
    versus scarcity, 30, 35, 102, 144
    and uniqueness (*see under* uniqueness)
Ratchford, Fannie, 15
Ray, Gordon, 133, 134
Reese, William S. (bookdealer), 175

Index

Regenstein, Mrs. Joseph, 116
Research Libraries Information Network (RLIN), 188
Reynolds, David. *Beneath the American Renaissance* (1988), 35n
Rice, Ann. *The Vampire Lestat*, 232
Richardson, Samuel. *Pamela*, 27–28, 28n31
Ricketson, Daniel, 29
Ridley, Jasper, 186
Ringelnatz, Joachim, 206
Roberti, Ercole de, 65, 66
Roederer Library, 114
Rose, Stuart, 197
Rosenbach, A.S.W. (bookdealer), 109, 110, 111, 113–14, 116, 117
Rosenbach, Philip, 115, 116
Rosenthal, Robert, 116
Rosenwald, Lessing, 114, 115; collection, 116
Rossi, Lorenzo di, 59, 62–63, 66
Rothkopf, Carol, 188
Rothschild, Loren, 200
Rowfant Club, 201
Rowland Library, 21
Roxburghe Club, 53, 123, 125
Roxburghe sale, 125
Royal Geographic Society, 73
Royal Library (Windsor), 192
Rubeis, Antonio de, 59
Ruskin, John, 53
Russian literature, 210–15

S

Sadleir, Michael, 30, 31n5
Santayana, George, 196
Scarisbrick, J.J., 186
Schelhorn, Johann Georg. *Amoenitates literariae* (1725, new ed. 1730), 17, 18
Schlosser, Mary, 188
Schumann Library, 114
Schwarz, Alan, 189
Schwarz, Susie, 186, 187, 191–92
Sebald, W.G., 217, 218
Sénancour, Étienne Pivert, *Obermann*, 220
Servius. *Commentaries*, 57
Sessler (firm), 125
Shackleton, Ernest H., 69, 71, 72, 73, 76, *Aurora Australis* (1908), 69, 70, 71–79
Shade, William Henry Taylor. *Buckeyeland and Bohemia* (1895), 36–37n11
Shakespeare, William
    folios, 20, 84, 163, 184, 239
    manuscripts, 174
    plays, early editions of, 132
    titles, 236
Shapero, Margo, 121
Shaw, Alice Howard, 121
Shelley, Mary. *Frankenstein*, 159
Shoemaker, Jack, 40
Siebert, Frank T. (collection), 151
Silver, Louis, 116
Silver, Rollo, 233
Sinclair, Isaac. *Gedichte*, 206, 210
Slater, J.H., 15
Small, Elden. *Songs at Twilight* (1919), 36–37n11
Smith, Clark Ashton, 229
Solzhenitsyn, Aleksandr, 212–15
Sontag, Susan, 152
Sotheby's (auction house), 15, 97, 99, 100, 158, 188
Sowerby, Millicent. *Rare People and Rare Books*, 23, 24, 25
special collections
    accessing, 235–36, 237–38, 240–41, 244
    acquiring, 205–210, 236
    contents of, 225–226, 232, 241–43

special collections *continued*
  development of, 169, 224–26, 228–29, 232–34
  donations to, 175, 178–79, 180, 181–82, 226, 227, 228
  Harris Collection of American Poetry and Plays, 226
  housing and organization of, 162, 224, 232, 243–44
  processing, 240, 241, 244
  trends in, 180, 234
  value of, 236, 237, 242–43, 244
Spiegelman, Art. *Maus*, 232
Spillane, Mickey, 198
Spira, Johannes de, 57
Spoor, John A., 15
St. Louis University, 158
St. Martin's Press, 233
Stanford University, 104, 236; University Library, 51
Stanley, Colonel, 20
Stanton, Elizabeth Cady, 118, 119, 120, 121
Starkey, George, 208
Stein, Gertrude, 228
Stern, Peter, 91
Stewart, Alan, 189
Stinehour, Christopher, 43, 44
Stoddard, Helen, 215
Stone, Herbert S., 121
Stone, Lucy, 121
Stoneman, William, 193
Stoppard, Tom, 132
Stow, John. *Survey of London* (1754), 185
Stratemeyer, Edward, 184
Strauss, Richard, 159
Streeter, Thomas, 130
Sweynheim and Pannartz, 57
Swift, Jonathan, 159
Swinburne, Algernon Charles, 21

T

Tanazaki, Junichiro, 84
Tàpies, Antoni, 218
Taylor, Robert, 130
Third and Elm Press, 233
Thoreau, Henry David, 29n; *Walden*, 120
Tolkien, J.R.R. *The Hobbit* (1937), 152
Tolstoy, Leo, works, 210–11
Toniolo, Federica, 64
Torquemada, *Meditationes*, 57
Transcendentalists, 118
Trillin, Calvin, 7
Trotsky archive, 213
Tura, Cosimo, 59, 61–62, 65
Turnbull Library, 77
Turner, Lana, 85

U

UNICEF, 9
Unicorn Press, 233
University of Chicago, 197, 198
University of Illinois, 158
University of Michigan, 104
University of North Carolina, 160
University of Texas, 158, 165
used book trade
  bookstores, 173
  future of, 106–7
  and Internet, 104, 105, 135, 145–56
  U.S. *versus* English, 165

V

Van Dyke, Marjorie, 110n
Veblen, Thorstein, 185
Venice
  book printing in, 57, 64
  woodcuts in, 63–64
Victorian English fiction, 30–31
Vienna, book collections in, 205–7, 209–10

Index

Virgil, 57
Vollard, Ambroise, 113
Von Zelowitz, John, 43
Voynich, Wilfrid Michael, 23, 24, 25

W

Wagener, Richard, 46
Walden, 119, 120
Wallin, Andreas. *Dissertatio academica de bibliomania* (An Academic Thesis on Bibliomania), 27
Wal-Mart, 7; effect on book market, 102, 103
Wandrei, Donald, 229
Warnock, John, 198
Washington University, 157
Watergate papers, 161
Weil, Susan, 110n
Weissman, Stephen, 200, 212
Wellman, Manley Wade, 229
Wetscherek, Hugo, 210
Wharton, Edith, 120; *Ethan Frome*, 120–121
Whitman, Walt, 34, 226

Wild, Frank, 71; "An Ancient Manuscript" (book chapter), 73, 76
Williams, William Carlos, 227–28
Williams College, 162
Wise, Thomas James, 15; *The Ashley Library Catalogue*, 26
Wolfe, Heather, 189
Wolff, Robert, 30, 31n5
woodcuts
  English, 155
  Italian, 57, 58, 58, 59–62, 60, 63–65, 66, 66–68
  modern, 165
Wren, Christopher, 185
Wrenn, John Henry, 15
Wyeth, N.C., 184

X

Ximenes Rare Books, 13, 200

Z

Zatta, Antonio, 208
Zeitlin (bookdealer), 125

This book has been designed by Scott Vile at the Ascensius Press, South Freeport, Maine. The type is Adobe Janson, first issued in digital form in 1985 by Linotype. The typeface, though named Janson, was designed by Hungarian punchcutter Nicholas Kis c. 1690.

Aa Bb Cc Dd Ee Ff Gg Hh Ii Jj Kk
Ll Mm Nn Oo Pp Qq Rr
Ss Tt Uu Vv Ww
Xx Yy & Zz

Aa Bb Cc Dd
Ee Ff Gg Hh Ii Jj
Kk Ll Mm Nn Oo Pp Qq
Rr Ss Tt Uu Vv Ww Xx Yy & Zz